T0330180

Varieties of Green Business

Varieties of Green Business

Industries, Nations and Time

Geoffrey Jones

*Isidor Straus Professor of Business History,
Harvard Business School, USA*

Edward Elgar
PUBLISHING

Cheltenham, UK • Northampton, MA, USA

Published by
Edward Elgar Publishing Limited
The Lypiatts
15 Lansdown Road
Cheltenham
Glos GL50 2JA
UK

Edward Elgar Publishing, Inc.
William Pratt House
9 Dewey Court
Northampton
Massachusetts 01060
USA

A catalogue record for this book
is available from the British Library

Library of Congress Control Number: 2018944046

This book is available electronically in the **Elgar**online
Business subject collection
DOI 10.4337/9781788114141

ISBN 978 1 78811 413 4 (cased)
ISBN 978 1 78811 414 1 (eBook)

Typeset by Columns Design XML Ltd, Reading
Printed and bound by CPI Group (UK) Ltd, Croydon, CR0 4YY

Contents

Tables

Preface

This book provides rich new empirical evidence on green business as it examines its variation between industries and nations, and over time. It demonstrates the deep historical origins of endeavors to create for-profit businesses which were more responsible and sustainable, but also how these strategies have faced constraints, trade-offs and challenges of legitimacy.

Based on extensive interviews and archives around the world, the book asks why green business succeeded more in some contexts than others. It tells the remarkable stories of the creation of alternative firms, processes and technologies, while also exploring episodes of slow and non-linear progress, failed category creation and contested outcomes. It integrates the stories of well-known business leaders with many stories of entrepreneurial actors whose ambitions, struggles and achievements are much less celebrated. By drawing lessons from failure as well as success, from the unknown as well as the celebrated, I hope to make the experience of the past more accessible to those seeking a more sustainable future.

Boston, Massachusetts
January, 2018

Acknowledgements

The majority of chapters in this book have only appeared in earlier versions as Harvard Business School Working Papers. A version of Chapter 1 was also published in Patrick Fridenson and Takeo Kikkawa (eds.) (2017), *Ethical Capitalism: Shibusawa Eiichi and Business Leadership in Global Perspective*, Toronto: University of Toronto Press. A version of Chapter 5 was published in *Business History*, vol. 58 in 2016. A version of Chapter 8 was published in *Enterprise & Society*, vol. 18 in 2017. I am grateful to the editors of these journals and volumes for agreeing that the heavily revised versions of the original essays can be published here.

I would like to acknowledge the fundamental contributions of my coauthors in this book, Ben Gettinger, Emily Grandjean, Simon Mowatt and Andrew Spadafora. They have been a team of extraordinarily dedicated collaborators. Sanjay Bansal, Loubna Bouamane, Annelena Lobb and Mayuka Yamazaki also contributed significantly. I was privileged to have many discussions about green business with Ann-Kristin Bergquist while she was Visiting McCraw Fellow at the Business History Initiative at the Harvard Business School. I am very grateful to Auckland University of Technology for offering a visiting fellowship which enabled me to conduct many interviews in New Zealand along with Simon Mowatt on the organic food industry. Lila Stromer performed wonderful copy-editing on draft chapters. The research for this volume has been generously funded by the Division of Research and Faculty Development at the Harvard Business School, to whom I am most grateful.

1. Varieties of business responsibility*

I INTRODUCTION

The belief that capitalist enterprises have a wider responsibility to, and for, society and the natural environment beyond exclusively making profits for their owners has a long history. One recent study has traced the history of what is now called "corporate social responsibility" (hereafter, CSR) concepts in the United States back to the eighteenth century.[1] This reflects the fact that although the term CSR was coined in the second half of the twentieth century, many core concepts can be found in earlier traditions of business paternalism and philanthropy. It is equally evident that an understanding of what business is, or should be, responsible for has remained diffuse and contested.[2]

This book is primarily concerned with how some business leaders have pursued sustainability in different industries, countries and time periods. The purpose of this opening chapter is to place this story in a broader context. It considers the different varieties of business responsibility which can be seen in the history of capitalism. The chapter proceeds chronologically. Section II examines the emergence of concepts of business responsibility during the opening era of modern industrialization. Section III looks at the further development of concepts of business responsibility as a result of the Great Depression. Section IV explores the evolution of concepts of business responsibility in Asia and Latin America. Section V looks at the highpoint of business responsibility in postwar Europe and in the United States, and Section VI looks at business responsibility in the era of quarterly capitalism after 1980. Section VII turns to green businesses, and places the remaining chapters of the book in context. Section VIII offers conclusions.

II BUSINESS RESPONSIBILITY IN THE ERA OF MODERN INDUSTRIALIZATION

As capitalism emerged in the Western world, it had an ambiguous relationship with the social values of the dominant religion, Christianity.

Famously, the German sociologist Max Weber associated the advent of modern capitalism with the Reformation in the sixteenth century, arguing that the ascetic, rational and individualist nature of Lutheran and Calvinist beliefs set them apart from Catholic and Orthodox Christianity, and shaped behavior. He identified the "Protestant work ethic" that encouraged people to work hard, be frugal and strive for success as proof of personal faith. In other words, it shaped entrepreneurs whose values were aligned with "the spirit of capitalism."[3]

Weber set off a famous debate among historians on the cultural basis of entrepreneurial success, which has continued to the present day; but this debate also overshadowed other issues concerning Christianity and the morality of capitalism. In the Gospel of Luke in the New Testament, Jesus was recorded as saying that "it is easier for a camel to go through a needle's eye than for a rich man to enter the kingdom of God." This hardly provided a compelling incentive to engage in capitalist endeavors. Medieval European societies struggled with the tensions between riches and religion, and the tensions did not go away as the modern world emerged. In 1776, Adam Smith, in *The Wealth of Nations*, argued that the market was value-neutral and that its invisible hand promoted public good out of private self-interest. He considered the science of economics as "the great antidote to the poison of enthusiasm and superstition."[4] However these observations were made within the context of his earlier book, *Theory of Moral Sentiments*, published in 1767, which sharply differentiated between individualism and egoism, and emphasized that competition took place within the context of mutual cooperation.[5] Other writers stressed the role of God in business and economic affairs. Thomas Malthus, a Christian minister, published *An Essay on the Principle of Population* in 1798, putting God and morality together in a central place in political economy.

As the Industrial Revolution took hold during the eighteenth century, the institutionalization of economic activity in the form of firms expanded. The concept of the corporation as a legal person separate from its owners was an invention of Western societies, originating in Roman law during the first two centuries AD, developed during the Middle Ages in both Church and civil law, and further codified by the British and American common law tradition.[6] The responsibilities of such corporations were less clear. At first, the family ownership of almost all corporations blurred the issue, as the personal values of founders and owners were expressed in their firms. The Christian values of founders helped shape a wider societal role for firms in the form of industrial paternalism and welfare capitalism. In Britain, a succession of entrepreneurs – from Josiah Wedgwood in the eighteenth-century pottery industry, to George Cadbury and William Lever in the late-nineteenth century, of the chocolate and soap industries, respectively – provided houses, villages, and health and recreational facilities for their workers. Self-interest coexisted with religious concerns in these endeavors, as entrepreneurs sought to build loyal and stable workforces inculcated with the values of industrial capitalism. Economics also mattered. It was the firms in especially favorable market positions, including Lever and Cadbury, which offered extended welfare benefits. Most large British firms did not.[7]

Mixed motives are evident in the literature on nineteenth-century paternalism in both Britain and the United States.[8] Lever built an exemplary model industrial village in 1888 for his employees at Port Sunlight, outside of Liverpool in Britain. However, in order to counter the threat of socialism, he also appointed a Wesleyan minister as the company's welfare officer and minister at the church he built in 1904; this was a blatant strategy to keep ideological dissent under control. In an extraordinary departure from convention, he even confined membership of his church to his employees.[9] George Cadbury, a Quaker, built a garden village around a new chocolate factory in Bournville, which was four miles outside of the crowded industrial city of Birmingham; this seemed to go above and beyond concerns to build a stable and docile workforce. In 1900 he even donated the village to a separate trust. Six years later, Cadbury articulated his "theory of giving":

> Begin at home with your work people, see to their comfort, health ... See that your workshops are light and well-ventilated ... give your people the advantage of living where there is plenty of space. This was our main object in removing from Birmingham into the country. It was morally right and proved financially to be a success, because the business had room to expand.[10]

The balance between morality and profits can be debated as much in the Cadbury case as in others, but the evidence of fervent religious views driving an agenda concerning responsibility is strong. However, it is important to note, as a study of another British Quaker – chocolate manufacturer Joseph Rowntree – has stressed, religiously motivated concerns for the welfare of employees was positioned within the context of seeking efficiency for a business growing in scale.[11] As one author observed, "the Quaker business ethic legitimized but also tempered capitalism by defining the proper means and ends of business."[12]

Debates on the motives of the American corporate paternalists of the nineteenth and early twentieth centuries in using their wealth to support philanthropic ventures, and engaging in sophisticated urban and social planning, are similar to the debates on the British paternalists. The prominent examples of welfare capitalism are well-known figures in American business history. These include, for example, the Houghton family, who built the glass company Corning in the town of Corning, New York; Milton Hershey, of the Hershey chocolate company; and George Pullman, the railcar manufacturer, who built a large town outside of Chicago in 1880 for his workers. Company towns became a feature of the American industrial landscape as the century progressed, though, as Green has suggested, they fell ostensibly into two types: paternalistic and downright exploitative.[13]

Major differences between the United States and Europe were the growing scale of American businesses and the enormous wealth of successful business leaders, such as Andrew Carnegie and John D. Rockefeller. An underlying driver of this philanthropy might have been the huge income and wealth inequality which had emerged in the United States by the early twentieth century: by the 1920s inequality had reached levels not to be seen again until the early twenty-first century.[14] These wealth disparities were fully understood, and provoked much criticism of "robber barons" and the abuse of power by "trusts" such as Rockefeller's Standard Oil. However, size also stimulated thoughts of responsibility among business leaders. "I was taught," wrote Henry J. Heinz, the founder of the Heinz Company, "that a certain responsibility goes with ... any large business affecting many people."[15]

Andrew Carnegie, who built a huge steel business, took the concept of charity to the next level. Believing that "hoarding millions is avarice, not thrift," he went beyond offering his workers good conditions and guaranteed employment to propose what he termed *The Gospel of Wealth*. Carnegie insisted that entrepreneurs had a responsibility to use their wealth to promote social good not by leaving money to their families but by funding public institutions, such as schools and libraries, which would offer further opportunities for others. Carnegie gave away almost all of his personal fortune of $10 billion (in today's dollars), and laid down the framework of modern American philanthropy by establishing the Carnegie Foundation in 1911, beginning "the art of spending money for the common good."[16] The foundation was a new form of institution designed to administer large resources and deliver them to multiple recipients. Carnegie had been distressed by sectarian divisions in Scotland, and initially showed little interest in religious matters, but by the time he began his large philanthropy projects, he was an active Presbyterian. Among the first big projects was the donation of thousands of organs to churches.[17]

Carnegie began a distinctly American view of the responsibility of business leaders: if they made a lot of money, they should give it away to promote the public good. This reflected the idiosyncratic American system that was at once highly individualistic yet also had a strong sense of community, and that was committed to making profits yet also believed in pursuing social justice. The Rockefeller Foundation was created in 1913. Between 1915 and 1930, as Zunz has noted in his study of American philanthropy, the number of foundations in the United States grew from 77 to 200.[18] More foundations followed, with the Ford Foundation created in 1936, and the hotelier Conrad Hilton establishing his foundation in 1944. There were strong religious beliefs behind many of these initiatives: the Rockefellers were Baptists; the Guggenheims, Jewish; and Hilton, a Roman Catholic.

Multiple authors have pointed out that business philanthropy was about more than giving away money; for example, American philanthropy has been seen as an investment in shaping the future. "Individual Americans return to society some monetary gain," Zunz observed, "with the motivation that it might benefit them in the long run."[19] Harvey and coauthors, using the example of Carnegie, employed the term entrepreneurial philanthropists to describe people who deployed financial wealth to achieve high social rates of return. From their perspective, Carnegie and subsequent philanthropists sought to deflect criticisms of huge wealth and establish their legitimacy, which would in turn enable them to engage "in the business of world making."[20]

By the 1920s, there were strong traditions of business responsibility in major industrial nations, including the United States and Britain, and in both countries some manufacturers practiced large-scale paternalism. In the United States, Carnegie started the tradition of creating philanthropic foundations. The motives for these acts varied, and religious and ethical motivations were clearly articulated, but other rationales were also present. Paternalism created stable labor forces, and philanthropy gave legitimacy to great wealth created in business.

III THE GREAT DEPRESSION AND ITS AFTERMATH

During the interwar years, the emergence of the concept of management as a profession took hold. This reflected and coincided with the growth of large corporations that increasingly dominated business activity. In the United States, the creation of business schools attached to prestigious universities, such as Columbia, Harvard and Dartmouth, led to a push to make management a profession on a par with law or medicine.[21] This was a particular concern of Wallace Donham, a lawyer who became dean of the Harvard Business School in 1919, and who strove to make the school as prestigious as the longer-established Harvard Law School. He wanted to develop a code of ethics for managers, and spoke abroad on multiple occasions on the broader responsibilities of business.[22] In 1927, in the Harvard Business School alumni newsletter, he warned, "Unless more of our business leaders learn to exercise their powers and responsibilities with a definitely increased sense of responsibility towards other groups in the community, our civilization may well head for one of its periodic periods of decline."[23]

The Great Depression and the consequent public criticism of Wall Street, in particular, and unfettered capitalism, in general, prompted extensive discussion of the responsibility of managers. Donham's ideas evolved further. In 1933 he published a widely cited article in *Harvard Business Review* in which he maintained that business had the responsibility to be ethical, and he warned that if it was not that governments would impose unwise and unnecessary laws on it. He wrote:

> The solution of problems of business ethics, the task of learning how to conduct business so as to add to general security and happiness, must be undertaken primarily by business leaders. Their object must be to do the job so well that the law and the policeman are unnecessary.[24]

During the 1930s, within the context of President Franklin D. Roosevelt's New Deal, there was extensive debate on the responsibility of business. In 1932 Adolphe Berle, the corporate lawyer who became an adviser to Roosevelt, coauthored with Gardiner Means *The Modern Corporation and Private Property*. This landmark study laid out the problems of separating ownership and control in large modern corporations. A key component of the argument, although subsequently overlooked, was that the growth of professional managers had broken what he considered the historic link between capitalism and social and moral responsibilities to the societies in which firms were based. Berle's view of what had transpired in the past may not have been historically accurate, but it is evident that the emergence of limited liability and the joint stock company proved a considerable challenge for business leaders who sought to combine wealth accumulation with a wider societal role. As their companies went public, managers assumed a fiduciary responsibility to shareholders and the creation of shareholder value.

Berle's solutions were regulatory and legal. He designed the new Securities and Exchange Act, which was designed to force disclosure of corporate information to make managers more responsive to social good.

During the 1930s, Berle debated with E. Merrick Dodd, a Harvard University law professor, who argued that it should be formally recognized that large corporations were social institutions that had responsibilities to multiple stakeholders beyond shareholders. Berle was less confident that managers would ever be fit to exercise such responsibilities, and called for formal government regulations to oblige them to meet broader responsibilities.[25]

In the United States, there were also important regulatory and institutional developments to facilitate corporate giving. In 1917 US law was changed to permit individuals to deduct charitable donations from their income tax. The primary motivation was to encourage gifts to charities related to the war effort. It was much more contested whether corporations could make such charitable donations, but then the 1935 Revenue Act permitted corporations to deduct charitable donations from their taxes. Corporate donations rose sharply thereafter. In the United States, a number of intermediate organizations emerged that were crucial to corporate philanthropy. In particular, the Young Men's Christian Association (YMCA) pioneered methods of corporate fundraising between 1905 and 1916.[26]

There were echoes of American debates on the responsibility of business in many other Western countries, although they were framed within their distinctive cultures, traditions and political systems. In Britain, the Christian churches continued to play a role in making the case for the ethical responsibility of business. A book written by a Post Office executive and published by the Student Christian Movement in 1922 described a new generation of managers who "may provide a priesthood in industry, just as there is a priesthood in worship."[27]

As in the United States, there was much discussion of the professionalization of management. Quaker business families, such as Rowntree and Cadbury, were especially important in the so-called management movement. The former family produced three of the most important interwar writers: Seebohn Rowntree, Oliver Sheldon and Lyndall Urwick.[28] Sheldon's *The Philosophy of Management*, published in 1923, included a chapter entitled "The Social Responsibility of Management," which discussed in detail the responsibilities of business to the well-being of their broader communities and to maintaining high ethical standards.[29]

Meanwhile, beyond debates on societal responsibilities, some American business leaders saw their responsibilities extending also to international diplomacy. Among the more famous examples were Henry Ford's Peace Ship during World War I, and the efforts by T.J. Watson, the chief executive of IBM, to head off mounting tensions in Europe in

the late 1930s. In 1937 Watson, also the president of the International
Chamber of Commerce, arranged a personal meeting with Adolf Hitler to
discourage him from planning another war. Watson was rewarded by
Hitler's promise that there would be no war, as well as a special Nazi
medal decorated with swastikas. As is well known, Watson had no more
success than Ford, who received a similar medal from the Nazi regime;
after the German invasion of France in 1940, Watson returned his
medal.[30]

The continued growth of big business, the drive to make management
a profession on par with the law and medicine, and the shock of the
Great Depression contributed to a deepening of the discussion on the
responsibilities of business to society. Harvard Business School deans,
among others, were among those calling for business leaders to be more
responsible to their societies, even for happiness. They also articulated
concerns of enhanced government intervention if business was perceived
to be acting badly or being responsible for social woes. However, other
voices asserted that public corporations were legally bound to be
responsible only to their shareholders. This began a debate that remains
unresolved.

IV BUSINESS RESPONSIBILITY IN ASIA AND LATIN
AMERICA

The previous sections have focused on the theory and practice of
business in the industrialized West. Asia and Latin America lagged
behind the West in modern industrialization, but nevertheless some of the
most radical concepts of business responsibility were developed in those
regions as modern business enterprises began to develop. This can be
explained by several factors, including philosophic and religious beliefs,
the extent of social deprivation and wealth inequality, and institutional
voids which resulted in few public policies to address such deprivation.[31]

Japan was forced to open its long-closed economy by American naval
forces in 1853, an event which led within 15 years to the overthrow of
the feudal Tokugawa regime which had ruled the country for two and a
half centuries. During the decades after the installation of the Emperor
Meiji in 1868, Japan became the first non-Western country to achieve
substantial modern industrial growth. As in the West, the business
leaders of the era articulated highly divergent views on business
responsibility. Yataro Iwasaki and Shibusawa Eiichi represented two
extremes, even though both were highly successful businessmen.[32]
Iwasaki was a major shipping entrepreneur and the founder of the

Mitsubishi Group.[33] Shibusawa was a serial entrepreneur, founder of nearly 500 companies and the creator of the modern Japanese banking system. In a context in which Meiji Japan was threatened by expansionist Western imperial powers, both men were aware that Japan's sovereignty rested on modernizing the economy. The views of the two men on the functions of capitalism, however, diverged. Iwasaki was a profit maximizer concerned about growing the wealth of his family. Shibusawa developed the concept of *gapponshugi*, which Kimura has translated as seeking to develop a business "by assembling the best possible people and funding to achieve the mission and with the aim of pursuing the public good."[34]

Shibusawa's ideas developed within a specific chronological and country context. Traveling to the Paris Exposition in 1867 as a member of a group of delegates, just as regime change was underway at home, Shibusawa encountered and was impressed by French accounting and asset management systems, and especially the joint stock system. Returning to Japan, he established the county's first joint stock corporation.[35] However he framed these and other reforms within the concept of Confucianism, the basic principle of the samurai and the ruling elite of the old regime. Confucianism was concerned with the behavior and relationships of lords to their vassals and parents to children. Shibusawa transferred Confucian concepts of morality to the emergent modern business sector, and he embedded these ideas in the hundreds of companies he started, as well as in numerous business associations.[36]

Shibusawa's views changed over time, not least because he was an international traveler who was well aware of, and interacted with, discourses beyond Japan. In 1907, for example, he publically criticized John D. Rockefeller for holding on to his wealth instead of returning it to society. Yet his views had a consistent basis that realizing public good and accumulating private wealth were not contradictory. Shibusawa's justification for business responsibility was secular, unlike almost all of his Western contemporaries, and reflected Confucian philosophy. It might be seen, as a result, as a precursor to the present day, in which the case for business responsibility is typically framed in secular terms, even if individuals hold strong religious views themselves.

China lagged behind Japan's modernization, but the new business leaders who began to develop manufacturing and other businesses in the late nineteenth century sometimes pursued wider social and cultural roles, especially in their local cities and regions. The influence of Confucian traditions was again significant. The case of Zhang Jian, who in the late nineteenth century founded the Dasheng Cotton Mill in Nantong, provides an important example. Zhang, who has been described "as one of the best known Confucians of his day,"[37] invested extensively in local educational, welfare and cultural facilities in an extensive program aimed at modernizing a formerly backward area. He was well aware that these activities increased his social status and influence. He carefully handled his favorable image in local newspapers, while reducing his actual financial commitments by charging for the schools and libraries he founded and often handing over facilities his family founded to the local government.[38]

In nineteenth-century British India, it was not Confucianism but religious traditions which often shaped the views of business leaders about responsibility to society. In the middle of the century, a locally owned modern cotton textile industry emerged in Mumbai (then known as Bombay). The owners were from the small Parsi community, who followed Zoroastrian beliefs about the importance of doing good works in the material world.[39] The most prominent Parsee business leaders were the Tata family, with whom Shibusawa had a close business relationship due to cotton trading.[40] "In a free enterprise," Jamsetji Tata, the group's founder noted, "the community is not just another stake holder in the business but in fact the very purpose of its existence."[41] The Tata family developed a distinctive corporate culture characterized by the concept of service to the wider community and high ethical standards. The long-term commitment to wider social responsibility was equally strong in the Godrej family, also Parsee, whose business group was founded by Ardeshir Godrej in 1897.[42]

However, more radical views of business responsibility also emerged that were associated with the noted independence campaigner and supporter of passive resistance, Mohandas Gandhi. Gandhi's economic views are most closely associated with the concept of rural self-sufficiency and opposition to modern industrialization. However, he also developed a trustee model of capitalism and ethical capitalism. In a speech to textile industrialists in 1928, Gandhi told them to hold all their "riches as a trust to be used solely in the interests of those who sweat for you."[43] Gandhi argued that the combination of self-interest and benevolence would lead to sustained economic development, which would integrate successful entrepreneurs into nation-building and the relief of poverty.[44] The sources of Gandhi's ideas of trusteeship were highly eclectic. He was influenced by aspects of Jain and Hindu traditional philosophies and practices, and also by Western thinkers such as John Ruskin and Henry David Thoreau. As with Shibusawa, there was also a secular component; Gandhi, a trained lawyer, transferred legal concepts of trusteeship from the law.[45]

Gandhi worked closely with a number of Marwari business leaders, who had developed the most influential business community by the interwar years. These included G.D. Birla and Jamnalal Bajaj.[46] Bajaj, a manufacturer who supported Gandhi's independence struggle against colonial rule, affirmed a trustee model of capitalism, emphasizing the responsibilities of firms to all stakeholders as well as the adoption of the highest ethical standards. Bajaj and his family pursued an ambitious social agenda focused on addressing the needs of the disenfranchised in society, especially the Untouchables (the lowest in India's caste system) and women, as well as rural development and environmental sustainability.[47]

Like the Quaker families Cadbury and Rowntree, who strictly avoided businesses related to war out of their pacifist convictions, Bajaj insisted that it mattered how businesses made profits as well as how funds were used. During the 1930s, he refused to follow his peers in diversifying beyond sugar refining into the lucrative business of alcoholic drinks because Gandhi forbade consumption of alcohol. Bajaj's belief that the use of handmade cloth was essential to solve the poverty of the Indian countryside and to provide employment opportunities for rural women to facilitate their emancipation also led him to avoid textile manufac-turing.[48] Bajaj was, it should be stressed, hardly typical. A recent study has observed that while many Indian business leaders of the time donated to schools and temples, the fact that they also engaged in extensive corruption suggests that their motives were primarily "to appease the gods they believed in" rather than demonstrate a commitment to trustee or stakeholder capitalism.[49]

In the Islamic world in Asia and elsewhere, strong beliefs about the importance of charity were manifested in a unique legal institution known as *waqf*. These institutions were founded throughout the Islamic world, represented by buildings and mosques, and services in hospital and medicine; more recently they have been associated with the growth of Islamic financial instruments.[50] Traditional Islamic practices also inspired the creation of businesses. To give an early example from India, in 1906 Hakeem Hafiz Abdul Majeed established Harmdard clinic in Delhi to provide wide access to *unani* medicines. It developed into a significant pharmaceutical business manufacturing natural and herb-based products. The venture became a *waqf* in 1948, and successor firms remain active today in India, Bangladesh and Pakistan.[51]

There was no equivalent to Shibusawa or Bajaj among the business elites in Latin America, where substantial economic growth, especially in the southern cone of the subcontinent, occurred from the late nineteenth century. However, business leaders were influenced by the Roman

Catholic Church and especially the Social Catholic Doctrine, dated from Pope Leo XIII's 1891 encyclical letter, *Rerum novarum*, which condemned both capitalism and socialism. An example is provided by what became one of the largest Colombian business groups, Fundación Social (FS). Originally a savings fund for workers founded by a Spanish Jesuit immigrant priest in 1911, the FS was firstly launched as a foundation. It then started successive businesses to make profits, which were channeled to social action programs in education and provided credit for low-income housing and community development in poor, conflict-torn communities. The FS financial companies pioneered low-income credit practices from the 1910s.[52]

Elsewhere in Latin America, businesses often engaged in giving discrete donations to churches, sports teams, schools and other causes, while family foundations provided further sources of financial support.[53] A study of the growth of philanthropy in Venezuela and Mexico points to the importance of families who built large business groups, such as Mendoza in the former and Zambrano in the latter, and the influence of the American business philanthropy role model.[54]

It was thus in Asia, and to some extent in Latin America, that the most radical concepts of business responsibility developed in the late nineteenth century and first half of the twentieth century. Both Shibusawa and Gandhi moved far beyond ideas of philanthropy and paternalism toward concepts of stakeholder capitalism, in which high ethical standards were seen as an integral component. They can be seen as pioneers of a belief that capitalism should be sustainable, and that pursuing public gain was, and should be, compatible with the pursuit of private gain. Various religious beliefs, from Zoroastrian and Jainism to Roman Catholicism, and secular philosophies such as Confucianism, were important, if not exclusive, motivating factors.

V STAKEHOLDER CAPITALISM IN THE POSTWAR DECADES

World War II saw a sharp improvement in the reputation of big business in the United States, which was hailed as playing an essential role in the Allied victory. The corporations themselves invested heavily in reinforcing this improved public image.[55] Berle, among others, hailed US corporations as accepting that they had a wide range of social and other responsibilities.[56] The new dean of the Harvard Business School, Donald K. David, insisted that business needed to expand its wider role in American society. In 1946 he called for firms to move beyond serving shareholders to acknowledge the "public responsibilities of enterprise."[57] Three years later, in a landmark article in *Harvard Business Review*, he insisted that American business had a responsibility to show it was a superior system to Russian-style socialism. This meant avoiding a narrow focus on profits and, among other things, treating employees fairly, combating racial discrimination and assisting in the development of poorer countries.[58]

There remained a significant religious dimension to discourses on business responsibility. In 1953 the National Council of Churches, an interfaith organization, funded a book by Howard Bowen entitled *Social Responsibilities of the Businessman*. Bowen identified the multiple stakeholders in a business, and argued that managers needed to serve all of them. Firms made "commercial goods and services," Bowen argued, but they also impacted the conditions in which such goods were made – including in providing employment and in marketing and advertising practices – and managers also had responsibility for these "social products."[59]

During the same era, large American businesses ramped up their corporate philanthropy. These were prosperous and confident years for large American corporations, which dominated innovation and led the world in high-tech industries. During the 1950s, General Electric invested heavily in social programs in local communities and in education, and was encouraged by new laws that made corporate giving to charities tax-deductible. A new generation of firms established foundations, and firms in particular invested directly in higher education. Alfred Sloan (president of General Motors) and other business leaders who sat on the Council on Financial Aid encouraged firms to give to universities.[60] During the 1960s, some American firms increased their corporate philanthropy further. The Minneapolis-based Dayton Hudson department store chain became noteworthy for giving away 5 percent of its pretax profits to philanthropy.[61]

The most radical exponent of the responsibility of corporations was the computer mainframe company Control Data Corporation and its founder, William C. Norris. The firm was founded in 1957 in Minneapolis and grew very rapidly, entering the Fortune 500 in 1965. Norris saw the responsibility of business as extending far beyond charitable giving, and made the case for businesses to identify social problems and to address them as opportunities. The company proactively sought to provide employment for people with physical disabilities and childcare for women employees, and it built factories in deprived inner city areas.[62]

The ambitious thoughts of Norris and other business leaders on business responsibility were not without critics. In 1958 the *Harvard*

Business Review published an article by Theodore Levitt, a marketing consultant who would later join the Harvard Business School faculty; he become the *Review*'s editor from 1985 to 1989. The article was entitled "The Dangers of Social Responsibility," and in it Levitt asserted flatly that companies were not designed to address social issues and were not equipped in such tasks.[63] In 1970 the economist Milton Friedman published his now-classic article in *New York Times Magazine*, in which he stated, "The social responsibility of business is to increase profits."[64] The new liberal era had not yet dawned, but the intellectual case was being made.

It is not so easy to track the development of concepts of responsibility in European businesses during the postwar decade. European firms initially had to reconstruct their business rather than debate wider responsibilities, and European business leaders were more discreet than their American counterparts in discussing their strategies. Many of the foundations founded in Germany and elsewhere during the postwar decade were more concerned with retaining family ownership than with philanthropic activity.[65] Europe lacked institutions such as the Harvard Business School, which could articulate theories of responsibility. Furthermore, European governments took responsibility for welfare and other issues in ways that the US government did not, reducing the perceived need for corporations to be involved in society. In Britain, France and elsewhere, large segments of the economy had also been nationalized.

Nevertheless, it is evident that a broadening view of the responsibility of large corporations was underway during the postwar decades. In the Netherlands, the executives of large corporations, including Philips, Shell and Unilever, articulated views on the wider responsibilities of companies. Unlike in the United States, there was limited interest in corporate philanthropy; instead, there was widespread support for concepts of trusteeship and the belief that firms had multiple stakeholders.[66] The consumer products company Unilever was at the forefront of such trends. Paul Rijkens, the Dutch chairman of Unilever during the immediate postwar decade, was a strong advocate of the social responsibility of corporations. He insisted that Unilever had responsibilities not only to shareholders but also to employees, consumers and the environment.[67]

Rijkens recruited like-minded figures to Unilever, including Pieter Kuin, who became a director in 1961. Kuin, an economist and active Catholic, published a series of important studies concerning the responsibilities of business.[68] In 1966 he told an international management conference in Rotterdam, "Management should never take up the cause of the rich against the poor, the privileged against the masses, the private against the public good."[69]

It would however be a mistake to suggest that Unilever became a consistent exponent of social responsibility. Rijkens's successors were less passionate about the subject, yet the corporate culture continued to insist that, in the words of an article in the house journal published in 1959, it was a "powerful force for good in the world."[70] During the 1960s, the firm's large Indian affiliate, Hindustan Lever, began a program of rural development that over time emerged as a textbook case of how a large Western multinational could use business to promote development. Seeking more reliable milk supplies, Unilever provided small farmers with guidance and knowledge of animal husbandry, and intervened with banks to get the farmers loans without corrupt payments.[71]

During the postwar decades, then, a belief in the importance of business responsibility was widespread in both the United States and Western Europe. It was an era when large corporations held stable positions in oligopolistic industries. Managers needed to pay limited attention to rates of return to investors, and were more inclined to see their businesses as serving multiple stakeholders. Confidence in what capitalism could achieve after victory over fascism in World War II, and a desire to assert the superiority of the West during the Cold War, encouraged an expansive view of capitalism's responsibilities.

VI BUSINESS RESPONSIBILITY AND QUARTERLY CAPITALISM

The decades since the 1980s have been ones with considerable paradoxes: (1) the pursuit of the wider corporate roles in society fell away in Western economies as investors acquired shorter time horizons, (2) finance theory followed Michael Jensen's strictures on agency costs and (3) globalization weakened the connection between firms and communities. Sometimes dubbed the Anglo-Saxon model of capitalism, so-called shareholder capitalism diffused elsewhere, including Continental Europe and Japan, along with globalized capital markets.

This trend did not stop firms from talking about business responsibility; instead, it became institutionalized as CSR, which grew as a virtual industry in itself. Mainstream corporations pursued CSR programs for multiple reasons, including enhancing their reputations, building their legitimacy and even gaining competitive advantages.[72] There was an extensive, if deeply under-researched, implementation of CSR by local companies in emerging markets such as Mexico.[73] Everywhere the relationship between rhetoric and reality was almost impossible to disentangle. There appeared to be a spectrum of strategies, with a small minority of corporations actively implementing broad concepts of corporate responsibility, a majority aiming to conform to regulatory and societal requirements and expectations, and some employing rhetoric cynically as a pure public relations device. The concept of CSR remained ill-defined and evidently interpreted in different ways among countries, even in a single region like Europe.[74]

The first decades of the twenty-first century saw an intensifying loss of the legitimacy of capitalism. As in the opening decades of the twentieth century, this reflected the perceived unfairness of wealth and income inequality, as well a series of scandals and shocks. The United States passed through a decade of corporate wrongdoing, including the Enron accounting fraud, the Madoff investment scandal and the Galleon Group hedge fund scandal. It was hard to find a country outside of the United States in which some major corporate misdeed was not revealed.[75] Low points of corporate behavior included the News Corporation phone-hacking scandal in Britain, the Satyam Computer Services fraud in India, and an ever-increasing list of once blue-chip manufacturing companies in Japan, including Olympus, Mitsubishi Materials, Nissan Motor, Takata, Toray, Toshiba and Kobe Steel, which were revealed to have engaged in accounting and standards fraud. Meanwhile, and at a system-wide level, the 2008 global financial crisis, which caused widespread economic and social dislocation in many parts of the world, was widely (and correctly) perceived to have been caused by systemic failures in the global financial system, including a willful lack of business responsibility in matters such as subprime lending and derivatives trading.

As in the earlier era, there was a new wave of business philanthropy, especially in the United States. This was largely funded by the huge fortunes made in financial services and, especially, high-tech industries. The Bill and Melinda Gates Foundation, created in 1995 by the founder of Microsoft, was symbolic of the new era of mega-foundations.[76] Business philanthropy spread beyond the United States, especially in emerging markets. In 2006 Mo Ibrahim, a pioneering African cell phone entrepreneur, established a foundation targeted at improving leadership and governance in Africa. There was a sudden emergence of business philanthropy in China after the Sichuan earthquake in 2008, in response to Internet activism and criticism of excessive wealth.[77]

There was also new re-evaluations of the responsibility of capitalism by management thinkers and others. The Harvard Business School Strategy professor Michael Porter developed the concept of "shared value." In a coauthored article with Mark Kramer, published in 2011, the authors argued that capitalism was "under siege" and being blamed for being "a major cause of social, environmental, and economic problems." In response, they called for a reinvention of capitalism. The starting point of their analysis was the view that not all profits should be regarded as equal. Instead, they argued that profits that serve social purposes should be seen as more important than other types of profits. An underlying assumption of this model was that conventional CSR was not sufficient; indeed, it was more of a problem than a solution for firms. Porter and Kramer argued instead that firms needed to get beyond the view that social issues are at the periphery of a business and instead see them at its core.[78] The shared value concept echoed Shibusawa's view that business activities that increase the public good are the most important virtue, and that profitability and societal responsibility were fully compatible. Empirical studies found it hard to demonstrate a positive correlation between corporate profitability and CSR, at least in the United States.[79]

There were also many criticisms of constraints faced by public companies which needed to report their earnings quarterly. In 2011 Dominic Barton, the global managing director of the management consulting firm McKinsey, fearing a rupture "in the social contract between the capitalist system and the citizenry," called for the need to rebuild capitalism around a longer-term vision and the replacement of what he termed quarterly capitalism. A longer-term capitalism, Barton suggested, would remove tensions "between creating value and serving the interests of employees, suppliers, customers, creditors, communities, and the environment."[80] It remained unclear, however, how such a longer-term capitalism could be achieved given the demands of global capital markets. In the United States there was a growing use of private capital markets, including venture capital, private equity and debt financing, but this was more related to securing greater freedom for risk-taking while retaining control, rather than the pursuit of wider stakeholder strategies.

There are some striking continuities between the present day and earlier historical periods with respect to beliefs about business responsibility to society. From nineteenth-century figures such as George Cadbury and Shibusawa Eiichi, through interwar Harvard Business School deans and Mohandas Gandhi, to Michael Porter and Dominic Barton today, a minority of business leaders and thinkers have argued both that business had broader responsibilities to society than making profits for owners, and that the pursuit of this responsibility need not involve a large trade-off with profitability. The motivation behind such beliefs has varied widely, but has often been underwritten by a belief that capitalism must be deemed legitimate if it was to be allowed to operate. Strikingly, these views have never achieved mainstream status.

VII   VARIETIES OF GREEN BUSINESS

The remaining chapters of this book will address the specific topic of business responsibility for the natural environment. Concerns about the impact of modern business and industrialization on the natural environment began early in the nineteenth century.[81] The response was a conservationist movement that had become institutionalized by the second half of the century. The world's first national park, Yellowstone National Park, was created in the United States in 1872. Environmentalist nongovernmental organizations (NGOs) followed, even earlier than the charitable foundations begun by Carnegie. In 1892 the Sierra Club was founded in San Francisco.[82] In 1907 US President Teddy Roosevelt, an active conservationist, used his presidential address to assert that "the conservation of our natural resources and their proper use constitute the fundamental problem which underlies almost every other problem of our National life." The approach taken by Roosevelt and organizations such as the US Forest Service were different to more romantic conservationists, in their optimism that modern technology could be harnessed to conserve the scarce resources of nature.[83]

Many of the individuals discussed in this chapter included ecological components in their arguments and actions. George Cadbury's garden village in Bournville included plentiful green spaces and gardens, and was designed as a self-sufficient sustainable community. Gandhi's views on rural self-sufficiency and critiques of overconsumption can be interpreted in ecological terms.[84] In his book *Social Responsibilities of the Businessman*, Bowen wrote that it could "be argued that obviously wasteful use of natural resources is morally indefensible, and that businessmen should be continuously searching for more economical methods of using them and striving to find reproducible substitutes."[85] However, Bowen added that there were limits to what could "reasonably be expected of businessmen" and that the "interests of future generations probably must be handled largely through government policy."[86]

The case studies in this book contribute to a growing scholarly literature on business, the environment, and green and sustainable entrepreneurship.[87] Although generally believed to be a recent phenomenon, current historical research has demonstrated that the first entrepreneurs concerned with sustainability, broadly defined, appeared in the nineteenth century. By 1980 the basic concepts of organic food, recycling waste, renewable energy, ecological architecture, green banking and other sustainable industries had been put in place, although none of these categories were very large. From the 1980s onward, there was significant growth. Solar and wind energy grew enormously in scale, as did recycling, the consumption of organic food and many other green industries. Books with titles such as *The Green Capitalists* and *The Ecology of Commerce* made the intellectual case that sustainability and profitability were compatible.[88] Like CSR, sustainability reports proliferated in big business.[89]

The greening of business in recent decades took place in the context of the mounting scientific evidence concerning the scale of human-driven climate change and other signs of environmental stress. As scientists described the new Anthropocene age, when the Earth's geology was for the first time fundamentally altered by human activities, governments introduced more wide-ranging environmental policies.[90] The number of national climate change laws and policies worldwide increased from around 60 in 1997 to 1,200 in 2017.[91] However, neither the increased number of laws nor corporate commitments to sustainability have stopped the continued deterioration of the natural environment.

As with the general concept of business responsibility, the history of green business as a whole has been neither linear nor evenly spread. Green businesses have appeared and evolved at different times, in different industries and in different countries. The following chapters provide rich new empirical evidence on the variety of green businesses. The limited existing literature on green business often explores positive cases. In contrast, the following chapters examine many situations in which progress was slow or reversed, and apparent success contained problematic outcomes. The settings deliberately varied in time, industry and place.

Chapter 2 is focused on the management of waste, which can be regarded as the first great environmental challenge. In preindustrial societies, the amount of waste – certainly in the rural areas in which most populations lived – was limited. The growing urban populations of industrialized countries in the nineteenth century began generating far more waste and recycled much less of it. This reflected the fact that rising incomes permitted people to waste more food and materials than in the past. Also, new materials such as glass and metal packaging were not biodegradable. The chapter explores the emergence of entrepreneurial firms in Germany and central Europe that sought to create profitable businesses out of conserving and returning waste resources to productive use, while maintaining public sanitation and in some cases offering nascent environmental protections. It draws on archives and secondary literature largely unfamiliar to English-speaking audiences. A number of these pioneering firms had strikingly modern views of ecological challenges and the need to overcome them.

Chapter 3 is concerned with solar energy in the formative period from the late nineteenth century to 1990. Modern industrialization rested on the use of coal and other fossil fuels. There was no understanding of the impact of fossil fuels on climate change until the late twentieth century, but there were concerns about their finite nature and about the sustainability of communities without access to coal. This chapter discusses early attempts to develop solar energy from parabolic troughs, the use of passive solar in architecture and the early growth of the modern photovoltaic industry after World War II.

Chapter 4 turns to finance. Shibusawa Eiichi, discussed earlier in this chapter, was an early exponent of the importance of functioning financial markets for capitalism to be productive. However, for most of the era of modern capitalism, banks and capital markets have been the problem rather than the salvation for green industries. Typically, the pursuit of sustainability has been riskier and less profitable than conventional businesses, making it unattractive for banks and capital markets to support. Beginning in the 1970s, and accelerating after 1980, a number of social banks were established. Chapter 4 examines why and how these banks were founded, and explores their impact. It then compares and contrasts the emergence of the much larger microfinance industry, primarily in emerging markets.

Chapter 5 is concerned with organic food. The impact on both human health and the health of the soil were two of the earliest environmental concerns in the nineteenth century. During the first half of the twentieth century, the principles of organic farming were developed. However, it proved challenging to persuade farmers to grow organic food and to encourage consumers to pay more for it. This chapter examines why, starting in the 1970s, organic agriculture and food consumption developed more in some countries than in others. The focus is on the limited growth of the New Zealand organic food sector in contrast with Denmark: they are similar countries in size and share significant export agribusiness sectors, but Denmark's organic food sector became significantly larger.

Chapter 6 examines why the organic wine industry has remained so small compared to the organic food industry. Even though the first organic wine ventures started in the 1970s in Germany and the United States, the organic wine industry developed slower than its organic counterparts in food and beverages, especially tea. Again, within this context, large variations in the growing and consumption of certified organic wine became apparent.

Chapter 7 looks at the growth of ecotourism in Costa Rica. Unlike the previous two chapters, this is a story of success, at least in terms of the size of the sector. This chapter explores why Costa Rica became one of the world's leading ecotourism destinations. It suggests that although Costa Rica benefits from biodiversity and a pleasant climate, the country's preeminence in ecotourism needs to be explained by more than its natural environment. While the government and NGOs have been important actors, this chapter draws particular attention to the critical role of small entrepreneurs, many of them expatriates.

Finally, Chapter 8 examines the impact of entrepreneurs who have offered alternative paths to reach their shared goal of a more sustainable world. Yvon Chouinard and Doug Tompkins were, respectively, founders of the prominent outdoor apparel brands Patagonia and The North Face in the United States. Chouinard pursued incremental sustainability strategies over decades at his firm. Tompkins, who went on to manage the fashion company Esprit, opted in 1989 to exit business entirely, having concluded that capitalism could never be sufficiently sustainable to significantly reverse environmental degradation. He and his wife, Kristine McDivitt Tompkins, who had been a highly successful CEO of Patagonia, purchased 1.5 million hectares of land in Chile and Argentina that they converted to protected areas and national parks.

VIII CONCLUSIONS

The belief that business has a responsibility for society and the natural environment in which it operates has a long history. It is striking how contemporary some of the views of Carnegie, Shibusawa, Gandhi and Donham sound. They were not prophets crying in a wilderness, but neither were they representative of general practice. During the late twentieth century, and especially after 2000, the rhetoric of corporate responsibility and sustainability became globalized. By 2018 there is hardly a large corporation anywhere in the world claiming in its published annual report that its primary purpose was solely to maximize the wealth of its shareholders. The reality, however, is often quite different. Plenty of negative social and environmental externalities from business remain, as do overall wide variations in what "corporate responsibility" means, the relationship between rhetoric and practice, and corporate motivations. This book shows both the potential for capitalism to make the world more sustainable, and the enormous challenges it continues to face in doing so.

NOTES

* This chapter appeared in an earlier version as Jones, Geoffrey, "Debating the Responsibility of Capitalism in Historical and Global Perspective," *Harvard Business School Working Paper* 14-004 (July 8, 2013). A later version was published as Jones, Geoffrey (2017), "*Gapponshugi* in Global Perspective: Debating the Responsibility of Capitalism," in Patrick Fridenson and Takeo Kikkawa (eds.) *Ethical Capitalism: Shibusawa Eiichi and Business Leadership in Global Perspective*, Toronto: University of Toronto Press, 144–69.

1. Carroll et al., *Corporate.*
2. Moon, *Corporate*, 3–5.
3. Weber, *Protestant.*
4. Quoted in Young, "Christianity," 43.
5. Werhane, *Adam Smith.*
6. Avi-Yonah, "Cyclical."
7. Gospel, *Markets*, 27–8.
8. Brandes, *American.*
9. Jeremy, "Enlightened."
10. Gardiner, *Life*, 120.
11. Fitzgerald, *Rowntree*, 217–76.
12. Dellheim, "Creation," 13–44.
13. Green, *Company.*
14. Piketty, *Capital.*
15. Cited in Carroll et al., *Corporate*, 81.
16. Zunz, *Philanthropy*, 1.
17. Carroll et al., *Corporate*, 85–7; Zunz, *Philanthropy*, 23.
18. Zunz, *Philanthropy*, 22.
19. Ibid., 296.
20. Harvey et al., "Andrew Carnegie."
21. Khurana, *Higher.*
22. Carroll et al., *Corporate*, 132–4.
23. Donham, "Social."
24. Donham, "Failure," 423; Carroll et al., *Corporate*, 179.
25. Carroll et al., *Corporate*, 169–71; Berle and Means, *Modern.*
26. Muirhead, *Corporate*; Hopkins, *History.*
27. Jeremy, *Ethics*, 365–6.
28. Wilson and Thomson, *Making*, 180.
29. Sheldon, *Philosophy*, Chapter 3.
30. Jones and Brown, "Thomas J. Watson."
31. Austin, Dávila and Jones, "Alternative."
32. Here and elsewhere Japanese names are shown in Western form, with first name first and surname last. Iwasaki and Shibusawa are the family surnames.
33. Wray, *Mitsubishi.*
34. Kimura, "Shibusawa," 124.
35. Ibid., 122–3.
36. Kikkawa, "Introduction," 6–8; Tanaka, "Harmony."
37. Juntao, "Confucian," 76.
38. Köll, *Cotton Mill*, 230–47.
39. Dobbin, *Asian*, 97.
40. Desai, "Origins," 307–18; Tripathi, *Oxford.*

41. *TATA Corporate Social Responsibility – A Century of Trust* (2010), accessed January 5, 2018 at https://www.slideshare.net/Odishadevelopment/tata-corporate-social-responsibility-a-century-of-trust.
42. Kananjia, *Godrej*.
43. Balakrishnan et al., "Multi-level," 137.
44. Ibid., 135–50.
45. Ibid., 137 n6.
46. Tripathi, *Oxford*, 260.
47. Nanda, *Gandhi's Footsteps*.
48. Jones, Kothandaraman, and Herman, "Jamnalal Bajaj."
49. Tripathi and Jumani, *Oxford*, 223.
50. Brown, *Islam*.
51. http://www.hamdard.in/legacy, accessed January 5, 2018.
52. Dávila et al., *Business Goals*.
53. Durand, "Business."
54. Puig, "Origins."
55. Marchand, *Creating*.
56. Berle, *Twentieth Century*; Carroll et al., *Corporate*, 199.
57. Spector, "Business," 318.
58. Ibid., 329; David, "Business"; Carroll et al., *Corporate*, 210–1.
59. Bowen, *Social*; Carroll et al., *Corporate*, 212–14.
60. Carroll et al., *Corporate*, 217–19; Heald, *Social*.
61. Carroll et al., *Corporate*, 246–8, 250–51.
62. Nicholas and Singleton, "Control Data"; Carroll et al., *Corporate*, 248–9.
63. Levitt, "Dangers."
64. Friedman, "Social."
65. Rey-Garcia and Puig, "Globalization."
66. Sluyterman, "Corporate."
67. Jones, *Renewing*, 247–8.
68. Kuin, *Management*.
69. Sluyterman, "Corporate," 328.
70. Jones, *Renewing*, 249.
71. Ibid., 173, 175.
72. Carroll et al., *Corporate*, Chapter 10; Carroll, "History."
73. Muller and Kok, "CSR."
74. Habisch et al., *Corporate*.
75. Balleisen, *Fraud*, Part V.
76. Zunz, *Philanthropy*, 284.
77. Luo et al.,"Mobilization."
78. Porter and Kramer, "Creating."
79. Margolis and Walsh, "Misery."
80. Barton, "Capitalism."
81. Guha, *Environmentalism*, 4.
82. Ibid., 49–54.
83. Kirk, *Counterculture*, 19.
84. Guha, "Mahatma."
85. Bowen, *Social*, 227.
86. Ibid.
87. Bansal and Hoffman, *Oxford Handbook*; Schaper, *Ecopreneurs*.
88. Elkington and Burke, *Green*; Hawken, *Ecology*.
89. Jones, *Profits*.
90. McNeil and Engelke, *Great Acceleration*.
91. Grantham, "Global trends."

REFERENCES

Austin, Gareth, Carlos Dávila and Geoffrey Jones (2017), "The Alternative Business History: Business in Emerging Markets," *Business History Review*, **91**, (3), 537–69.

Avi-Yonah, Reuven S. (2005), "The Cyclical Transformations of the Corporate Form: A Historical Perspective on Corporate Social Responsibility," *Delaware Journal of Corporate Law*, **30**, (3), 767–818.

Balakrishnan, Jaydeep, Ayesha Malhotra and Loren Falkenberg (2017), "Multi-level Corporate Responsibility: A Comparison of Gandhi's Trusteeship with Stakeholder and Stewardship Frameworks," *Journal of Business Ethics*, **141**, (1), 133–50.

Balleisen, Edward J. (2017), *Fraud: An American History from Barnum to Madoff*, Princeton, NJ: Princeton University Press.

Bansal, Pratima and Andrew J. Hoffman (eds.) (2012), *The Oxford Handbook of Business and the Natural Environment*, Oxford: Oxford University Press.

Barton, Dominic (2011), "Capitalism for the Long Term," *Harvard Business Review*, March.

Berle, Adolf A. (1954), *The Twentieth Century Capitalist Revolution*, New York: Harcourt, Brace.

Berle, Adolf A. and Gardiner C. Means (1932), *The Modern Corporation and Private Property*, New York: MacMillan.

Bowen, Howard Rothmann (1953), *Social Responsibilities of the Businessman*, New York: Harper.

Brandes, Stuart D. (1976), *American Welfare Capitalism: 1880–1940*, Chicago: University of Chicago Press.

Brown, Rajeswary (2014), *Islam in Modern Thailand. Faith, Philanthropy and Politics*, London: Macmillan.

Carroll, Archie B. (2008), "A History of Corporate Social Responsibility," in Andrew Crane, Abagail McWilliams, Dirk Matten, Jeremy Moon and Donald S. Siegel (eds.), *The Oxford Handbook of Corporate Social Responsibility*, Oxford: Oxford University Press, 19–46.

Carroll, Archie B., Kenneth J. Lipartito, James E. Post and Patricia H. Werhane (2012), *Corporate Responsibility: The American Experience*, Cambridge: Cambridge University Press.

Dávila, José Camilo, Carlos Dávila, Lina Grisales and David Schnarch (2014), *Business Goals and Social Commitment. Shaping Organizational Capabilities – Colombia's Fundación Social, 1984–2011*, Bogotá: Ediciones Uniandes.

Dellheim, Charles (1987), "The Creation of a Company Culture: Cadburys, 1861–1931," *American Historical Review*, **92**, 13–44.

Desai, Ashok (1968), "The Origins of Parsi Entrepreneurship," *Indian Economic and Social History Review*, **5**, (4), 307–18.

Dobbin, Christine (1996), *Asian Entrepreneurial Minorities: Conjoint Communities in the Making of the World Economy 1570–1940*, Richmond, UK: Curzon.

David, Donald K. (1949), "Business Responsibilities in an Uncertain World," *Harvard Business Review*, **27**, 1–8.

Donham, Wallace B. (1927), "The Social Significance of Business," *Harvard Business School Alumuni Bulletin*, July.

Donham, Wallace B. (1933), "The Failure of Business Leadership and the Responsibility of the Universities," *Harvard Business Review*, **11**, (4), 418–36.

Durand, Francisco (2005), "Business and Corporate Social Responsibility: The Peruvian Case," in Cynthia Sanborn and Felipe Portocarrero (eds.), *Philanthropy and Social Change in Latin America*, Cambridge, MA: Harvard University Press, 191–222.

Elkington, John and Tom Burke (1987), *The Green Capitalists*, London: Victor Gollancz.

Fitzgerald, Robert (1995), *Rowntree and the Marketing Revolution, 1862–1969*, Cambridge: Cambridge University Press.

Friedman, Milton (1970), "The social responsibility of business is to increase its profits," *New York Times Magazine*, September 13.

Gardiner, A.G. (1923), *Life of George Cadbury*, London: Cassell.

Gospel, Howard F. (1992), *Markets, Firms, and the Management of Labour in Modern Britain*, Cambridge: Cambridge University Press.

Grantham Research Institute on Climate Change and the Environment (2017), "Global Trends in Climate Change Legislation and Litigation: 2017 update," May 9.

Green, Hardy (2010), *The Company Town: The Industrial Edens and Satanic Mills that Shaped the American Economy*, New York: Basic Books.

Guha, Ramachandra (2000), *Environmentalism: A Global History*, New York: Longman.

Guha, Ramachandra (1998), "Mahatma Gandhi and the Environmental Movement," in Arne Kalland and Gerald Persoon (eds.), *Environmental Movements in Asia*, Richmond, UK: Curzon Press.

Habisch, André, Jan Jonker, Martina Wegner and Rene Schmidpeter (2005) (eds.), *Corporate Social Responsibility across Europe*, New York: Springer.

Harvey, Charles, Mairi Maclean, Jillian Gordon and Eleanor Shaw (2011), "Andrew Carnegie and the Foundations of Contemporary Entrepreneurial Philanthropy," *Business History*, **53**, (3), 425–50.

Hawken, Paul (1993), *The Ecology of Commerce*, New York: HarperCollins.

Heald, Morrell (1970), *The Social Responsibilities of Business, Company, and Community, 1900–1960*, Cleveland, OH: Western Reserve University Press.

Hopkins, Charles Howard (1951), *History of the Y.M.C.A. in North America*, New York: Association Press.

Jeremy, David J. (1991), "The Enlightened Paternalist in Action: William Hesketh Lever at Port Sunlight before 1914," *Business History*, **33**, (1), 58–81.

Jeremy, David J. (2009), "Ethics, Religion, and Business in Twentieth-century Britain," in Richard Coopery and Peter Lath (eds.), *Business in Britain in the Twentieth Century*, Oxford: Oxford University Press, 356–84.

Jones, Geoffrey (2005), *Renewing Unilever*, Oxford: Oxford University Press.

Jones, Geoffrey (2017), *Profits and Sustainability: A History of Green Entrepreneurship*, Oxford: Oxford University Press.

Jones, Geoffrey and Adrian Brown (2015), "Thomas J. Watson, IBM and Nazi Germany," *Harvard Business School Case 9–807–028*.

Jones, Geoffrey, Prabakar Kothandaraman and Kerry Herman (2017), "Jamnalal Bajaj, Mahatma Gandhi, and the Struggle for Indian Independence," *Harvard Business School Case 9–807–28.*

Juntao, Wang (2003), "Confucian Democrats in Chinese History," in Daniel A. Bell and Hahm Chaibong (eds.), *Confucianism for the Modern World*, Cambridge: Cambridge University Press, 69–89.

Kananjia, B.K. (1997), *Godrej: A Hundred Years, 1887–1997*, 2 vols., New Delhi: Penguin.

Kikkawa, Takeo (2017), "Introduction," in Patrick Fridenson and Takeo Kikkawa (eds.), *Ethical Capitalism: Shibusawa Eiichi and Business Leadership in Global Perspective*, Toronto: University of Toronto Press, pp. 3–13.

Kirk, Andrew G. (2007), *Counterculture Green: The Whole Earth Catalog and American Environmentalism*, Lawrence, KS: University Press of Kansas.

Köll, Elisabeth (2003), *From Cotton Mill to Business Empire: The Emergence of Regional Enterprises in Modern China*, Cambridge, MA: Harvard University Press.

Kuin, Pieter (1977), *Management is méér. De sociale verantwoordelijkheid van de ondernemer*, Amsterdam: Elsevier.

Khurana, Rakesh (2007), *From Higher Aims to Hired Hands: The Social Transformation of American Business Schools and the Unfilled Promise of Management as a Profession*, Princeton, NJ: Princeton University Press.

Kimura, Masato (2017), "Shibusawa Eiichi's View of Business Morality in Global Society," in Patrick Fridenson and Kikkawa Takeo (eds.), *Ethical Capitalism. Shibusawa Eiichi and Business Leadership in Global Perspective*, Toronto: University of Toronto Press, 121–43.

Levitt, Theodore (1958), "The Dangers of Social Responsibility," *Harvard Business Review*, **36**, (September–October), 41–50.

Luo, Xiaowei Rose, Jianjun Zhang and Christopher Marquis (2016), "Mobilization in the Internet Age: Internet Activism and Corporate Response," *Academy of Management Journal*, **59**, 2045–68.

Marchand, Roland (1998), *Creating the Corporate Soul: The Rise of Public Relations and Corporate Imagery in American Big Business*, Berkeley, CA: University of California Press.

McNeill, John R. and Peter Engelke (2014), *The Great Acceleration. An Environmental History of the Anthropocene since 1945*, Cambridge, MA: Harvard University Press.

Margolis, Joshua D. and James P. Walsh (2003), "'Misery loves companies': Rethinking social initiatives by business," *Administrative Science Quarterly*, **48**, 268–305.

Moon, Jeremy (2014), *Corporate Social Responsibility: A Very Short Introduction*, Oxford: Oxford University Press.

Muirhead, Sophia A. (1999), *Corporate Contributions: The View from 50 Years*, Report No. 1249-99-RR, Ottawa: Conference Board of Canada.

Muller, Allan and Ans Kok (2009), "CSR Performance in Emerging Markets: Evidence from Mexico," *Journal of Business Ethics*, **85**, (2), 325–37.

Nanda, B.R. (1990), *In Gandhi's Footsteps: The Life and Times of Jamnalal Bajaj*, Delhi: Oxford University Press.

Nicholas, Tom and Laura G. Singleton (2011), "Control Data Corporation and the Urban Crisis," *Harvard Business School Case 9–808–096*.

Piketty, Thomas (2014), *Capital in the Twenty-first Century*, Cambridge, MA: Harvard University Press.

Porter, Michael E. and Mark R. Kramer (2011), "Creating Shared Value," *Harvard Business Review*, **89**, nos. 1–2 (January–February), 62–77.

Puig, Nuria (2016), "The Origins of Modern Business Foundations in Spanish-speaking Countries: A Preliminary Study," in Paloma Fernández Pérez and Andrea Lluch (eds.), *Evolution of Family Business. Continuity and Change in Latin America and Spain*, Northampton, MA: Edward Elgar, 57–74.

Rey-Garcia, Marta and Nuria Puig (2013), "Globalization and the Organization of Family Philanthropy; A Case of Isomorphism," *Business History*, **55**, (6), 1019–46.

Schaper, Michael (ed.) (2005), *Making Ecopreneurs: Developing Sustainable Entrepreneurship*, Aldershot, UK: Ashgate.

Sheldon, Oliver (1923), *The Philosophy of Management*, London: Pitman.

Sluyterman, Keetie (2012), "Corporate Social Responsibility of Dutch Entrepreneurs in the 20th century," *Enterprise & Society*, **13**, (2), 313–349.

Spector, Bert (2008), "'Business Responsibilities in a Divided World': The Cold War Roots of the Corporate Social Responsibility Movement," *Enterprise & Society*, **9**, (2), 314–36.

Tanaka, Kazuhiro (2017), "Harmony between Morality and Economy," in Patrick Fridenson and Takeo Kikkawa (eds.), *Ethical Capitalism; Shibusawa Eiichi and Business Leadership in Global Perspective*, Toronto: University of Toronto Press, 35–58.

Tripathi, Dwijendra (2004), *Oxford History of Indian Business*, New Delhi: Oxford University Press.

Tripathi, Dwijendra and Jyoti Jumani (2013), *The Oxford History of Contemporary Indian Business*, Oxford: Oxford University Press.

Weber, Max (2011), *The Protestant Ethic and the Spirit of Capitalism*, Oxford: Oxford University Press.

Werhane, Patricia H. (1991), *Adam Smith and his Legacy for Modern Capitalism*, Oxford: Oxford University Press.

Wilson, John F. and Andrew Thomson (2006), *The Making of Modern Management, British Management in Historical Perspective*, Oxford: Oxford University Press.

Wray, William D. (1984), *Mitsubishi and the N.Y.K., 1870–1914*, Cambridge, MA: Harvard University Press.

Young, B.W. (1989), "Christianity, Secularization and Political Economy," in David J. Jeremy (ed.), *Religion, Business and Wealth on Modern Britain*, London: Routledge, 35–54.

Zunz, Oliver (2011), *Philanthropy in America: A History*, Princeton, NJ: Princeton University Press.

2. Business and waste management in Europe before 1945*

With Andrew Spadafora

I INTRODUCTION

This chapter examines the role of private business in the municipal solid waste industry in Europe from the late nineteenth century until 1945. Central and Northern Europe, and especially Germany, are the primary foci, as particularly interesting business models emerged there in response to the first big environmental problem faced by the world after the Industrial Revolution.

As industrialization spread, urban populations soared, causing a growing waste problem. The nature of waste also changed with the creation of new materials such as packaging. Manufacturing caused new types of industrial waste, such as spent coals.[1] In the twenty-first century, the problem of waste has not been remotely solved but remains a huge contributor to global warming and poses health threats to billions of people. Yet a few developed countries, including Germany and Sweden, have made great strides in recycling waste and recovering energy.[2] This chapter shows that it was during this early historical period that some foundations of this later success were laid down.

Historians have studied the growth of waste generated by industrial capitalism on both sides of the Atlantic. Most attention has been given to the response of municipal governments and their creation of publicly owned waste utilities.[3] A smaller and more recent literature has looked at for-profit businesses that remained active in the industry.[4] These businesses are less well known, however, because not only have historians paid greater attention to public sector waste-service providers, but also because these companies were often unable to achieve sustained profitability for long, and they often failed.

This chapter seeks to recover the largely forgotten early history of these waste entrepreneurs. It will explore what they did and why, and examine their struggle to create long-lasting businesses. Section II describes the emergence of waste as an environmental problem when industrialization spread and municipal waste departments were formed. The next sections examine the role of private business, in particular dimensions of the waste industry. Section III examines the role of the business in "dust-free" waste collection. Sections IV and V turn to the businesses of incineration and composting. Section VI looks at the changing role and organizational structure of scrap merchants. Section VII examines early recycling businesses. Section VIII considers the company built by the pioneering Berlin-based recycling entrepreneur Carl von der Linde, and briefly looks at the stories of other such ventures through the Nazi regime in Germany between 1933 and 1945. A final section concludes.

II WASTE AND MUNICIPALIZATION

Prior to the twentieth century, ordinary citizens in Europe and the United States generated little waste in an absolute sense. They practiced a "stewardship of objects," in which reuse was nearly universal owing to the pressures imposed by economic necessity under conditions of low incomes. The scarcity even of basic resources made it economical to reuse old metal, textiles, leather, wood and so forth in the production of new goods, while organic kitchen waste and animal carcasses were used for fodder, soap or glue; and bodily wastes as fertilizer. One factor promoting these preindustrial patterns of reuse in the home, farm or workshop was the relative simplicity of the materials from which most goods were made: without complicated alloys, synthetic or artificial materials, or the combination of multiple materials in a single product, collection and treatment of old materials for reuse was unproblematic. What could not be reused was generally burned for heat in fireplaces or was usually biodegradable.[5]

The above description is a better fit for the countryside than the cities. It was in the new industrial cities of the nineteenth century that waste first became a problem and a domain that attracted profit-seeking businesses. There appears to have been a common pattern of development in urban central Europe. Sanitation in the cities changed relatively little for centuries before the 1830s, when cholera epidemics induced health professionals and city officials to consider measures to improve urban water and sewerage infrastructure, but solid waste management efforts generally lagged several decades behind.[6] Government officials in the eighteenth and early nineteenth centuries generally dealt with the problem of solid waste by issuing municipal ordinances prohibiting inhabitants from dumping their household waste in the streets or public squares. Where these ordinances were actually observed, residents unloaded waste in unsanitary *Sammelgruben* (collecting pits) in the interior courts of their apartment houses. Small entrepreneurial disposal firms – often simply a single man with a horse and cart – emptied these periodically, and would contract with a household to transport its waste from the city to the outskirts, where the firm would then deposit it or, more often, sell it to local farmers as fertilizer.[7] Some German cities offered concessions to a smaller number of firms for wider-scale waste removal and street cleaning, based on the lowest bid for services. In a handful of cases, such as in Hamburg between 1850 and 1869, towns charged entrepreneurs for the right to pick up and resell the wastes in the countryside.[8] In other cases, such as in Nuremberg, local farmers themselves removed the waste.[9]

Three main factors led to the decline of such early, agricultural-based waste "recycling" systems during the second half of the nineteenth century: (1) it was subject to the growing critique by health professionals; (2) the rapid acceleration of urbanization in industrial cities led to increases in the quantity of waste that overwhelmed the existing infrastructure and local agricultural demand; and (3) the content of urban wastes changed. Farmers' use for urban waste diminished as the proportion of glass and metal packaging increased and as the cities' sewer systems expanded, thereby reducing the proportion of organic waste useful as fertilizer just as lower-priced chemical fertilizers were also becoming available.[10] The growing indiscriminate dumping of wastes not wanted by farmers raised questions both of space and of sanitation.

These factors prompted a response from municipal governments in Germany and elsewhere. A number of large cities, including Frankfurt, Mannheim and Dortmund, municipalized water provision, sewerage and street-cleaning functions.[11] However, small cities could not afford to provide services themselves, so they continued to use private firms. Even among large German cities, many continued to contract with or simply allowed private waste-service providers, while the private sector always provided service outside of the central city, even in those jurisdictions with municipal control. Berlin, for instance, was estimated to have some 60 such disposal firms in the early 1890s.[12] Yet, small traditional waste haulers tended to neglect their obligations in areas of the city best served by municipal sewers, as they had difficulties covering the cost of frequent pick-ups when they were no longer able to sell the waste in the countryside.[13]

There was increased municipalization in Germany and elsewhere after 1890. Many municipal waste departments were founded.[14] Nevertheless, many cities still opted to contract with a small number of private firms – or often a single firm, as in the cities of Leipzig, Dresden, and Chemnitz – to attain a uniform, regulated collection pattern and to ensure that certain hygienic standards were met.[15] By 1910, 77 German cities with populations above 25,000 had municipalized trash collection, while 44 had contracted with private firms and 48 had not made any specific arrangements.[16]

The disruption of the old waste collection and disposal system by economic, demographic and technological development, then, led to increased political involvement in the waste industry. There were also many experimental ventures by private business, especially after 1890. In a number of cases, these ventures can be seen as predecessors for modern waste collection and recycling enterprises.

III BUSINESS AND "DUST-FREE" WASTE COLLECTION

Practices changed both in collection and in disposal during the late nineteenth century. Among the more interesting strategies was the effort to keep cities cleaner through *staubfrei* (dust-free) collection. In 1895, Berlin, one of the fastest growing cities in Europe, decided to combat the plague of dust and ash generated in the streets by trash pick-ups and open-topped trash wagons by enacting an ordinance requiring all waste removal firms to adopt "dust-free" collection practices by using closed containers which the firms, not the residents, were now obligated to provide.[17] This commitment to dust-free collection put Berlin in the vanguard, as other German cities did not adopt this practice until at least the 1920s, while elsewhere, as in Britain, the spread of dust-free systems awaited post-1945 rationalization of waste management.[18]

Complying with the 1895 ordinance put many of the smaller Berlin firms out of business or forced them to raise prices to such a high level that the Wirtschafts-Genossenschaft Berliner Grundbesitzer (WBG), a recently formed group of the city's property-holders, entered the market as a cooperative waste disposal company, the Berliner Grundbesitzer GmbH. Initially intended simply to negotiate terms with the existing private firms, the WBG began to purchase its own containers and fleet of collection wagons. Shortly after 1895, four firms – the WBG, the Staubschutz GmbH, the Vereinigte Müllabfuhrunternehmer, and B. Röhrecke – dominated the market, all of which employed patented collection systems using one of two methods. In the *Sammelkastensystem* the firm provided trash cans that closely fitted into openings in a covered collection wagon, thereby avoiding spillage; in the *Wechseltonnensystem*, the collection wagons contained empty cans that were exchanged each time with households' full cans at the pick-up point.

The Staubschutz company, whose very name implied its commitment to the new dust-free mandate, represented the *Sammelkastensystem* in the city. Its emphasis on "the requirements of modern hygiene" and the avoidance of fire, dust and spread of spoiled and sickness-causing garbage quickly gained it market share.[19] Between its start of operations in 1895 and October 1898, the company expanded to supply collection services by multiyear contract to 2,750 properties in Berlin and to 600 in Charlottenburg, a neighboring wealthy suburb that subsequently became part of the city.[20] Aware that most Berlin waste was destined for dumping in the countryside, Staubschutz not only provided for a dust-free interface between individual garbage cans and its collection wagons but it also designed the wagons to allow for the direct loading of their separable containers onto trains or barges. The company was particularly successful in its cultivation of public clients and government ministries, boasting numerous state officials in its testimonials.[21]

The WBG, which by contrast used the *Wechseltonnensystem*, served 11,224 properties in Berlin in 1903, a number it claimed to be approximately half the total in the city.[22] The following year, the city's decision to require by ordinance that all wastes be transferred dust-free to the rail cars that carried them out of Berlin and to dumping grounds in the countryside had a radical effect on the WBG and other companies. Ultimately, the 1904 ordinance contributed to the WBG's market control by raising costs even further for the remaining for-profit firms, and it also required a risky program of major capital expenditures and acquisitions. Because of its collection system, which required the emptying of many thousands of small individual trashcans into open rail cars, the WBG could not comply with the ordinance without changing its system. It consequently bought Staubschutz GmbH, the only one of its main rivals that operated on the *Sammelkastensystem*, allowing for fewer, larger containers and thereby easier dust-free rail transfer, and it ordered thousands of new trash bins and the wagon systems suited to the new method. It also purchased two of its other largest rivals, the Berliner Abfuhrgesellschaft and Hermann Scheller, both of which had approached WBG about being acquired, presumably because of their inability to comply with the new ordinance.[23] In 1904 the firm counted 14,533 Berlin properties among its clients, and by the following year it served 23,284 separate properties.[24] By 1914 the WBG could count some 90 percent of

Berlin households as clients dispersed across 39,680 properties. Its continued positive earnings, effective management of strikes and maintenance of the lowest prices in the city allowed it to outcompete and purchase its remaining rivals. Overall, it acquired 31 other collection businesses across its two decades of operation.[25]

The WBG, then, grew as a highly successful cooperative business venture in waste, skilled in relations with the municipality and able to acquire and absorb competitors. However, World War I was a major exogenous shock. The company suffered from severe labor shortages as the war dragged on, and many employees left for the Front or for more pressing industrial service. Initial attempts in 1915 to substitute prisoners of war for German collection workers led to indifferent results, and the WBG was compelled to increase its fee by 25 percent to cover growing costs.[26] The year 1916 brought even greater difficulties, now including transportation problems: horses were requisitioned and horse fodder became scarce, as did railroad cars available for the removal of wastes from the city, while staffing problems continued and service fees increased again.[27] The next two years saw continually decreasing capacity and performance. After the German surrender in 1918, the cooperative despaired of its ability to provide anything resembling adequate services without workers or equipment and with the freeing of the war prisoners by revolutionaries in the winter of 1918–19, although it was still serving 37,701 households on the last day of 1918.[28]

Although the WBG barely survived the war, it did not survive the period of instability and inflation that followed. It failed in 1922.[29] Its successor, the Berliner Müllabfuhr AG (BEMAG), was a private firm, though with a substantial share of public ownership. The short-lived company embodied the tensions inherent in most waste collection services in major cities with the multiple goals of preserving city sanitation and public health, providing residents with efficient service and controlling costs. Building on the heritage of the monopolistic WBG, with which it had close connections, the businessmen behind BEMAG argued that a citywide private firm with special privileges and public oversight was the only effective way of reconciling these tensions. As a private company, the founders suggested, BEMAG would avoid the "bureaucratic narrowness" of municipal departments and benefit from decades of private-sector expertise in the industry. However, the simultaneous involvement of the city would extend from partial capitalization of the enterprise to supervision by city officials who could represent the public interest in matters of public health and hygiene, alleviating the traditional concerns of conflicts of interest between profit and health.[30] BEMAG's founders claimed that only a large firm, and not congeries of smaller competing firms, could represent the common interest. It was given a legal monopoly through a city ordinance requiring Berlin households to contract with the company for collection services.[31]

BEMAG inherited a very labor-intensive business. Managing an enterprise serving 60,000 properties required an office staff alone of approximately 220, mostly for making fee assessments and fee collections, and for book-keeping and filing. There were 35 inspectors who monitored the daily activities of the collection workers.[32] BEMAG needed the infusion of public capital in order to rebuild and modernize its collection infrastructure, especially to motorize collection vehicles. Motorization was seen as essential to achieve profitability.[33] However, it proved very difficult to make necessary investments and earn profits. As a result, the public ownership of BEMAG gradually increased from an initial 25 percent to over 85 percent in 1927. It was reorganized as a city government entity under the Nazi regime after 1933.[34]

The need to provide dust-free service, first in Berlin and then especially in the 1920s in other German cities, generated demand for the manufacture of new equipment to supply the collection companies. The most prominent firm to enter this market was the sheet metal products manufacturer Schmidt & Melmer, which became a producer of metal receptacles for the various systems and itself was a patent-holder for several of the most successful products.[35] The company managed to renew its success in selling trash container systems in various eras of Germany's turbulent history; pre-World War I success was duplicated in the 1920s with the new "Es-Em" system, a variant of the *Sammelkastensystem*, which was adopted in many large German cities and used in Hamburg, Frankfurt, Mannheim and many others until the 1950s.[36] There were many other firms not only producing equipment designed for collection systems but also garbage cans for nonsystematic collection. Peter Bauer Fahrzeugfabrik, of Cologne, produced both street-cleaning vehicles and various dust-free waste pick-up wagons, selling them to cities such as Cologne and Hamburg prior to World War II.[37]

The desire for dust-free waste collection, then, created an ecosystem of waste collection and engineering companies. In their pronouncements, they promoted a vision of the urban environment that was healthier, cleaner and more aesthetically appealing, and as such might be seen as presaging later concerns with environmental protection in some ways. However, as the case of BEMAG showed, the more mechanized the business became, the more difficult it was for the private sector to run a profitable operation.

IV SEEKING PROFITS IN INCINERATION

The initial and primary way that waste was disposed of in Berlin (and other German cities) was for companies, no matter the size, to dump collections in the countryside. However, a number of other methods were also used by private businesses. The first was incineration, a process pioneered in Britain in the 1870s. The process soon attracted the favorable attention of doctors and public health officials in Germany owing to its alleged elimination of materials seen as key contributors to epidemic diseases. The pioneering incineration plants in Britain became the destination of many German municipal inquiry commissions.[38]

Aside from their imputed sanitary advantage, advocates pointed out that incineration did not just "remove" garbage from space-deprived cities (or, in reality, only greatly reduce its weight and volume while producing air pollution in the process) but it also generated useful byproducts.[39] Principal among these were energy and clinker to be used as building material, for instance in the construction of roads. The first incinerator in Germany was built in Hamburg in 1896, after a major cholera epidemic of 1892 had raised alarms about dumping in the countryside. In Britain around the same time, emphasis shifted from incineration simply as a way of addressing the waste issue to generating electricity from the burning of refuse, with its relatively high concentration of leftover coals; the first incineration plant in Britain directly linked to an electrical power plant was constructed in 1897.[40]

The German plants at Hamburg and elsewhere benefited by being followers of the British experience.[41] However, local conditions varied and it was not a straightforward matter to transfer technologies between cities. Berlin had particular trouble owing to the low calorific content of the burned bituminous coal and the higher-than-usual levels of ash generated by Berlin residents; other cities such as Potsdam and Magdeburg faced similar problems.[42]

The incinerators were municipal projects, but city officials relied on entrepreneurial engineers to develop incineration facilities that took into account the specific needs of German cities (based in part on the calorific content of the refuse in these cities) for construction and operation of the plants.[43] Engineers developed other processes to increase the yield of useful materials from incineration.[44] The machinery manufacturer BAMAG-Meguin, which licensed the right to manufacture in Germany the proprietary system of a British company, supplemented its incineration equipment with salvage or recovery systems in the 1920s.[45] These included the magnetic separation of ferrous metals from the waste stream

and forced-air separation of paper for recovery.[46] The company principally targeted municipal governments. In its marketing, as with other
incineration engineering firms, BAMAG portrayed landfilling as out-
moded and unhealthy. Explicitly placing the use of its system in the
context of the movement toward "rational" management and efficiency
seen in the 1920s, the company contended that incineration with materials recovery should take its place alongside other municipal facilities
such as gas, water, and electricity plants and sewage systems. Conversion
from basic incineration to this combined recovery process was presented
as the "modern" approach to incinerating wastes. BAMAG also promoted
its waste recovery plants as capable of yielding income in the course of
providing their key service – the protection of public health. The
company emphasized the output of the incineration process in steam for
heating or electricity generation and in clinker for reuse in building
materials and road construction.[47]

Kurt Gerson, an enterprising engineer in Berlin, made it his personal
mission to improve on what he saw as the wastefulness inherent in
generating only two main byproducts from incineration, expensive steam
and equally expensive and unnecessary clinker-based building materials.[48] He founded the publicly traded company Müllverwertung AG in
Berlin in 1925, taking over the failed BEMAG incineration plant, on the
"Red Island" in Schöneberg, in order to produce not only clinker and
energy but also what he called *Müllwolle* (literally, garbage-wool) made
from cellulose and animal fibers within the refuse gathered for the
plant.[49] Gerson developed multiple processes designed to separate
organic and nonorganic wastes. The organic, fibrous elements of the
plant's waste input, when processed as *Müllwolle*, could be resold for use
in paper and paperboard making, lightweight building material (with
cement), tar-based chemicals and heating briquettes, while dust and ash
produced in the process could be set aside toward inclusion in synthetic
fertilizers or in macadam. Gerson also aimed to produce a form of
synthetic silk to be used for consumer products such as women's
stockings.[50] Gerson can be seen as a true pioneer of the much later
concepts of how to combine profitability and social value.

Gerson's company operated throughout the 1920s, employing approximately 35 workers and a small office staff.[51] However Gerson, who was
probably Jewish, lost control over the enterprise with the Nazi advent to
power. The same industrial site was occupied during the mid-1930s by a
firm known as Aretz Faserstoffplatten GmbH, run by Willi Aretz, a
chemist and Nazi Party member, who aimed to generate many of the
same products out of city waste. Though praised in the Nazi press for his

work in contributing to national recycling goals, the neighboring population complained about the intensifying pollution and odors. Aretz's firm was mainly known for its attempt to make building board for construction and a product known as *Bodenkulturmatte*, a dry, matte-like board made of organic materials that could be laid in small gardens to decompose, thereby fertilizing the soil. The poor quality of the building materials produced may have been the main reason for the firm's failure in 1937.[52]

V THE BUSINESS OF COMPOSTING

A number of businesses promoted innovative composting schemes rather than pulverizing waste. Composting was especially popular in the Netherlands where city governments ran facilities, and, after 1929, a state-controlled joint stock company, the Vuil Afvoer Maatschappij (VAM), ran them.[53] Composting had also gained a foothold in Germany around the turn of the century. In the late 1890s, one of the leading Berlin waste collection entrepreneurs, Bruno Röhrecke, tested various crops of vegetables, grains and flowers on land fertilized with composted Berlin waste. There were similar efforts in Cologne.[54] During World War I, there were multiple composting efforts; for instance, a facility was erected at Neumünster in 1915, which operated successfully for a decade but then faced decreasing prices as the fertilizing value of its product declined, leading it to go out of business in 1930.[55]

One of the most successful efforts to use composted waste for farming came from Arthur Schurig, an entrepreneurial farmer. After experimenting with crops and intensified mechanization on his farm, Schurig took the unusual step of returning to urban waste fertilization – on a massive scale. Starting in 1907, he purchased organic kitchen wastes from Charlottenburger Abfuhrgesellschaft, which sorted waste in the wealthy Berlin suburb of Charlottenburger (this venture is discussed later) to fertilize his estate in Etzin, just outside Berlin. As he expanded, he also used unsorted, previously composted Berlin garbage to create a loamy surface on moor and sandy soil for later planting. Given the chemical composition (especially of ash) of this fertilizer, the reclaimed land was especially suited to certain types of planting, such as hemp and sugar beets. Schurig became the largest vegetable producer in Germany, supplying markets throughout Berlin before his death in 1932.[56]

Composting attracted chemists, biologists and engineers, all of whom sought to create profitable businesses from their understanding of both agricultural science and the treatment of urban wastes. Franz Boerner, for example, established the company Franz Boerner Müllverwertung in Breslau in the 1920s. He sought to "completely solve the waste recovery question" while simultaneously improving agricultural soil by adding his patented chemical additive, Kulturin, to waste-based fertilizers.[57] Sympathizing with some critics of incineration, Boerner observed that focusing on production of agricultural fertilizers from waste would save the expense of adding extra coal to incinerators to deal with the large portion of household waste already constituted of ash, merely in order to gain costly clinker for building. Instead, he suggested employing a waste-sorting system, in which ash and other particulate matter in household waste was separated out, subjected to germicidal treatment and enriched with his Kulturin to generate effective fertilizer.[58] In a circular to prospective investors and customers, Boerner promised both high profits and the opportunity to provide a product that would serve the "common good of the German people."[59]

In neighboring Austria, a limited partnership known as the Edaphon-Müllverwertung Commanditgesellschaft (hereafter Edaphon) was established in Salzburg in 1930 to utilize the patented composting processes of the biologist Raoul Heinrich Francé, a former director of the Biological Institute of Munich. Although little is known about the actual operations of this firm, which were conducted by Salzburg businessman K. F. Höller, Francé was a highly public advocate for the need to make use of urban wastes in creating natural fertilizers for organic farming that preserved humus and soil biota endangered by modern chemically intensive agriculture. His research during the 1920s suggested that it was not just bacterial activity but also the activity of all soil organisms that enriched the soil with the requisite minerals for agricultural productivity and kept it aerated. The company marketed a nonsynthetic, sanitary and purportedly odorless fertilizer to organic farmers, which aimed to promote a regular nitrogen "cycle" through the right mix of soil-preserving organisms rather than by adding synthetic phosphates and nitrogen to the soil.[60]

Edaphon's method was to take in municipal solid waste, street sweepings and sewage as its raw materials. The company pitch was that the product "transforms garbage into something useful and contributes to the cleaning of cities."[61] For Francé, this use of waste, and especially the preservation of the soil that would result, was a duty so high that it called for religious language and metaphors of rebirth and resurrection. City wastes were, chemically speaking, just as much a part of the natural cycle as those that remained on the farm; indeed, they must "be included in the cycle of composition and decomposition. Their comparison with the fertilizers of the farm's own [internal] economy is therefore imperative and their orderly return to the soil a duty."[62] The composted fertilizer product itself was advertised using language with a very modern feel; an advertisement from the 1930s testified: "Edaphon Humus Fertilizer is a pure natural product and contains no artificial chemical salts."[63] In addition to the Salzburg plant, the company was able to license its process to plants in Munich and in Milan, Italy during the 1930s.[64]

Composting, then, served as the basis for several large businesses in the interwar years. It was also an activity with impassioned advocates, as demonstrated by the environmentalist, even religious, discourse of Francé and Edaphon.

VI SCRAP MERCHANTS

Sorting and reselling useful scrap material was the basis both of the traditional scrap industry and of the new recycling plants that sprang up in various cities beginning in the 1890s. Like the waste-to-fertilizer industry, the scrap trade had ancient roots but underwent substantial changes in the late nineteenth and early twentieth centuries. Prior to intensive industrial production and technological changes in such scrap-using industries as steelmaking and papermaking, scrap had been gathered on a small scale by large numbers of scavenger firms and by peddlers trading new goods for rag, bone, old metal and other worn-out objects from households. Paris was famous for its *chiffoniers* (rag-pickers), gathering old textiles for use in the paper industry, but the trade existed even in the smallest localities. There were an estimated 7,500 chiffoniers in the city in 1884, who formed a sort of open guild and established procedures for sorting useful scrap from trash containers on the streets. Even more than in the organized sorting facilities discussed shortly, the health risks to these independent workers were very high, particularly from infected rags.[65]

In Germany, such scavengers were known as *Naturforscher*, or naturalists, and they generally specialized in a particular product such as rags or glass. As in Paris, they operated on the streets and also in dumps, and in some cases were hired by small-scale entrepreneurs, who leased the right to sort through stored garbage from the disposal firms.[66] In Vienna, such work tended to be carried out by women, who worked 12 hours a day for low wages.[67] The work was low status and risky, and there were low barriers to entry, making it either a practice turned to in desperation or an area in which poor but entrepreneurial individuals could rapidly shape a successful business. In Germany, Jewish minorities often owned scrap firms.[68]

Although the industry continued to contain numerous small firms well into the middle decades of the twentieth century, scrap collection and dealing was powerfully affected by the pace and scale of late nineteenth-century industrialization, which led to the formation of larger scrap companies and more extended trade networks. Technological changes in the paper industry in the mid-nineteenth century allowed for rapid growth in productivity and a search among papermakers for ever-larger quantities of cotton and linen rags, old paper and other fibrous materials – eventually including wood pulp toward the end of the century, when cellulose from wood began to replace rags as the favored input for the industry. Scrap metal was second only to rags in the late nineteenth century and soon grew to be the dominant branch of the scrap industry, as the open-hearth process allowed for higher temperatures in steel-making, which burned away phosphorus and other impurities and allowed for greater use of scrap iron (up to 90 percent), as compared to the Bessemer process (the initial technology used to mass-produce steel from molten pig iron). Scrap businesses were not always started by poor or marginal entrepreneurs; sometimes they developed out of existing mer-chant enterprises that became engaged in a sideline trade in scrap material. This was the case for one of Denmark's largest scrap busi-nesses, H.J. Hansen A/S.[69] Founded in 1829 by J.J. Limkilde, a small dry goods merchant in Odense, the business prospered under his son in the mid-nineteenth century and began to carry on a trade in rags, bone and scrap iron with its often-rural customers. However, the scrap trade likely generated less than half of the firm's business until the 1890s:[70] bought by H.J. Hansen in 1888 and taking his name, the firm quickly expanded its rag trade beyond exchanges with customers to buying from an army of small peddlers and reselling rags to Odense's Dalum Paper Factory, and eventually to other papermakers in Jutland.[71]

The number of firms making iron and other metal products in Denmark more than doubled between 1888 and 1897, to some 462. Odense became the country's second major industrial city after Copen-hagen, and H.J. Hansen attempted to meet the expansion of demand for scrap. Expanding its industrial customer network into Germany, Norway, Sweden and, to a lesser extent, Britain, the firm met competition within Denmark principally from the two large Copenhagen firms: Petersen & Albeck, and Joseph Levin. Hansen did well during World War I as prices of old metal shot up. Crisis conditions proved lucrative for scrap recycling, but the firm also weathered a subsequent dramatic drop in prices. The firm's diversified product lines – having kept the dry goods business and expanded into the wine trade – were key to survival. In 1929 it was still the third largest scrap dealer in Denmark. By then, the early days of low barriers to entry had given way to an oligopolistic structure in which large firms such as H.J. Hansen specialized in particular product lines and pursued large-scale contracts with industrial clients.[72]

In scrap metal particularly, some major corporations developed their own scrap divisions or subsidiaries – among them giant German steel producers Thyssen, which treated the scrap business as an opportunity for vertical integration.[73] More easily recognizable as a modern recycling business was the subsidiary of the large family-owned Berlin/Essen chemical company Th. Goldschmidt. In 1889 it developed the "first technically practicable and economically exploitable method of the de-tinning of cans," allowing the firm to recoup the valuable tin used to coat new packaged food products.[74]

Goldschmidt's de-tinning business, like other early recycling efforts, probably owed its existence solely to economic rather than ecological reasoning. It first used electrolysis in a process patented by the chemist and partner in the company, Hans Goldschmidt, but it required a great deal of electrical power. After 1905 the firm switched to a second process involving chlorine, which made large-scale can-processing possible. Despite the dangers of toxicity in the latter process – recovered tin could not be used in cans and caused a number of injuries and illnesses at the firm, including among the Goldschmidts themselves – this second process was used until 1943. The firm became multinational, owing to its need to secure a supply of used cans sizeable and steady enough to make mass processing possible. It expanded into London, Paris and Glasgow, and operated purchasing networks throughout Western Europe and the United States. Unlike other scrap businesses, world wars were very difficult for Goldschmidt because of the complete disruption of its international purchasing networks; its Essen de-tinning facility was also destroyed in 1943. Nevertheless, the de-tinning subsidiary was also protected from the large price swings that threatened other scrap businesses because it was part of a large diversified firm. It was able to ride out the first net losses in the 1920s when secondary metal prices dropped and concerns about the potential exhaustion of tin mines in Bolivia and Indonesia led can manufacturers to redesign their products so as to reduce the amount of tin used, causing Goldschmidt to redouble its efforts to expand its supply networks for used cans.[75]

VII SALVAGE AND EARLY RECYCLING BUSINESSES

Firms like Goldschmidt's de-tinning business or Schurig's agribusiness, which did not do their own direct scrap collection, relied on others to provide them with the right sort of materials. The newest types of firms in the recycling industry around 1900 were those that became involved in the large-scale collection and sorting of waste. There were parallels between these firms and the expanding scrap business; for example, they took their cue as much from the need to process waste as a quasi-environmental problem of pollution in the cities as from the desire to increase economic efficiency, and they aimed to produce a profitable business model in doing so, a goal that usually remained elusive.

Perhaps the first such facility in the world began operating in Hungary in 1895. Budapest's city waste collection had been municipalized, but much of what was gathered found its way to the privately owned sorting facility originally on the outskirts of the city under contract to the city. The plant sorted and sold waste products, generating its own electricity. The firm contracted with another firm in Munich which opened a more sophisticated operation in the suburb of Puchheim in 1898.[76]

Presorting of waste at the Munich plant was done by sieve and then hand-sorting on conveyor belts. Workers were provided with uniforms and gloves that were washed and disinfected once per week; the floors were disinfected twice daily; and an infirmary was opened reported to counter the outbreaks of infection which had occurred during the first decades of the plant's operation. The recovered materials, particularly bones, rags, paper and glass, were treated and disinfected before being resold. Kitchen garbage was boiled and used as fodder for the firm's own piggery. Although the plant burned down in 1901, it was rebuilt; and the city of Munich renewed its contract with the company several times. Financially, the firm was dependent on the payment of a subsidy. The resale of the recovered scrap accounted for about three-quarters of the cost of wages, quite aside from overhead. The firm also earned regular income from its own agricultural operations, including the piggery.[77] This operation may have been the most successful of the early recycling facilities in central Europe, and it lasted until World War II.

Sorting facilities were not the only enterprises that aimed to solve the waste problem through reuse; collection firms, too, became involved in several German cities and elsewhere, including Sweden.[78] Among the Berlin collection ventures, Staubschutz GmbH sought early on to provide salvage or recycling services for both agricultural and industrial reuse of wastes. Using sieves to separate the dust and ash from the larger items, as in Budapest and Munich, the company also more innovatively added forced-air systems to further remove ash and collect it, after which the remaining waste was sent through a steam chamber for disinfection. Workers specializing in particular product, such as bones and metals, processed it as it passed by on conveyor belts, while an air circulation system partially improved conditions for them, and organic wastes remained on the belt for final collection and agricultural use. The company emphasized that its disinfection process differentiated it from other contemporary sorting systems.[79] Compared to competing disposal solutions, such as incineration, the company claimed to base its salvage efforts on the "economically most rational foundations" and that it used the simplest, most proven methods, allowing it to provide the best solution for the intensifying urban waste problem and to receive the active approval of the German Agricultural Society.[80]

Subsequently, and just after the outbreak of World War I, the WBG undertook an exploratory study of waste recovery in Berlin based on a bipartite source-separation system that would keep food wastes separate from all other forms.[81] A number of local experiments were conducted, and subsequently its successor, BEMAG, committed to widen its remit beyond collection to "the disposal of waste hygienically and cheaply for the general public, and to create from these waste materials the greatest economic value possible."[82] Attempts were made to introduce the creation of heat and electricity, fertilizers, tar products and building materials from the wastes.[83] As noted earlier, however, the venture struggled to be profitable, and was largely publicly owned by the late 1920s.

VIII RECYCLING, CARL VON DER LINDE AND CAG

Prior to World War I, all but one of the companies that institutionalized salvage efforts as part of the management of urban wastes adopted a single-stream approach, using machinery to separate useful items from one another after they were collected from households. The exception lay in the sizeable and wealthy Berlin suburb of Charlottenburg, then with a population of about 250,000. Following earlier developments in New York City,[84] the city hired the firm Charlottenburger Abfuhrgesellschaft (CAG) to introduce the *Dreiteilungssystem*, or three-way source-separation system, for the recycling of household wastes. The entrepreneur behind CAG, Carl von der Linde, always maintained the system was not directly copied from New York.[85]

Experimentation from 1900 onward showed the adequacy of the system, so city government officials were persuaded that a source-separation and recycling system was preferred over any other method of waste management because it appeared to offer the best chance of recovering valuable materials from the waste stream, thus achieving efficiency. Citizens were obliged by city ordinance to separate their waste into the three categories: dust and ashes; garbage (organic waste, including animal and vegetable matter); and dry, bulky rubbish that was potentially commercially reusable. CAG provided residents with three corresponding bins in apartment house courtyards, or a tripartite container for an individual household complete with removable sacks. These wastes were collected by separate carts at least weekly, and taken by train either to a dump in the case of the ashes or to the firm's sorting facility in Seegefeld, where the rubbish was further processed much in the manner of the Munich-Puchheim facility. The firm used recovered organic materials in a piggery, resold scrap materials, and incinerated residual materials for power generation.

Von der Linde wrote about the waste business and about his own firm. He saw his venture as a means of husbanding scarce resources and opposing disposal practices that wasted materials, and he shared with younger peers like Gerson a mix of economic, social and incipient ecological goals. In a pair of pamphlets from 1902 and 1906, von der Linde showed himself to be aware of the environmental damage to groundwater and surface water, and to human habitation, caused by dumping of waste. He was concerned about the ways in which urban life had separated city-dwellers from what he considered the more natural conditions of the farm. On farms, he observed, the three waste categories were never mixed but always kept separate for their proper uses.[86] He condemned ocean dumping for being unsanitary, for "pollution" of the water, and for the disfigurement of the coast.[87] In discussing the reasons he advocated the three-way source-separation system, he observed that one of its advantages was the ability to bury the ash and dust that had been presorted from the organic matter or garbage in pits outside of the cities, without raising concerns about vapors and water contamination.[88]

Von der Linde's major motivation was not pollution prevention or concern over urban lifestyles, but finding ways to prevent the waste of resources that were mistakenly regarded as useless, much like the chemist tasked with finding all possible uses for byproducts of existing processes – a heroic figure in the Germany of his day to whom von der Linde made an explicit appeal.[89] He argued that Germany, in particular, needed to learn to depend on an intensive use of its *own* resources, rather than (for example) on colonies, and that waste was one such resource, useful for fodder, various industrial employments and fertilizer.[90] The three-way separation system was key to the plan. He concluded: "Thus each product finds its interested party, be it only for combustion for the production of energy."[91] He also emphasized the benefits to health that arise from avoiding the mixing of wastes and the putrescence such mixing produces in otherwise unobjectionable items, and observed that the extra incentive given the private entrepreneur by the possibility of reselling the separated organic matter as fodder would induce him to move the waste faster and more effectively, preventing offense and health hazards.[92]

Von der Linde's business case for the CAG and its source-separation system depended at least as much on showing the inadequacies of the alternative systems of waste management, in the areas both of health and economic sustainability, as it did on providing positive indications that the three-way system itself could function. Though he was generally positive toward the most traditional system, on the collection of city wastes for agricultural use, he pointed out the high and increasing incidence of broken shards, paper, rags and boxes as impediments to effective use and to farmers' demand for useful waste.[93] Although this approach – around 1900 still the preeminent solution in France and most other European countries, aside from Britain – had been subject to hygienic objections, von der Linde argued that these objections did not require abandoning agricultural use of waste so much as abandoning the unhygienic ways of treating it prior to its direct application as fertilizer and for improving swamp or marshland.[94]

Some entrepreneurs, Von der Linde recognized, had attempted to remedy the first problem of agricultural usage, that of sharp and bulky objects, at the same time as they tried to resell the other useful goods to be derived from the total waste stream by operating sorting facilities on the Munich model. Generally, however, he argued that the cost of sorting made the "purer" waste for agricultural use expensive enough that it could only be employed in the general vicinity of the plant because the subsequent additional transportation costs raised its price to unprofitable levels.[95] He saw the sorting systems, though preferable to incineration as long as sanitary conditions were properly considered, as too expensive, even aside from the attempt to produce marketable fertilizers. The expense was because the rag-pickers generally removed the best wastes prior to collection. However, the bigger issue was that only some 12 percent of the total waste stream constituted of recoverable materials after removal of ash and garbage, while 100 percent of it had to pass through single-stream collection and processing, dirtying the other recoverables and breaking some of them along the way. Thus, the single-stream system was never been able to operate without substantial subsidy.[96]

Incineration, meanwhile, received von der Linde's intense opposition. In 1902, while CAG was still very much in the experimental stage, he observed that a city's selection of incineration was complicated by the substantial differences in composition among a city's wastes, by having the highest costs of all the procedures, and by the concerns expressed by some that valuable material was irremediably destroyed in the process.[97] A few years later, von der Linde had evolved into an active opponent of incineration, as he flatly stated, calling it the "barbarism of destruction."[98] He insisted both that it was uneconomical and, rejecting the usual claim that incineration was the most hygienic procedure, that it *created* health problems. No private business, he observed, had by itself successfully carried out an incineration operation across a period of years; instead, they merely sold equipment and whole incineration facilities to municipal entities that were not compelled by the market to cover costs.[99]

He was particularly intent on dismissing the claims made for energy recovery. He argued, for example, that if the incinerator in the wealthy city of Wiesbaden, with its higher calorific trash content, was unable to produce the amount of electricity claimed by major incineration proponents, then surely other cities with less energy-rich wastes would fail to cover their costs through energy recovery.[100] Advocates of incineration had taken to calling it a form of recovery or recycling, he observed, prefiguring later twentieth-century debates, but for von der Linde such claims were illegitimate as long as incineration either required subsidies or preserved less "value" than what would be preserved by the same amount of waste used more efficiently for agricultural purposes.[101] He attributed the success of the incineration method in Britain to the general prosperity of its cities, to the greater quantities of unburned coals left in British waste, to the relative backwardness of the methods of employing waste in the competing use of agriculture there, and finally to the marketing skills of the incinerator producers.[102] Despite the common suggestion that incineration was the most hygienic practice, he argued that it was in fact more hazardous to health than other methods, not just because of the air pollution it generated but also because the facilities were located *within* the cities and, when not in operation, garbage piled up around the incinerators closer to population centers than to ones outside the city in the countryside.[103]

Von der Linde's confident predictions that his own method would need no subsidies were not borne out in practice when his firm passed from the experimental stage to full-scale operations. He had the support of the local community, as well as a citizen group called the Verein für Gemeinnützige Abfallverwertung (Association for Nonprofit Waste Recovery), which was a 30 percent shareholder in the CAG. This association was set up in 1903, possibly by von der Linde. The firm conducted extensive public relations work through brochures and newspaper articles aimed at persuading residents to sort their trash, offering instruction in schools, and even providing tours of the facility in Seegefeld. However the firm ran into a raft of challenges that prevented it from ever reaching profitability.[104]

In its early experimental days, the firm's operations seemed to bear out von der Linde's convictions. He recognized from the outset the problem CAG would face in persuading those who handled urban households' trash, primarily servants and housewives, to separate their household wastes. In the absence of the municipal ordinances requiring separation, as occurred in New York City, von der Linde attempted to promote separation indirectly in his sample of about 500 Charlottenburg residences by offering small payments to the porters of large apartment buildings for separated wastes.[105] He lobbied the city government to pass ordinances or differential fees for removing unseparated and separated wastes, as these could level the playing field with other waste companies that did not recover value from the waste stream. While waiting for success on this front, the payments to porters worked reasonably well, and the company also made efforts to ensure that its receptacles were handy and aesthetically pleasing to maximize their use by residents.[106] Initially, the CAG aimed to recycle only dry rubbish, which was easier to put back into immediate industrial use, but success with these products induced the firm to collect and recycle the animal and vegetable matter as hog fodder.[107] The facility, which organized the presorted wastes, was operating successfully and employing 60 people in 1902, but it burned down in 1904.[108]

During the experimental phase of CAG's operations, von der Linde observed that there were households that made no objection to separating their wastes, but only as long as the proceeds from the collection and processing were directed not to the apartment buildings' porters or to the firm but to the "common good." Consequently, the Association for Nonprofit Waste Recovery contracted with the CAG to receive a set amount in exchange for taking over supervision of the "agitation for separation and oversight over its proper execution."[109] When the city of Charlottenburg selected the CAG to run its entire waste management operation beginning in 1907, the wholly owned subsidiary that processed the separated wastes was known as the Allgemeine Müllverwertungs-Gesellschaft mbH.[110] The contract was to run for 15 years, while the city retained the right to supervise all operations, and the firm was obliged to put aside a high deposit of 200,000 marks against the possibility that it did not fulfill its obligations. These obligations were, in general terms, the exact execution of the system as described, including the provision of the tripartite bins, regular pick-up service and objection-free disposal, and keeping the infrastructure sanitized and intact.[111] In return, the CAG received its desired monopoly status as residents were required by police ordinance to use the three-way separation system and therefore to separate their wastes in the home.[112]

More trouble than a fire was in store, however. Although the company prospectus for 1908 expected a profit of 600,000 marks, in fact the firm was nearly 500,000 in debt, a situation which worsened by about 50,000 marks the following year. The city had to raise its collection fees for residents and offer the firm a guaranteed interest rate on its debt. Some of these early woes were due to unexpected circumstances: the first year saw a very high rate of death among the company's pigs, which frequently ingested needles, glass and pottery shards inadvertently left in the food matter used to feed them. This was not simply bad luck – it reflected the need to change the cultural norms that governed household waste disposal: residents sometimes sorted in a haphazard manner. The costs of running three separate collection wagons also made Charlotten-burg service the most expensive in Germany. Not enough waste was generated in the city confines to make the costs of the collection and sorting profitable. There was little financial viability in the recycling industry and in the volume of consumer wastes. With the help of subsidies from the city, the firm survived well into World War I, during which it was feted as a model contributor to the cause of extending the usefulness of scarce resources. However, the withdrawal of most of its man- and horsepower during the war caused the firm to close its doors in 1917.[113]

CAG was the best known of the firms that introduced source-separation of household wastes, although there were efforts to introduce a *Zweiteilungssystem*, or dual-sorting system, in Potsdam and in Hamburg.[114] During World War I, a federal regulative ruling permitted state and municipal governments of a certain size to require separation of organic food matter and other kinds of refuse as a means of ensuring provision of animal fodder under the Allied blockade. Only the state of Hesse formally did so by 1916, although a private entrepreneur, the engineer Simon Gumpertz, who founded the firm Hamburger Abfall-verwertung (HAV), spearheaded an effort in Hamburg. Beginning in April 1915, HAV contracted with the city to collect household wastes separated by the citizens into organic and other wastes. Despite difficul-ties due to the declining caloric value of household waste during the hard years after 1916, the firm survived until 1922. It was ultimately felled by increasing costs during the hyperinflation period, by competition from other collection firms not as heavily regulated by the city, and by the decreasing willingness of consumers to separate their wastes once the peacetime conditions no longer made such practice seem like a patriotic duty.[115]

During the 1920s, interest in recycling waned, although there were some efforts such as Gerson's Müllverwertung AG. However, in the following decade, there was a resumption of it due to the peculiar circumstances of the Nazi regime. Although the regime advocated a certain vision of environmental protection,[116] the primary interest of the government was the promotion of national autarchy.[117] The Nazi state did not nationalize the scrap industry or other recycling businesses, but after 1936 it controlled them to such a degree that business conditions radically changed even before the start of World War II. When Jewish ownership of scrap businesses was banned, major gaps opened up in the personnel and especially the leadership of a sector the Nazis considered essential.[118]

Because of the importance of the scrap business to the rearmament program, the Nazi Party deferred slightly more than usual to industry expertise; it employed its customary expansion of bureaucratic controls but without putting state officials or Nazi Party members in charge of confiscated businesses, and the state, in fact, extended some economic protection measures intended to secure the sector's survival. Be that as it may, the industry was largely reorganized by administrative command. Aside from the expulsion of Jewish and other "undesirable" workers, the largest changes occurred under the "Four-Year Plan" of 1936, which involved the official designation of a local monopoly collection area for each small firm or individual scrap dealer substantial enough to secure a living for the firm's employees, who were required to ensure the "complete" return of old material to new uses within their territory. Those operating within the monopoly area had to visit its households during the first ten days of each month and pay for scrap at state-set prices, after which they were allowed to expand beyond their local territory to the surrounding 50 km^2 area during the remainder of the month. Larger firms were required to buy from these local or smaller dealers, though they were also allowed to have their own employees collect under the same regulatory conditions. The bureaucratic nightmare of this intensive regulation led to many disputes about the borders of firms' areas of operation and to disconnects between supply and demand. By 1939 the head of the waste management regulatory agency confessed that only the scrap metals and rags were being used adequately, while much of the collected paper and bones were unused and spreading disease instead.[119]

During World War II, there was at first a relaxation of efforts to collect scrap as Nazi victories abroad generated a steady stream of plundered material.[120] However, as the German army's advance was checked and as Allied air attacks began to take effect, a renewed urgency for intensified recycling led to further attempts to increase control over the scrap industry and to maximize its efficiency. The Nazi leadership attempted to generate efficiencies through organizing the larger companies into a close alliance, forcing them to share patented technologies, processes and trade secrets with their former rivals, and promoting a sole focus on materials useful to war production. The Nazis also tried imposing forced labor obligations on Jews and on convicts, and initiated a successful campaign of child labor by organizing schoolchildren to take over visiting residences for scrap sales and all manner of scavenging, including in dumps. All households in cities of more than 35,000 people were required to sort their wastes according to the *Zweiteilungssystem* to support state-run piggeries and thus to ensure the meat supply; compliance was ensured by police surveillance more intrusive than in pre-World War I Charlottenburg. Since this was a state program, firms already engaged in organic waste recycling were put out of business and their employees had either to join the program or find other work. With veterinarian monitors employed as well, the project appears to have been a success; the Nazis were good at feeding pigs with garbage.[121]

IX CONCLUSIONS

This chapter has explored how a number of Central and Northern European entrepreneurs built substantial businesses that aimed to make positive social and environmental contributions to their societies. These firms had strikingly modern views of environmental challenges, and they prefigured many later twentieth-century recycling processes. These businessmen were neither conservation activists nor could they have benefited from greenwashing their businesses as environmentally friendly in the century before mass public engagement with environmentalist ideas. Instead, they were driven by a desire to keep city and countryside healthy and unpolluted and to avoid the gratuitous waste of resources. The profit motive encouraged technological innovation and left a legacy of scientific and engineering knowledge of waste materials and their processing and utilization, which benefited later recyclers. These firms represent a neglected stage in the evolution of business responses to the waste problem – in terms of scale, diversification, the involvement of scientists and engineers, and the social and environmental motives of their founders.

In an era of municipalization, these entrepreneurs demonstrated the potential for fruitful interactions between business and city government. For public authorities and citizens looking to reuse their wastes and to recover some of the cost of providing municipal waste services, they were offered a variety of alternatives appropriate to cities' differing waste streams and preferences. At the same time, the entrepreneurs benefited from municipal legal ordinances that created the conditions for new entrepreneurial endeavors, such as dust-free collection that would not otherwise have been profitable.

The historical experience seen here revealed the challenges of achieving profitability in large-scale recycling. Entrepreneurs faced a difficult terrain when building their businesses. Despite collaborative relationships with municipal governments, they often struggled to survive over the longer term. Although they paid low wages, these labor-intensive businesses were sometimes unable to cover even their variable costs. They encountered exogenous turbulence and shocks, and prices for recycled commodities were volatile. These recovered resources often faced competition from virgin materials. There was a tension between the cyclicality of demand for recycled materials and the continuousness of waste production. While collection services had to function at all times and for all waste products, the profitability of processing and reselling any given recovered resource depended on many factors, including the season, the point in the business cycle, the volume of salvaged material collected by competitors and scrap drives, and the availability of substitutes. All these factors made the business difficult or uncertain without subsidies or guaranteed minimum prices, at least insofar as it was geared to fix the waste collection problem, which was why public actors became involved.

Governments could not only be allies but also competitors or threats. Entrepreneurs needed to negotiate contracts with local authorities, which sometimes replaced them entirely with government-owned entities. Wars depleted companies' personnel and assets and introduced new nonprofit competitors even as they raised the prices of recovered resources. The Nazi dictatorship in Germany after 1933 removed waste businesses' independence, and expropriated many of their owners while distorting scrap markets and reorienting the industry solely around war production.

Quite apart from the lack of sustained profitability, these enterprises were never a panacea for the overall waste problem from an environmental perspective. Ironically, even the more environmentally friendly activities such as incineration with energy recovery or recycling depended on large amounts of waste. Yet, despite this inherent contradiction, it can be asserted that the businesses considered here laid important organizational, technological and scientific foundations for the efforts of later generations to manage waste in a more environmentally positive fashion.

NOTES

*   This chapter appeared in an earlier version as Jones, Geoffrey and Andrew Spadafora, "Waste, Recycling and Entrepreneurship in Central and Northern Europe, 1870–1940," *Harvard Business School Working Paper*, No. 14-084 (March 2014).
1. Jones, *Profits*, 138.
2. Ibid., 312–23.
3. On the United States, see especially Melosi, *Garbage*; Melosi, *Sanitary City*; Strasser, *Waste and Want*; Wines, *Fertilizer*; Hickman, *American Alchemy*. On Europe, see especially Barles, *L'invention*; Jugie, *Poubelle-Paris*; Isabella et al., *Per una storia*; Sæveraas, *Fra*; Schmidt, *Nürnberger*; Breer et al., *Asche*.
4. Zimring, *Cash*; Stokes et al., *Business*; Jones, *Profits*, 138–44.
5. Strasser, *Waste*, Chapter 1.
6. Münch, *Stadthygiene*, Part I; Evans, *Death*, esp. Chapter 2.
7. Curter, *Berliner*, 19; Frilling and Mischer, *Pütt*, 25; Evans, *Death*, 129.
8. Evans, *Death*, 130–31.
9. Schmidt, *Nürnberger*, 17.
10. Rüb, "Müll," 22; Frilling and Mischer, *Pütt*, 125; Popp, *Festen*, 3.
11. Stokes et al., *Business*, 14.
12. Curter, *Berliner, Gold*, 27; Schmid, "Der lange," 31.
13. Frilling and Mischer, *Pütt*, 26; Evans, *Death*, 135.
14. Köster, "Private," 173–4.
15. Hösel, *Unser*, 201.
16. Münch, *Stadthygiene*, 111.
17. Curter, *Berliner*, 25–7.
18. Stokes et al., *Business*, Chapter 2.
19. Federal Environment Ministry, Dessau, Germany, Sammlung Erhard Collection (hereafter Erhard Collection), Sign. A 715, *"Staubschutz" Gesellschaft mit beschränkter Haftung: Förderung der staubfreien Verladung und Beseitigung bezw. Verwerthung von hauswirtschaftlichen Abfällen, Kehricht (Müll) und dergleichen* (Berlin, March 1900), 3.
20. Ibid., 6.
21. Ibid., 4–6.
22. Erhard Collection, Sign. A 747, *IX. Annual Report of the WGB*, 1903. All materials are in the German language.
23. Erhard Collection, Sign. A 748, *X. Annual Report of WGB*, 1904.
24. Erhard Collection, Sign. A 749, *XVI Annual Report of WGB*, 1910.
25. Erhard Collection, Sign. C V 13, *XX. Annual Report of the WGB*, 1914.
26. Erhard Collection, Sign. C V 14, *XXI. Annual Report of the WGB*, 1915.
27. Erhard Collection, Sign. C V 15, *XXII. Annual Report of the WGB*, 1916.
28. Erhard Collection, Sign. C V 17, *XXIV. G Annual Report of the WGB*, 1918.
29. Erhard Collection, Sign. A 279, *Berliner Müllabfuhr, A.-G.*, n.d. (ca. 1923), 4.
30. Ibid., 2–3.
31. Ibid., 3, 5.
32. Ibid., 5.
33. Ibid., 4, 6–7.
34. Hauser, "Berliner," 26.
35. Hösel, *Unser*, 169.
36. Frilling and Mischer, *Pütt*, 53; Stokes et al., *Business*, 31–2, 61.

37. Frilling and Mischer, *Pütt*, 45ff.
38. Jones, *Profits*, 141; Lindemann, "Verbrennung."
39. Lindemann, "Verbrennung"; Münch, *Stadthygiene*, 54–5.
40. Lindemann, "Verbrennung," 97.
41. Frilling and Mischer, *Pütt*, 73–5, 126.
42. Curter, *Berliner*, 28–30; Fodor, *Elektrizität*, 53–4.
43. Lindemann, "Verbrennung," 97.
44. Stellberger, "Müllstandort."
45. Erhard Collection, Sign. C IV 111, letter of 8 April 1927, from BAMAG-Meguin to Heinrich Erhard.
46. Erhard Collection, Sign. D II, BAMAG-Meguin company pamphlet.
47. Erhard Collection, Sign. A 271, Bamag-Meguin Aktiengesellschaft, "Die Verwertung von Hausmüll als die Zukünftige Müllbeseitigung für Mittlere und Grosse Städte," Berlin, 1927.
48. Stellberger, "Müllstandort"; Windmüller, *Kehrseite*, 178–84.
49. Jones, *Profits*, 142.
50. Erhard Collection, Sign. C IV 113, "Müllverwertung Aktiengesellschaft: Die Gersonschen Verfahren der Müllverwertung," n.d. (ca. 1925), 2.
51. Erhard Collection, Sign. C IV 113, "Gutachten: Das Gerson'sche Verfahren und seine praktische Ausnutzung in der Müllvernichtungsanstalt zu Schöneberg."
52. Stellberger, "Müllstandort"; Windmüller, *Kehrseite*.
53. Hösel, *Unser*, 186.
54. Lindemann, "Verbrennung," 95, 104n18.
55. Hösel, *Unser*, 186.
56. Rüb, "Grenzen," 93–8; Köstering, "'Der Müll," 23–4; Jones, *Profits*, 142.
57. Erhard Collection, Sign. D II b, undated letter from Franz Boerner, ca. 1925.
58. Ibid.
59. Ibid.
60. Erhard Collection, Sign. C V 8, "Edaphon Dünger," typescript, February 1930.
61. Ibid.
62. Ibid.
63. Erhard Collection, Sign. D II, "Über Müllverwertung und Edaphon-Humus-Düngung," 1947.
64. Ibid.; Jones, *Profits*, 145.
65. Silberschmidt, "Müll," 620–21.
66. Ibid., 630; Frilling and Mischer, *Pütt* 107.
67. Fodor, *Elektrizität*, 19–20.
68. Huchting, "Abfallwirtschaft," 260.
69. This company remains a prominent business in Denmark today.
70. Nevers and Petersen, *Købmænd i 175 år*, 27.
71. Ibid., 37–47.
72. Ibid., 54–5.
73. Fear, *Organizing*, 471.
74. Köstering, "Hundert Jahre."
75. Ibid.
76. Jones, *Profits*, 141.
77. Fodor, *Elektrizität*, 47.
78. Ibid., 12; Silberschmidt, "Müll," 638.
79. Erhard Collection, Sign. A 715, *"Staubschutz" Gesellschaft mit beschränkter Haftung: Förderung der staubfreien Verladung und Beseitigung bezw. Verwertung von hauswirtschaftlichen Abfällen, Kehricht (Müll) und dergleichen* (Berlin, March 1900), 18–19.
80. Ibid., 20.

81. Erhard Collection, Sign. C V 21, Wirtschaftsgenossenschaft Berliner Grundbesitzer eGmbH, "Betrifft Zweiteilung des Mülls. Anlagen zu unseren Schreiben an den Herrn Oberbürgermeister der Stadt Berlin vom 13 November und 14 December 1914."
82. Erhard Collection, Sign. A 279, "Berliner Müllabfuhr, A.-G.," 7.
83. Ibid., 8.
84. Jones, *Profits*, 140. Erhard Collection, Sign. A 106, Carl von der Linde, *Müllvernichtung oder Müllverwertung, insbesondere das Dreiteilungssystem: Ein Beitrag zur Hygiene des Mülls mit Rücksicht auf ihre volkswirtschaftliche Bedeutung* (Charlottenburg: Adolf Gertz, 1906), 19.
85. Fodor, *Elektrizität*, 10–17; Silberschmidt, "Müll," 591, 638–9; Windmüller, *Kehrseite* 167–71, 174; Curter, *Berliner*, 30–31; Köstering, "Der Müll," 16–18; Jasner, "Frühe"; Frilling and Mischer, *Pütt*, 126–8; Von der Linde, *Müllvernichtung*, 23–9.
86. Erhard Collection, Sign. A 716, von der Linde, *Die Müllfrage und ihre Lösung nach dem neuen Separations-System der Charlottenburger Abfuhrgesellschaft m.b.H.* (Charlottenburg: Adolf Gertz, 1902), 1, 4.; Von der Linde, *Müllvernichtung*, 20.
87. Von der Linde, *Müllvernichtung*, 3.
88. Von der Linde, *Müllfrage*, 6.
89. Ibid., 2.
90. Ibid., 1.
91. Von der Linde, *Müllfrage*, 7.
92. Von der Linde, *Müllvernichtung*, 33.
93. Ibid., 5; Von der Linde, *Müllfrage*, 1.
94. Ibid., 11.
95. Ibid., 6.
96. Ibid., 6–8; Von der Linde, *Müllfrage*, 3.
97. Von der Linde, *Müllfrage*, 2.
98. Von der Linde, *Müllvernichtung*, 2.
99. Ibid., 12.
100. Ibid., 13–14.
101. Ibid., 12.
102. Ibid., 10.
103. Ibid., 9, 16.
104. Fodor, *Elektrizität*, 10–17; Silberschmidt, "Müll," 591, 638–9; Windmüller, *Kehrseite*, 167–71, 174; Curter, *Berliner*, 30–31; Köstering, "Der Müll," 16–18; Jasner, "Frühe"; Frilling and Mischer, *Pütt*, 126–8.
105. Von der Linde, *Müllvernichtung*, 22–3.
106. Ibid., 29.
107. Ibid., 32; Von der Linde, *Müllfrage*, 7.
108. Ibid., 7.
109. Von der Linde, *Müllvernichtung*, 29–30.
110. Ibid., 37.
111. Ibid., 36.
112. Ibid., 34.
113. Fodor, *Elektrizität*, 10–17; Silberschmidt, "Müll," 591, 638–9; Windmüller, *Kehrseite*, 167–71, 174; Köstering, "Der Müll," 16–18; Jasner, "Frühe"; Frilling and Mischer, *Pütt*, 126–8.
114. Frilling and Mischer, *Pütt*, 129–34.
115. Ibid.
116. Brüggemeier et al., *Nazis*; Uekötter, *Green and the Brown*.
117. Huchting, "Abfallwirtschaft."
118. Ibid.
119. Ibid.
120. Ibid.
121. Gerhard, "Breeding Pigs."

REFERENCES

Barles, Sabine (2005), *L'invention des déchets urbains: France, 1790–1970*, Seyssel, France: Champ Vallon.

Breer, Ralf, Stephan Mlodoch and Hanskarl Willms (2010), *Asche, Kehricht, Saubermänner: Stadtentwicklung, Stadthygiene und Städtereinigung in Deutschland bis 1945*, Iserlohn: SASE.

Brüggemeier, Franz-Josef, Mark Cioc and Thomas Zeller (eds.) (2005), *How Green were the Nazis? Nature, Environment and Nation in the Third Reich*, Athens, OH: Ohio State University Press.

Curter, Maria (1996), *Berliner Gold: Die Geschichte der Müllbeseitigung in Berlin*, Berlin: Haude & Spener.

Evans, Richard (2005), *Death in Hamburg: Society and Politics in the Cholera Years, 1830–1910*, New York: Penguin.

Fear, Jeffrey (2005), *Organizing Control: August Thyssen and the Construction of German Corporate Management*, Cambridge, MA: Harvard University Press.

Fodor, Etienne de (1911), *Elektrizität aus Kehricht*, Budapest: Julius Benko.

Frilling, Hildegaard and Olaf Mischer (1994), *Pütt und Pann'n: Geschichte der Hamburger Hausmüllbeseitigung*, Hamburg: Ergebnisse Verlag.

Gerhard, Gesine (2005), "Breeding Pigs and People for the Third Reich: Richard Walther Darré's Agrarian Ideology," in Franz-Josef Brüggemeier, Mark Cioc and Thomas Zeller (eds.), *How Green were the Nazis? Nature, Environment and Nation in the Third Reich*, Athens, OH: Ohio State University Press, 129–46.

Hauser, Evelyn (2004), "Berliner Stadtreinigungsbetriebe," in Tina Grant (ed.), *International Directory of Company Histories*, vol. 58, Detroit, MI: St. James Press.

Hickman, H. Lanier (2003), *American Alchemy: The History of Solid Waste Management in the United States*, Santa Barbara, CA: Forester Press.

Hösel, Gottfried (1987), *Unser Abfall aller Zeiten: Eine Kulturgeschichte der Städtereinigung*, Munich, Germany: Jehle.

Huchting, Friedrich (1981), "Abfallwirtschaft im Dritten Reich," *Technikgeschichte*, **48** (3), 252–73.

Isabella, Caterina, Giuseppe Rubrichi and Franco Sensi (1997), *Per una storia della nettezza urbana a Roma dal 1870 al 1960*, Gorle and Bergamo, Italy: CEL.

Jasner, Carsten (2003), "Frühe Alternative: Das Charlottenburger Dreiteilungsmodell," in Susanne Köstering and Renate Rüb (eds.), *Müll von gestern? Eine umweltgeschichtliche Erkundung in Berlin und Brandenburg*, Münster, Germany: Waxmann, 115–20.

Jones, Geoffrey (2017), *Profits and Sustainability: A History of Green Entrepreneurship*, Oxford: Oxford University Press.

Jugie, Jeanne-Hélène (1993), *Poubelle-Paris, 1883–1896: la collecte des ordures ménagères à la fin du XIXe siècle*, Paris: Larousse.

Köster, Roman (2017), "Private Companies and the Recycling of Household Waste in West Germany, 1965–1990," in Hartmut Berghoff and Adam Rome (eds.), *Green Capitalism? Business and the Environment in the Twentieth Century*, Philadelphia, PA: University of Philadelphia Press.

Köstering, Susanne (1992), "'Der Müll muss doch heraus aus Berlin!'," *WerkstattGeschichte*, **3**, 16–26.

Köstering, Susanne (2003), "Hundert Jahre Entzinnung von Konservendosen: Ein Wettlauf zwischen Altstoffrueckgewinnung und Rohstoffeinsparung," in Susanne Köstering and Renate Rüb (eds.), *Müll von gestern? Eine umweltgeschichtliche Erkundung in Berlin und Brandenburg*, Münster, Germany: Waxmann, 151–64.

Lindemann, Carmelita (1992), "Verbrennung oder Verwertung: Müll als Problem um die Wende vom 19. zum 20. Jahrhundert," *Technikgeschichte*, **59**, (2), 91–107.

Melosi, Martin (2005), *Garbage in the Cities: Refuse, Reform, and the Environment*, rev. ed., Pittsburgh, PA: University of Pittsburgh Press.

Melosi, Martin (2000), *The Sanitary City: Urban Infrastructure in America from Colonial Times to the Present*, Baltimore, MD: Johns Hopkins University Press.

Nevers, Jeppe and Jens Åge Petersen (2004), *Købmænd i 175 år: H.J. Hansen, 1829–2004*, Odense, Denmark: H.J. Hansen Holding A/S.

Münch, Peter (1993), *Stadthygiene im 19. und 20. Jahrhundert*, Gottingen, Germany: Vandenhoeck & Ruprecht.

Popp, Camillo (1930), *Die festen städtischen Abfallstoffe*, Munich, Germany: Oldenbourg.

Röhrecke, Bruno (1901), *Müllabfuhr und Müllbeseitigung*, Berlin: Kommissionsverlag von R. Skrzeczek.

Rüb, Renate (2003), "Müll und Städtehygiene um 1900," in Susanne Köstering and Renate Rüb (eds.), *Müll von gestern? Eine umweltgeschichtliche Erkundung in Berlin und Brandenburg*, Münster, Germany: Waxmann.

Rüb, Renate (2003), "Grenzen eines tradierten Systems: Vier Jahrzehnte Mülldüngung bei Nauen," in Susanne Köstering and Renate Rüb (eds.), *Müll von gestern? Eine umweltgeschichtliche Erkundung in Berlin und Brandenburg*, Münster, Germany: Waxmann, 87–100.

Sæveraas, Siv, (2006), *Fra boss til bruk: BIR 1881–2006*, Bergen, Norway: BIR.

Schmid, Ingrid (2003), "Der lange Weg zur Kommunalisierung der Bein Westberliner Müllabfuhr," in Susanne Köstering and Renate Rüb (eds.), *Müll von gestern? Eine umweltgeschichtliche Erkundung in Berlin und Brandenburg*, Münster, Germany: Waxmann, 31–8.

Schmidt, Alexander (1999), *Die Nürnberger Abfallwirtschaft und Stadtreinigung, 1899–1999*, Nuremberg, Germany: ASN.

Silberschmidt, W. (1919), "Müll: Mit Hauskehricht," in A Gärtner (ed.), *Weyls Handbuch der Hygiene*, 2nd ed., Vol. 2, Leipzig, Germany: Barth.

Stellberger, Olaf (2003), "Müllstandort Rote Insel in Schöneberg: Experimentierfeld der Müll-Moderne," in Susanne Köstering and Renate Rüb (eds.), *Müll von gestern? Eine umweltgeschichtliche Erkundung in Berlin und Brandenburg*, Münster, Germany: Waxmann, 125–38.

Strasser, Susan (1999), *Waste and Want: A Social History of Trash*, New York: Metropolitan Books.

Stokes, Raymond G., Roman Köster and Stephen C. Sambrook (2014), *The Business of Waste: Great Britain and Germany, 1945 to the Present*, Cambridge: Cambridge University Press.

Uekötter, Frank (2006), *The Green and the Brown: A History of Conservation in Nazi Germany*, Cambridge: Cambridge University Press.

Windmüller, Sonja (2004), *Die Kehrseite der Dinge: Müll, Abfall, Wegwerfen als kulturwissenschaftliches Problem*, Münster, Germany: LIT.

Wines, Richard A. (1985), *Fertilizer in America: From Waste Recycling to Resource Exploitation*, Philadelphia, PA: Temple University Press.

Zimring, Carl A. (2005), *Cash for your Trash: Scrap Recycling in America*, New Brunswick, NJ: Rutgers University Press.

PRIMARY MATERIALS

Federal Environment Ministry, Dessau, Germany, Sammlung Erhard Collection.

3. "Power from sunshine": The business of solar energy before 1990[*]

I INTRODUCTION

This chapter examines the business history of solar energy from the late 1800s to 1990. Although solar energy had had a long history by 1990, it remained unimportant as an energy source. It was most significant in the United States, where it accounted for a mere 0.022 percent of electricity generated. Among the major developed countries, it was next highest in Italy (0.002 percent), Spain and Portugal (0.0004 percent in each), and Japan (0.0001 percent). It was inconsequential elsewhere, as combustible fuels (primarily coal and oil), nuclear energy and – in a handful of countries, including Brazil, Canada and Sweden – hydropower dominated the generation of electricity.[1]

The lack of importance of solar energy in 1990 does not, however, mean that the early history of the industry lacks significance. The idea of capturing energy from the sun emerged well before World War I. Frank Shuman, an early American pioneer, published an article on the future importance of "power from sunshine" in the journal *Scientific American* in 1911.[2] The story of how difficult it was to compete against typically subsidized conventional alternatives reveals the scale of the challenge of competing against conventional incumbents, even after it became apparent that they had large environmental costs.

Solar is complex because it involves multiple technologies. The major technology used until World War II employed parabolic dish collectors to drive steam-powered plants. A number of architects also employed passive solar in their buildings. After World War II, the new photovoltaic (hereafter, PV) cell technology was born, which converted solar radiation directly into electricity.

Section II explores the early history of parabolic solar collection. Section III discusses the early use of passive solar in architecture. Section IV explains origins of the PV solar industry in the United States. Section V examines the effects of rising oil prices on the industry, and Section VI the entry of big business into PV solar energy. Sections VII and VIII examine developments in Japan and Europe, respectively. Section IX concludes.

II THE EMERGENCE OF THE PARABOLIC SOLAR INDUSTRY

The idea of using the power of the sun for heating and lighting is intuitive. Passive solar energy has been used as a form of light and heat since early mankind. From the eighteenth century, science was applied to capturing solar power more systematically. In the 1760s, Swiss scientist Horace de Saussure built an insulated rectangular box with a glass cover that became the prototype for solar collectors to heat water.[3] In 1839, Edmund Becquerel, a French experimental physicist, discovered the PV effect while experimenting with an electrolytic cell made up of two metal electrodes. He found that certain materials would produce small amounts of electric current when exposed to light.[4] In 1878 a solar-powered steam engine was invented by August Mouchot, a French mathematician, after he received funding from the French government to work on an alternative source of energy. Concerned that fossil fuels would eventually run out, he created the first solar steam-powered plant using parabolic dish collectors. The French government supported his experiments in the colony of Algeria, but his solar generator remained a one-off.[5] Solar energy was also successfully employed in the late nineteenth century to power water desalinization plants in Chile's Atacama desert.[6]

It proved extremely challenging to develop the commercial use of solar energy at a time when coal was cheap and widely available, and the environmental costs of fossil fuels were not understood. The first entrepreneurial endeavors in solar, then, took place in locations where using the sun rather than coal made financial sense. During the 1890s, several solar water heater companies were started in California, which lacked domestic coal supplies. The first hot water heaters were bare metal tanks turned toward the sun.[7]

In 1908 William J. Bailey, a former mechanical engineer at the Carnegie Steel Company, invented a solar collector with copper coils and an insulated box, which became the standard design.[8] Aubrey Eneas adopted Mouchot's technology to heat boilers more evenly and efficiently, producing a greater volume of steam. He developed large solar collectors to power steam engines and pumps for agricultural irrigation water in California and Arizona during the 1900s, but weather damage ended the venture. During the 1920s there were large sales of solar water heaters in Miami, Florida, but the leading company failed in 1926 following a hurricane and the end of the Florida's building boom.[9]

It was in the developing world, rather than the developed, in which more ambitious schemes were launched. An early attempt at harvesting energy from the sun was initiated in 1870s by William Adams, a British colonial official in India, who had worked in the British Patent Office, and encountered new research on energy systems, including Mouchot's research. In the introduction to his book, *Solar Heat: A Substitute Fuel in Tropical Countries*, published in Bombay (now Mumbai) in 1878, Adams wrote of Mouchot's discoveries:

> This idea may be, and probably is, purely Utopian, but very important discoveries have been made in striving for the impossible; and if no further success is achieved than that of utilizing the rays of the sun for driving stationary steam engines, an important addition to physical science will have been made, and a great commercial revolution will have been effected.[10]

Adams came up with a plan to use concentrated sunlight to make the kind of high-pressure steam needed to run modern steam engines. After his first boilers imported from Britain were installed and running, Adams spent a few months perfecting his technology to increase their steam production capacity. However, the colonial government was extremely skeptical that solar heat could be scaled up for large commercial purposes. The government engineers noted that the limited power storage capacity of Adams's machines meant that workers had to arrive well before dawn to get the boilers started, and be sent back home whenever the sun was not strong enough. In response to this criticism, Adams argued – unsuccessfully – that solar energy could supplement coal that was imported from Britain. However, it was too costly.[11]

Adams's frustration prompted him to abandon experiments and instead to focus on writing his book. His research, however, sparked the interest of officials in other British colonies with hot climates and no fossil fuels. Aden (in contemporary Yemen), for example, faced both these issues as well as a scarcity of potable water, which had to be distilled from seawater and purchased at an expensive price. Local engineers successfully adapted Adams's apparatus and used it to produce drinking water until cheap oil from the Arabian Peninsula appeared after World War II.[12]

The greatest progress in the use of solar power was in the British protectorate of Egypt, where American entrepreneur Frank Shuman established a solar business. Shuman was a Philadelphia inventor who built a small solar collection plant in his backyard in 1907. He became convinced that only scaling would enable solar to compete with coal. He warned in the journal *Scientific American* in 1911 that after fossil fuels were exhausted, solar would "remain as the only means of existence of the human race."[13] Moving first to London to raise capital, Shuman launched a solar venture in Egypt, which the British colonial administration supported as a way to bolster irrigation of the vital cotton crop in a country without coal. A solar plant was built, and it had successful operation through World War I, after which it was then dismantled for parts and scrap metal.[14]

The concept of capturing energy from the sun, then, had early appeal. Entrepreneurs and inventors created products, whether household boilers or parabolic arrays in the desert, which turned the idea into a reality. However, the cost differential with conventional fuels was such that these products were only viable in circumstances in which cheap coal or other fossil fuels were not readily available. Scaling was the solution, as Shuman realized, but the cost differentials were so great that there was no business case to support this process.

III SOLAR HOUSES

As urbanization spread in the nineteenth century, architects largely ignored rather than enjoyed the natural environment. Houses and cities became massive consumers of energy and drivers of pollution.[15] During the interwar and immediate post-World War II decades, a few visionary architects began to consider ways to capture the energy of the sun. Shortages of conventional fuels, and sometimes concerns about their sustainability, motivated these efforts.

The first engineered passive solar houses of the modern era were built in Germany after World War I, when the Allies occupied the Ruhr area, which included most of Germany's coal mines.[16] During the 1930s, American architect George F. Keck began experimenting with the basic principles of passive solar houses.[17] He designed the all-glass "House of Tomorrow" for the Century of Progress Exposition at the 1933 World's Fair in Chicago,[18] and noted that it was warm inside on sunny winter days even prior to the installation of the furnace. Following this, he gradually started incorporating more south-facing windows into his designs for his clients. In 1940 he designed a passive solar home for real estate developer Howard Sloan, in Glenview, Illinois. Referred to as the "solar house" in the *Chicago Tribune*, it became the first house to carry this name. Sloan continued to build passive solar houses, contributing to the emergence of a solar house movement in the 1940s.[19] It was also in this period that iconic American architect Frank Lloyd Wright experimented with engineered passive solar design with his Solar Hemicycle House, built in 1943.[20]

During World War II, the threat of depleted energy sources further stimulated interest in solar homes in the United States. In addition, technology advances in the glass industry allowed homebuilders in cold climates to use larger window areas. In 1945 the Libbey-Owens-Ford Glass Company, which in the previous decade had experimented with double-glazing windows in order to retain heat, initiated a large-scale solar house project after receiving numerous letters from prospective home buyers interested in energy-efficient houses. The company planned to build solar houses in all 48 states, and selected local architects to design these houses via a jury composed of editors, university deans and other key personalities in the building industry.[21] The project was launched but encountered harsh criticism. F.W. Hutchison, a refrigeration engineer working at Purdue University, built two houses which were identical except one had much greater window area than the other. They were observed over three heating seasons. Hutchinson concluded that passive solar houses "may be net money losers in terms of heating costs."[22] Ultimately, the solar house movement failed to create a community of solar architects or to launch a widespread solar house movement. Instead, architects began to focus on all-electric cooling and heating.[23]

Passive solar was once again employed by a new generation of modernist architects who became influential in mid-twentieth-century America. Carl Koch was a Harvard-educated architect who studied under Walter Gropius, the founder of the Bauhaus movement. Koch traveled to Sweden on a fellowship in 1938, and was struck by how Swedes had begun to prefabricate houses. He began working on building houses that were not only significantly cheaper but also functional and pleasant homes. Upon returning to the United States in 1941, Koch's first undertaking was a community housing project called Snake Hill, in Belmont, Massachusetts. Koch developed the project on a rocky hillside previously regarded as uninhabitable as a way to design an inexpensive home for himself and his family, who moved into one of the complex's five original houses.

This experience inspired Koch to pursue a career in creating quality affordable housing for families. He believed that the best post-World War II housing solution for the shifting and expanding American population was the creation of demountable, prefabricated housing. Koch developed the "Techbuilt House" in 1954, designed with prefabricated components that could be custom-assembled to create houses that were not only unique to the needs of the clients but also affordable because of mass production. He designed houses with post-and-beam construction that allowed for the large expanses of glazing. Koch's houses were designed around a common family "hearth" and celebrated the connection to the outside through large expanses of windows that made effective use of passive solar heat. In his 1958 book on his architectural work, Koch wrote of his hopes that in the future, "atomic or solar energy" would provide the cheap electricity needed for heating and cooling.[24]

The concept of bio-climatic architecture was developed during the 1950s by Victor and Aldar Olgyay, twin brothers who had opened an architecture practice in Hungary in 1938, and who then moved to the United States ten years later. They asserted that each climatic region demanded different architectural forms, in contrast to the homogenization that seemed to be spreading with modern architecture. In contrast to Koch and Wright, the brothers had more sharply defined ecological concerns. They particularly encouraged the use of passive solar energy. The brothers were prolific authors, but while they designed multiple buildings, cost considerations constrained the application of bio-climatic architecture.[25]

The Olgyays, Koch and the other architects were important figures in the history of architecture in the United States. There were important contemporaries in other countries, including Hassan Fathy, in Egypt.[26] Yet by the 1960s the momentum behind solar houses had been lost, probably – as architectural historian Daniel Barber has argued – because of the consensus that conventional energy and other resources were abundant.[27] Although the oil prices rises of the 1970s would again bring this assumption into question, the general impact of ecological architects who often employed passive solar was to remain very limited before the end of the twentieth century, when the emergence of certification programs helped mainstream the concept of greener buildings. Even then, cost considerations largely confined ecological buildings to the public sector and large commercial buildings.[28]

IV PV CELLS AND THE NEW SOLAR INDUSTRY

The solar industry was reinvented through the development of the PV cell after World War II. PV cells converted solar radiation directly into electricity: when photons of sunlight struck the cell, electrons were knocked free from silicon atoms and drawn off by a grid of metal conductors, which yielded a flow of direct current. The new technology had its origins at Bell Laboratories, the research facility of the US telephone utility AT&T where there were a series of innovations, from the invention of a silicon solar battery in 1946 to the creation of the first solar cell which could generate significant electric power in 1954.[29]

There was an initial wave of excitement over the potential of solar power, both PV and other technologies. A World Conference on Solar Energy, held in 1955 in Tucson and Phoenix, Arizona, was partly sponsored by the nonprofit Stanford Research Institute, which studied the many potential uses of solar energy.[30] The overall conclusion was that the costs were too high, yet the fact that officials from Britain's Colonial Office were in attendance indicated the interest in solar as a cheap source of energy in poor tropical countries.[31] The International Solar Energy Society was founded after the Arizona conference. In 1954 the Rockefeller Foundation awarded the University of Wisconsin-Madison (hereafter, UW-Madison) a $250,000 grant for research on solar energy. The lead researcher was a chemistry professor named Farrington Daniels, who, as his wife later described, "sought solace in the sun, the poor man's atomic power plant."[32] Daniels had strong humanitarian feelings, and harbored a sense of guilt over his earlier involvement in the Manhattan Project that had developed the atomic bomb. In 1948, in the first of many speeches, he stressed the need for humans "to conserve our resources, control the birth rate of the world's population and increase the efficiency of our utilization of sunlight."[33]

On receipt of the Rockefeller grant, a facility was established in a wooden shack, which was grandly named UW-Madison's Solar Energy Lab. The Rockefeller Foundation's mandate was to focus on bringing solar energy to developing countries, as it was assumed that it was wholly impractical to use it in the United States. The focus was using solar energy to power simple home appliances. Daniels traveled to Mexico, hoping to establish solar cookers as a substitute for cooking with wood, charcoal or cow dung; and to the South Pacific islands of Tahiti and Rangaroa and to Ecuador's Galapagos Islands, hoping to supply drinking water with simple solar stills that could be built from local materials. There were many difficulties. The problem with the solar cookers was an inability to store energy for later use. However, Daniels had greater success in promoting solar water heaters around the world.[34] He continued as a vocal supporter of solar energy; for example, when in the mid-1960s the Solar Energy Society almost went bankrupt, he became its president and borrowed on his own life insurance to help the society survive. The society moved its headquarters to Australia, as at the time the Australian government had a large research program.[35]

Daniels's focus on the potential of solar for developing countries was to become a theme for other researchers over following decades. Interestingly, the governments of many developing countries at the time considered efforts to interest them in solar energy as a ploy for rich countries to retain their hold over existing energy sources.[36] It was not until much later, and after dramatic falls in the cost of solar panels, that enthusiasm for the potential of solar energy and off-grid electricity spread, especially in Africa.[37]

Daniels did not concern himself at all with PV technology. However, this new technology did come to the attention of the new US space program because of its potential solution to power satellites. This was a rare instance, in the context of low and often falling costs of fossil fuels, in which it made financial sense to invest in PV solar technology. However, the market was niche and the technology new, so it was left to small entrepreneurial firms based in Los Angeles, such as those founded by Leslie Hoffman and Alfred Mann, to develop the PV satellite market. Mann sold his company, Spectrolab, to a conglomerate called Textron in 1960, and left the solar business, but a number of future solar entrepreneurs had started their careers at his firm. The annual market for solar cells was worth only a tiny $5 million to $10 million in the mid-1960s.[38]

Experiments to extend the use of PV technology ran into massive cost roadblocks. The International Rectifier Corporation, founded in 1947 and based in El Segundo, California, became a large manufacturer of semiconductors and subsequently began making PV cells. In 1960 it supplied a 9,200-cell solar battery to the weather satellite TIROS 1. In the same year, it launched the first-ever solar car. A 1912 Baker Electric car had 10,640 silicon solar cells mounted on the roof via a detachable 26-square foot panel. It employed a solar conversion system pioneered by Charles Escoffery, chief chemist at International Rectifier. The automobile was proudly advertised as a "smog free car." The company asserted that solar was both safe and sustainable, given the finite nature of fossil resources and the risks of nuclear waste disposal.[39] However, the automobile's solar panel cost $20,000 ($160,000 in today's dollars), and it took a week of charging to get enough power to drive for three hours, at 20 miles per hour.[40] The solar car remained a one-off experiment.

V OIL PRICE INCREASES IN THE 1970s

The oil price increases in 1973–74 and in 1978–79 ended the era of cheap oil that had characterized the postwar decades, and raised major concerns over the security of oil supplies. Governments everywhere began to reconsider energy supplies and consumption, but there were policy variations among countries. Energy conservation programs, enhanced investment in nuclear power and a renewed interest in solar energy were now all on the table.

In some countries, alternative energy sources were looked at with renewed interest, especially because of growing environment concerns. In 1972 the United Nations held its first Conference on the Human Environment, in Stockholm, Sweden,[41] and it launched an Environment Program. Although few tangible results emerged from this, the potential of solar energy became more widely discussed than previously. One report in 1977, for example, lauded the potential of solar energy for the Mediterranean region. This energy resource, the report observed, was renewable, "clean" and well distributed. "Solar energy," it continued, "is the only possible solution for countries which are poor in fossil energy but which do not wish to be totally dependent either on oil or on the atom for their supplies."[42]

The United States was replete with domestic coal, oil and nuclear energy, but the rise in oil prices stimulated a new interest in alternative energy. In 1974 the Ford Foundation produced a major report entitled *A Time to Choose: America's Energy Future*. Solar energy did not feature prominently in the report, but it was mentioned as the "world's most abundant renewable energy resource."[43] The authors were especially impressed with the prospects for solar heating and cooling in buildings, and asserted that the technologies for more fundamental use of solar in the generation of electricity were on the threshold of taking off – if the government provided as much investment as it had earlier for nuclear energy.[44]

However, this level of support for solar was not forthcoming. The most significant government initiative was the Solar Energy Research Development and Demonstration Act of 1974. The Solar Energy Research Institute (eventually renamed the National Renewable Energy Laboratory) began operating in 1977 in Golden, Colorado. Nevertheless, funding for solar remained modest, and the focus remained on defense and space uses. Congressional hearings in 1978 were noteworthy for their identification of the problems that would beset US government policy for decades. A representative of the Worldwatch Institute told the Committee on Government Operations, "There is no substitute for money. While competing energy sources have financially benefitted from the diligent efforts of scores of highly-paid lobbyists, solar energy has not."[45] A consulting engineer on the faculty of the School of Architecture, at the University of Southern California, noted that the growth of the United States had "been based on cheap energy."

> We have done everything we can to make it easy to build cheaply, and inefficiently and then to subsidize it by operating with cheap energy ... These same policies prevent us from going into more energy efficient scenarios, as for example, solar technology. We are always asked, why don't we go solar, and then, what kind of a payoff is there?[46]

In the same year, a set of public policies aimed at stimulating demand for alternative energy proved important for both the solar and wind energy businesses in the United States. The Public Utility Regulatory Policies Act (PURPA) of 1978 introduced the concept of feed-in tariffs by requiring utility companies to buy electricity from nonutility facilities that produced electric power, including solar energy and wind energy. The 1978 Energy Tax Act also offered a 30 percent investment tax credit to residential consumers for solar and wind energy equipment, and a 10 percent investment tax credit to business consumers for the installation of solar, wind and geothermal technologies.[47]

The utility commissioners of individual states were left to implement this new federal legislation. Only the state of California took the initiative, and it did so on a large scale. In 1978 Governor Jerry Brown, advised by state architect Sim van der Ryn, took the most radical measures to promote alternative energy. In that year Brown established a SolarCal office under van der Ryn, along with a $200 million solar and conservationist program. Van der Ryn was particularly interested in building energy-efficient public buildings, in which he installed solar energy. The state also offered a 55 percent credit against state income tax to people who bought solar energy systems. This credit was given both to consumers and house builders in order to encourage the use of multiple solar designs in houses. The program was designed to expand the market sufficiently to capture scale economies and eventually lower prices.[48]

US federal government support for solar rose to a new dimension under the administration of President Carter. Carter had entered office concerned about energy consumption and supply; in April 1977 he labeled the energy problem "the moral equivalent of war" but initially was not especially concerned about alternative energy sources. However, the Iranian Revolution and the second oil shock in 1979 resulted in a swathe of measures designed to stimulate domestic production, develop synthetic fossil fuels, constrain oil consumption, and develop both solar and wind power. In 1979 the Carter administration announced a $3 billion program of research for the solar industry.[49] By the next decade, the United States represented 80 percent of the still tiny world market for solar energy.

VI BUILDING A TERRESTIAL MARKET AND THE ENTRY OF BIG BUSINESS

The rise of federal and state government investments in solar energy provided a useful backdrop for a new generation of American entre-preneurs who sought to build a market for solar beyond the space program. This turned out to be an expensive proposition, both in terms of the capital and the time needed to develop technologies. Entrepreneurs found themselves seeking funds from large corporations. Surprisingly, the largest oil companies emerged as key investors.

Start-ups in 1973 began the new era. The first company was founded by Elliot Berman, a New Jersey-based industrial chemist, who developed a new, cheaper type of solar cell based on organic materials such as dyes. While working as a US defense contractor at a company that made cameras for spy satellites, Berman became interested in providing solar electrical power to the rural poor in developing countries. In view of the high cost of silicon cells, he suggested to the company that it needed to invest in a new type of solar cell, made from the photographic film on which he was working. When his company would not take up the idea, he left to found his own company, but he failed to secure funding. A chance conversation led Berman to Exxon, which had just begun to consider alternative energies in the expectation that conventional energy prices would raise substantially over the following decades. Berman moved his lab into the oil company, and started developing this new technology. The organic cells he was proposing would take years to develop; in the meantime, he decided to buy conventional silicon solar cells with which he commercialized an interim product.[50] Berman first tried to purchase these cells from a small company named Centralab, but the company only sold rejects from the space program, which was far from enough to meet his needs. He then decided to fly to Japan, to meet with the Japanese electronics company Sharp which had been producing solar cells for over a decade. Unfortunately, Berman and representatives from Sharp (discussed below) could not agree on a price, and thus no agreement was reached.[51]

Berman realized he needed to manufacture these silicon solar cells himself. In April 1973, he launched Solar Power Corporation as a fully owned subsidiary of Exxon. This was the first company established to specifically manufacture terrestrial PV cells in the United States. Berman did not use the expensive pure semiconductor-grade crystalline silicon employed in the space industry, but instead used cheaper silicon wafers rejected by the semiconductor industry.[52] Berman initially believed that the US Coast Guard would be his primary customer, but this did not work out.[53] Instead, Berman started manufacturing solar cells to be used on Exxon's offshore platforms in the Gulf of Mexico. According to Berman:

> We went and visited some Exxon platform in the gulf. What we learned, which everybody down there knew, but nobody at the headquarters knew, is you have one platform that's loaded with power, and that's where all the crews live. However, most of the platforms are unmanned and have no power.[54]

At the time, the system for powering platforms relied on large lead-acid batteries, each weighing several hundred pounds and costing over $2,100 each. When these batteries were exhausted, the crew would simply dump them in the waters, which had a devastating effect on marine life. In 1978 the Environmental Protection Agency outlawed such disposing of batteries in the ocean, which added a sense of urgency for oil companies to come up with new ways to power their platforms. This was the first of a number of investments in solar energy by US oil companies.

A second large US oil company to become interested in solar was Mobil. As with Exxon, the origins of its involvement lay outside the company. A researcher named Abraham Mlavsky worked at an investment and holding company called Tyco, in Waltham, Massachusetts, which, during the 1960s, was engaged in semiconductors and energy conversion. Mlavsky developed the process for producing a continuous thin ribbon of silicon that could be separated into suitable lengths, processed into solar cells and then placed in modules. In 1971, in search of lighter weight solar cells, NASA gave Tyco the opportunity to produce solar cells from ribbon silicon, but Tyco was unable to achieve suitable conversion efficiencies. NASA resumed interest two years later, and in 1974 Mobil and the Tyco joined forces to begin developing advanced silicon solar cells. Mobil-Tyco spent years attempting to develop efficient production, and by the end of the 1980s they had cut the cost of fabricating crystalline silicon solar cells in half.[55]

The entry into solar by Atlantic Richfield Oil Company (ARCO), a third US oil company, came through the activities of another start-up, launched in 1973. Joseph Lindmeyer and Peter Varadi, two Hungarian-born engineers, were working on space solar cells for a satellite company called Communications Satellite Corporation (COMSAT), which was US-government sponsored but privately owned. In 1973 Lindmeyer and Varadi set up their own company, Solarex. They targeted the terrestrial market, perceiving solar as a decentralized energy source, and explicitly sought not to rely on government business, which Varadi perceived as "dangerous because the direction of government spending can make a 180 degree turn." They also saw the potential not of the "small local market" but of a "large global market (with) at least 1.6 billion people without electricity who would require decentralized access to electricity."[56] Varadi was particularly interested in the potential of PV to power water pumping in developing countries, "where water was needed for people and animals and for irrigation."[57]

The company did well but struggled to build a market beyond watches and calculators until the second oil crisis. Solarex's big breakthrough came in 1979 when it obtained equity funding from three large companies. Holec, a Dutch electrical company, and Leroy-Somer, a French electric power generating company, invested to obtain Solarex's expertise and license in manufacturing PV cells. Leroy-Somer saw solar as a means to power the water pumps they operated in West Africa.[58] The most significant investment for Solarex was a $7 million investment from Amoco. With an apparently booming PV market due to supportive US government policies, Solarex spent this investment on a new "breeder" plant powered by PV cells to produce PV cells. To show its support, Amoco installed Solarex PV panels on one of the service stations located at its head office in Chicago.[59] In 1980 an article in the *New York Times*, on the subject of innovation in America, singled out three companies as exemplars of innovation; Solarex was one of them, along with Apple and Genentech.[60]

During the early 1980s, the combination of declining oil prices and the withdrawal of federal government support resulted in Solex experiencing difficulties as the PV market stalled. In 1983 Maryland Bank, with which Solarex had a $7 million debt, demanded full repayment within three months after becoming alarmed by a reporting mistake by the Solarex chief financial officer. Solarex could not repay the money or refinance. Efforts to find new investors proved fruitless. Amoco acquired full control of Solarex, which joined Solar Power as an oil company-owned venture.[61]

Acquisition by an oil company was also the destiny of another entrepreneurial start-up by a former employee of Spectrolab, Bill Yerkes. Yerkes, a mechanical engineering graduate of Stanford University, worked for Chrysler and Boeing, with which he built the Boeing Kent Space Environment Laboratory in support of the Apollo lunar landings. After moving to Los Angeles, Yerkes became chief executive officer of Spectrolab – still owned by Textron – where he was responsible for developing the solar technology that, along with space batteries, was left behind on the moon by Apollo 11. During his time at Spectrolab, Yerkes and his wife had opted to live an alternative, environmentally friendly lifestyle for nearly two years, living in a 24-foot house trailer in which all appliances, including an electric composting toilet, were powered solely by PV cells, despite the presence of adjacent power lines.[62]

Yerkes was sacked when Hughes Aircraft acquired Spectrolab in 1975. He resolved to build his own solar company, founding Solar Technology International in 1975 with $80,000 of his own money as seed capital. He achieved major advances in production that became standard for the industry and which reduced costs. However, it proved hard to raise further necessary capital, so in 1977 he sold his company to ARCO, another large US oil company, to form ARCO Solar.[63] ARCO's investment in solar reflected the firm's longstanding commitment to environment issues under its founder, Robert O. Anderson, who was one of the founders of the environmentalist organization, Friends of the Earth.[64] Going into commercial production in 1980, ARCO built the first production facility of greater than 1 million watts (MW) capacity. ARCO was involved in several high-profile PV projects, including utility-scale plants in California. Internationally, ARCO developed partners and sold PVs for off-grid applications in more than 80 countries.[65] The firm's sales reached $40 million in 1988, and it became the largest PV manufacturer in the world.[66] However, Yerkes himself became increasingly unhappy. ARCO imported managers who had no understanding of solar technology and who pursued technological options in thin-film silicon, which he considered unviable. He left the firm in 1985, returning to Boeing.[67] Table 3.1 shows the US oil companies that invested in and/or sold off solar energy companies from 1970 to 1983.

Table 3.1   Major US oil company investments in solar energy, 1970–83

Date	Firm	Strategy	Outcome
1973	Exxon	Creates Solar Power	Solar Power sold to Solarex in 1984
1974	Mobil	Joint venture with Tyco	Venture sold to Applied Solar Energy in 1994
1977	ARCO	Acquires Solar Technology International (Solar)	ARCO Solar sold to Siemens in 1990
1979	Amoco	Invests in Solar Power (100% in 1983)	Amoco acquired by BP in 1999

Source: Author research

This period also saw the renewal of parabolic solar endeavors. The biggest was LUZ International, created by Arnold Goldman. Goldman had become wealthy after selling his word-processing start-up, and in 1977 he moved from the United States to Israel to finish a book on philosophy and social theory. Goldman envisaged the creation of a utopian city, which he named LUZ, after the biblical city in which Jacob dreamed of a ladder ascending to heaven; in Goldman's case, LUZ would have a wall that would gather sunlight to provide energy. He advocated a new type of intellectualism he called biocosmology, which would allow humans to "clearly see the relationship between the whole and the particulars of daily life."[68] After trying and failing to get venture capital funding for developing solar energy in Israel, Goldman switched his attention to America, with the idea that PURPA provided the prospect of supplying an energy grid. Between 1984 and 1990, LUZ raised $1 billion, with which Goldman built nine reflective solar collectors in the Mojave Desert that focused sunlight on oil-carrying receiver pipes. The oil was heated as it circulated through the pipe to create the steam for turbine generators. LUZ sold its electricity using the feed-in tariffs, and earned returns for its investors through careful use of tax credits.[69]

The United States became the world leader in solar energy. LUZ made successful use of tax concessions and PURPA. Large investments by oil companies encouraged a rapid growth of PV production in the United States. "The oil industry is generally considered the Big Bad Wolf for PV," Varadi later noted, yet "the oil companies provided money, which no other investor did, for the establishment of the first terrestrial solar cell and module factories."[70] Table 3.2 shows the history of PV production in the United States from the mid-1970s through the mid-1990s.

Table 3.2   US PV solar production, 1976–95

Year	Annual Production	Cumulative Production
	Megawatts	
1976	0.3	0.3
1977	0.4	0.7
1978	0.8	1.6
1979	1.2	2.8
1980	2.5	5.3
1981	3.5	8.8
1982	5.2	14.0
1983	8.2	22.2

Year	Annual Production	Cumulative Production
	Megawatts	
1984	8.0	30.2
1985	7.7	37.9
1986	7.1	45.0
1987	8.7	53.7
1988	11.1	64.8
1989	14.1	78.9
1990	14.8	93.7
1991	17.1	110.8
1992	18.1	128.9
1993	22.4	151.4
1994	25.6	177.0
1995	34.8	211.8

Source: Earth Policy Institute, "Climate, Energy, and Transportation" webpage

In 1995 the US production of 34.8 MW was by far the largest share of total world production, which was 78 MW. Japan was the second most important country, with 14 MW.[71]

As Table 3.3 shows, US companies were also prominent among the largest PV manufacturers, again with only Japanese firms as substantive competitors.

The size of the US manufacturers, however, did not translate into profits. A major problem was that solar had sustained profitably only in niche markets in which conventional fuels could not compete, such as in space satellites and on offshore oil platforms, or when there were tax concession and subsidies. During the 1980s, oil companies accounted for 70 percent of all the solar modules sold in the United States.[72] In other markets, solar energy was vulnerable both to the shifts in the price of alternative fuels and to changing public policies. During the 1970s, both factors favored the rapid build-up of solar energy in the United States, but during the following decade they eroded the conditions that had favored the spread of solar. The world price of oil, which had peaked in 1980 at more than $35 per barrel, fell to $10 per barrel by 1986. The price of oil and natural gas remained far below previous heights for the next two decades. This coincided with ideological shifts in the United States that resulted in reduced support for renewable energy.

Table 3.3 PV solar manufacturer rankings and world market share, 1988

Company	Country	World production (%)
ARCO Solar	United States	17.5
Solec/Sanyo	Japan	16.5
Solarex	United States	10
ASE (RWE Schott Solar)	Germany	8
Kyocera	Japan	5.5
BP Solar	United Kingdom	4.5
Photowatt	France	2
Sharp	Japan	2
Helios	Italy	1.5
Top 9 total production as % total		67.5
WORLD TOTAL PRODUCTION (MW)		33.9

Source: Author estimate based on Haller and Grupp, "Demand," 502; 1988 world capacity from World Solar

The election of Ronald Reagan as president in 1980 brought the Carter solar program to an abrupt end. During fiscal year 1981, the Reagan administration cut solar funding by $79 million and reduced the solar energy budget to about $193 million for fiscal year 1982, in favor of nuclear energy. Reagan rejected recommendations of the Solar Energy Research Institute (SERI), which suggested that the United States could implement a program to increase its share of renewables in energy production. Instead, the staff of SERI was cut from 950 to 350 employees.[73] The vocal support for solar of environmentalists and antinuclear activists, such as actress Jane Fonda, proved a liability in the new political context, as solar became polarized within the American political system.[74] Solar tax credits, however, escaped the Reagan budget axe. These credits included a 40 percent residential credit for homeowners on the first $10,000 invested in solar equipment and conversion; a 15 percent residential credit for landlords; a 15 percent business investment credit; and a tax credit for industrial development bonds for state renewable resource programs. In California, however, the Republican governors who succeeded Jerry Brown after 1982 began to close down credits and subsidies.[75]

The changing price of oil and shifts in public policies resulted in divestments and closures. Some entrepreneurs at the time understood this risk. Varadi later commented on his own policy regarding Solarex:

> We never relied on government money or programs, we were constantly going after customers, where the real money is. For example, Solar Power Corp, who was our main competitor when we started, had to shut down because they were depending on federal funding and the government was also their main customer. We made it a point to not work exclusively with government agencies at Solarex.[76]

Solar companies in the United States became pawns in the market for corporate control, as each owner who failed to make the business profitable responded by selling to another. In 1984 Exxon sold the Solar Power Corp. to Amoco-owned Solarex. Six years later in 1990, ARCO, then the largest PV manufacturer in the world but not the most profitable, sold its solar business to Siemens.[77] Five years later, Siemens sold the business to Shell. Mobil sold its solar business to German-owned Applied Solar Energy (ASE) in 1994.[78] Amoco retained control of Solarex, although its consumer product and other divisions were sold off, as was most of its international business. In 1996 the solar business was placed into a joint venture with Enron, and three years later the British oil company BP acquired the whole of Amoco.[79]

The changing environment also resulted in the end of LUZ. The company had survived the Reagan decade. By 1990 it had built and installed those nine solar power stations in California. For the tenth project, it had hoped that investors from previous projects would continue as before. However, LUZ had previously been exempt from Californian property tax, and this exemption suddenly stopped. It was a fatal development. LUZ filed for bankruptcy in 1991, although its stations have continued to generate electricity and serve as the world's largest solar site.[80]

VII THE RISE OF THE JAPANESE SOLAR INDUSTRY

During the 1970s, Japan lacked both the huge space program and the governmental investment in renewables that drove the growth of the American PV industry. Instead, in Japan, electronics firms that perceived the potential of solar for commercial use took the lead.

The industry was created and shaped by three electronic corporations based in the Kansai region, at a considerable distance from Tokyo and with a tradition of independence from the government bureaucracy based in Tokyo. The pioneer venture was Sharp. This company originated before World War I, and was founded as a metalworking shop by Tokuji Hayakawa, who had a desire to make people happy. The company pioneered the Japanese production of radios during the 1920s, and after World War II it diversified into televisions. In 1953 it launched the first commercial television set, and over the following years it also made refrigerators and washing machines. In 1961 Sharp began to invest in new product development in electronics, and this took the firm into electronic calculators, optical semiconductors, computers and solar cells. Sharp's engineers focused on developing marketable applications for solar cells. This led to the use of Sharp solar cells in the No. 1 Tsurumi light buoy in Yokohama Port in 1963.[81]

Sharp developed the world's first electronic calculators, and then office products during the 1970s. It continued to invest in PV as part of its business portfolio. Japan's modest space program provided a market for some cells. In 1976 the Japanese satellite *Ume* was launched with Sharp's solar cells on board. However, Sharp's primary focus was commercial applications. In 1976 Sharp introduced the world's first solar-powered calculator. In 1979, at its R&D facility near Nara, the company built a hybrid house that was powered and heated by solar panels. None of these activities generated profits, and the continued investment appears to have been motivated by the personal vision of Hayakawa. He wrote in his 1970 biography:

> I believe the biggest issue of the future is the accumulation and storage of solar heat and light. While all living things enjoy the blessings of the sun, we have to rely on electricity from power stations. With magnificent heat and light streaming down on us, we must think of ways of using those blessings. This is where solar cells come in.[82]

A different approach was taken by the Kyocera Corporation, which was founded as Kyoto Ceramic Co. Ltd. in 1959 by Kazuo Inamori. Kyocera's original product was a ceramic insulator for use in television picture tubes. The company quickly adapted its technologies to produce an expanding range of ceramic components for electronic and structural applications. In the 1960s in the United States, the NASA space program, the birth of Silicon Valley and the advancement of computer technology created demand for semiconductor integrated circuits, for which Kyocera developed ceramic semiconductor packages. In the mid-1970s, Kyocera began expanding its material technologies to produce a diverse range of applied ceramic products, and it invested in solar.

Inamori's interest in solar originated in his growing awareness of environmental problems. Japan's rapid industrialization during the 1950s and 1960s resulted in growing pollution. Inamori noted that the water from his own factories polluted rivers and killed fish, and by the late 1960s he was already investing in water purification technology, even though it forced up the costs of his still medium-sized company.[83] These environmental issues led him into solar after a fortuitous encounter with a new technology in the United States. As he later described:

> From various media articles, I knew that some [Japanese] companies such as Sharp and US companies had been developing solar cells and that solar power was, though weak, a most ideal alternative energy source. Japan had no energy sources and had to import everything including coal, oil and natural gas, and I thought it was a weak point of the nation ... I became friends of a president of Tyco, a venture company based in Boston. I learned that Tyco had successfully developed a technology to pull out a single crystal sapphire—being a ceramist I had some expertise in crystallization of minerals. When I heard about this, with this technology, I thought it would enable us to create various shapes of sapphire.[84]

Inamori's encounter with Tyco came just as the oil shock was hitting Japan, and he realized the implications for making solar cells.

> Till then, solar cell was produced by pulling out [a] single crystal silicon in a [cylindrical] shape and slicing the silicon cylinder into pieces, like creating wafer[s] for semiconductor[s]. But Tyco people told me that, if using their method, there would be no need to make silicon in a cylinder shape and no need to slice it. They said they would be able to produce solar cells much less expensively by pulling out silicon in a film form.[85]

Inamori considered producing solar cells using the method, but concluded that a single company could not handle mass production. He then contacted the heads of Sharp and Matsushita, leading electronics companies, and they established a joint venture called the Japan Solar Energy Corporation.[86]

The Japanese government, like the US government, became interested in solar energy after the oil shocks. In 1974 Project Sunshine was launched to explore alternative energy sources. This turned out to be at best ineffective, for the focus was on solar thermal energy, even though Japan frequently had cloudy skies.[87] At worst, the government programs were environmentally damaging, as the ocean thermal energy conversion technology developed by the project facilitated stratospheric ozone depletion.[88] Although Project Sunshine sponsored considerable R&D into renewable energy, the government also made no effort to translate research into actual products. The Japanese government's reaction to the energy crisis was to work toward securing stable oil supplies and to promote the development of nuclear power, which it insisted was a clean energy source. There were yet further obstacles because the country's ten electric companies monopolized the energy market, and none had interest in solar, wind or any other renewable energy.[89]

Inamori, who was concerned to keep his distance from government, recognized the futility of the Japanese energy policy. He mobilized his engineers at Kyocera to work on the development of solar cells, but it proved a lengthy and costly process to pull out silicon in a film form by a roller. The company also tried to develop a market by creating various products such as solar-powered batteries for portable radio and road signs. In 1979 the company received its first large order, which was for panels to power a microwave telecom relay station located in the Peruvian Andes.[90] As the memory of the oil shocks faded, and costs stubbornly refused to come down, the solar joint venture stumbled, and Kyocera became its sole owner. Inamori again found a foreign technology that could help. Wacker, the German electronics company, had a developed multicrystal silicon wafer. Inamori scrapped all his firm's existing production facilities and shifted to a multicrystal approach, which produced silicon ingot via molding. This would in time become a major production method for making solar cells. Inamori established the Shiga Yohkaichi Factory in 1980, and manufacturing of solar cells started with mass production of multicrystalline silicon solar cells two years later. In 1993 Kyocera achieved a 19.5 percent world record efficiency with single crystal silicon solar cells.[91]

By then a third Kansai-based electronics company, Sanyo, had developed an even larger solar business. It also employed solar cells in its calculators but did not use crystalline silicon, instead Sanyo used thin-film technology. This was not as efficient at converting sunlight into electricity but performed well when applied under electronic light. The huge growth of the solar-powered calculator market resulted in Sanyo emerging as the world's largest solar cell manufacturer by 1986.[92]

Over the following years, Japan became the largest solar cell-producing country in the world, accounting for 40 percent of the world's production at its peak, before being replaced by Europe, and then China, as the largest manufacturer.

VIII SOLAR ENERGY IN EUROPE

In Europe, as in Japan, there was an early interest in the potential of PV solar energy from large electronics companies. In Germany, the electronics giant Siemens conducted experimental research from the 1950s. During the second half of the 1950s, Kees Daey Ouwens, a young engineer at Philips, the leading Dutch electronics company, did experimental research on solar cells, powering a transistor radio with them in the garden of Philips's physics laboratory. However, interest in the technology waned after the discovery of the large gas field at Groningen in 1959. During the 1970s, Ouwens continued to work on solar at Eindhoven University, which hosted conferences on renewable energy, especially its use in developing countries. In 1981 a Dutch company, Holecsol, was founded to produce solar cells.[93]

As elsewhere, the rising oil prices of the 1970s increased interest in alternatives to fossil fuels. France, like the United States, became engaged in solar energy research. In 1975 the Centre national de la recherché scientifique, the state research agency, built a 1000-kilowatt solar furnace at Odeillo, the world's largest, high up in the French Pyrenees, while the French space agency began research on thin-film solar cells in Toulouse.[94] French oil companies also looked to the solar industry. The Compagnie Française des Petroles (CFP), the largest French oil company, began investing in solar energy research in 1975 (along with US firm Photon Power), but this was soon abandoned. In 1983 CFP returned to solar by establishing Total Énergie, in Africa, with a mission to develop renewable energy resources. It began manufacturing solar modules in South Africa in 1996, and by the end of the decade had acquired large franchises in Morocco and had developed a European business.[95] Photowatt, a firm established by EFL Acquitaine, an oil company, and by Compagnie General des Eaux, a utility company, struggled until a scientist, Claude Rémy, took control in 1979.[96] By 1988 it accounted for about 2 percent of world production and was ranked as one of the top nine solar firms in the world.

In Italy, there was considerable scientific interest research in solar power, associated especially with Giovanni Francia's experiments with concentrating-type solar thermal employing flat mirrors. Ansaldo, the large electrical machinery company, began PV production during the 1970s, although subsequently withdrew because of unprofitability. The national electric utility Enel built the world's first large concentrating-type plant in Sicily in 1980, but it was closed down after some years of tests.[97] There were also start-ups. In 1981 Franco Traverso founded Helios Technology, near Padua, to manufacture PVs. Traverso was a mechanical engineer whose father owned a small plastics company, and he became "fascinated by the idea of producing energy from the sun." He met a professor from the University of Padua who had worked in silicon technology and had contacts in the United States; these contacts provided the technology for the new venture. Traverso sought his first customers among the owners of country houses in remote rural areas in which solar power offered a solution as a source of electricity, and he used residues from the semiconductor industry as raw materials before inventing a means to recover silicon from used electronic devices.[98] Helios was one of the world's top nine solar producers by 1988, albeit with a small output. Six years later, Photowatt held 2.6 percent of the world market, and Helios 1.4 percent.[99]

A number of small firms were also founded in Spain. From 1977 to 1982, a socialist government led by Felipe Gonzales took some legislative steps to promote renewable energy, although it allocated few financial resources. It did seem to stimulate some interest in the solar business. In 1981 Isofoton was founded in Malaga from a university project led by a professor from the Polytechnic University of Madrid; the project was to build PV cells using silicon wafers technology. In 1983 the firm Atersa was created as a result of the merger four years earlier between two small solar distributors. It developed a small manufacturing business that included installation of PV systems to provide electricity, water pumps and public lighting systems in rural areas. In 1984 the long-established engineering firm of Abengoa, based in Seville, which had provided equipment for electricity grids, built some of the components for a solar platform that began a growing investment in the industry. Felipe Benjumea, the son of the founder, started working in the company in the early 1980s, and he developed an interest in environmental issues, particularly global warming. He decided to invest in renewable energy and to make "greenness" the new core philosophy of the company. Absent of government support, however, the business was largely abroad, beginning with a contract for equipment for the Weizmann Institute of Science, in Israel.[100]

In Britain, a solar industry was slow to develop. An official report by the National Physical Laboratory, the government's measurement standard's laboratory, expressed skepticism about the prospects of solar energy as early as 1952. As a nuclear power, British governments were highly motivated to invest in civilian use of nuclear energy, despite evidence of the risks, including the disastrous fire at the Windscale nuclear plant in October 1957 which spread contamination across Europe.[101] In 1960 the former chief scientist at the Ministry of Fuel and Power noted that he "had been interested in the use of solar energy" but was "not very successful in arousing interest elsewhere." He added that he "[did] not think anyone ever expected that solar energy would be of any serious interest in the United Kingdom, but it has possibilities in sunnier climes."[102] The Tropical Products Institute of the Department of Scientific and Industrial Research, another government department, was indeed interested in the potential for tropical colonies. It even set up a flat-plate solar water heating apparatus on the roof its building in London.[103] Individual enthusiasts within the government continued to make the case for solar power. In the early 1960s, Sir Reginald Plunkett-Ernle-Erle-Drax, a prominent retired admiral in the Royal Navy, campaigned for more research into solar, with little success, finally campaigning for at least research on the use of solar to heat open-air school swimming pools.[104] Modest research efforts continued over the following decade, primarily focused on experimental research developing solar arrays for satellites.[105] In 1975 the Department of the Environment funded the first instrumented solar space heating system in Britain in the new town of Milton Keynes, which was closely monitored over the following five years.[106]

The high oil price of the 1970s stimulated greater interest in solar in Britain, as elsewhere. The country's Department of Energy commissioned a study on the potential of solar energy, which was published in 1976. It concluded that if sufficient investment was made, it was possible to envisage solar energy contributing 2 percent of the country's energy needs within 25 years.[107] In 1977 the Department of Energy launched a £3 million research program to evaluate further solar heating technologies. It was renewed in 1980, but enthusiasm for solar was constantly dampened by the realities of the country's weather. Britain received almost half as much sunshine as Israel or Australia, and mostly in summer, and too little in the middle of the winter.[108] A strategic review of renewable energies in 1982 divided potential energy sources into four categories. It considered onshore wind and tidal energy "strongly placed," passive solar was considered having economic potential but lacking established routes to deployment, solar water heating was regarded as "promising" and active solar space heating as a "long shot." The use of PV solar in Britain was ruled out as inconceivable.[109] In 1980 an estimated 19,000 British homes had solar heating systems, mainly for heating water, but the installation cost was high – between £300 and £1,500 – and consumer lobbyists complained about unscrupulous traders who overpromised results.[110]

The discovery of oil and gas in the North Sea was as fatal as the weather for the development of the solar industry in Britain. BP found gas off the coast of East Anglia in 1965. Ten years later, the large Argyle and Forties oilfields were discovered. By the early 1980s, Britain had become a net exporter of oil, and by the mid-1990s of gas. The government, controlled by the right-wing Conservative Party between 1979 and 1997, had few concerns about the environmental effects of fossil fuels.

It was Germany that became the first European country to adopt a formal renewable energy policy. This originated in 1974 and was primarily initially focused on research. Government spending on solar began modestly, given that boosting nuclear and coal production were the core priorities. The equivalent of €10 million was spent on solar energy in 1974. This had risen to (the equivalent of) €60 million in 1978, and peaked at €150 million in 1982.[111] The Chernobyl nuclear power station accident in 1986 had a huge impact on Germany, and stimulated increased support for alternative energies. In 1990 the government launched a 1,000-roof program for PVs, under which the federal government provided 50 percent of the investment costs plus another 20 percent from the state (Lander) governments. Some 2,250 roofs were equipped with PV modules. In 1991 a feed-in tariff was introduced that required utilities to connect alternative energy generators to the grid and to buy their electricity at agreed rates set at 80 percent of the historical average retail price. The program was capped at 5 percent. This provided incentives to investors, although less for solar because of its high expense. The feed-in tariff rates were less than the cost of producing PV cells, although several Lander governments continued to support solar installations for special purposes, such as schools.[112]

The German policy for renewables provided the context for further investment by Siemens in the solar industry. In the early 1980s, Siemens was part of the first terrestrial application of solar power, and it participated in a European Union (EU) project to install a solar power plant using monocrystalline solar cells on the Greek island of Kythnos. Siemens developed the first thin-film technology based on hydrogenated amorphous silicon. In 1990 Siemens acquired ARCO Solar, taking over its investment in thin-film technology based on copper indium diselenide. The size of the German market could not match that of the United States at that time, so Siemens proceeded to close down its domestic production in favor of its US plants, and focused on supplying markets in the developing world. By 1996, based on crystalline silicon wafer technology, Siemens Solar Industries accounted for one-fifth of the total installed PV capacity worldwide.[113] The other two manufacturers in Germany were divisions of other big companies: Nukem (a uranium services company) and DASA (an aerospace company). In 1994 these firms spun off their solar divisions to form a new company, ASE.[114]

By then, the German policy regime for solar and renewables was modest when compared to what would come later, but the foundation had been built. The structure of electricity distribution facilitated further experimentation with solar energy. Four large companies, including RWE, generated four-fifths of the country's electric power, while the remainder was generated by a thousand or so local electric utilities that were typically owned by the towns they served.[115] This structure provided an opening for local environmental activists to lobby city councils for a system whereby the private owners of solar systems could feed the electricity they generated into the public grid, receiving sufficient funds in return to maintain their systems and make a small profit. It was approved by the government of the Lander of North Rhine-Westphalia in 1994, after several towns had already taken this route. It then spread after that. By 1997, 42 German towns had such systems.[116]

As in the United States (although somewhat later), European oil companies had become interested in solar energy during the 1970s as they pursued the then fashionable strategy of diversification. Shell made unsuccessful forays into nuclear energy and coal during the decade.[117] The company entered solar heating in 1979 with the acquisition of a 50 percent interest in the Australian company Solarhart. This Perth-based company, originally a plumbing and ironworks venture, had developed a solar heating business in the 1950s, and built a nationwide dealer network selling solar water heaters.[118] Two years later Shell acquired Holecsol. In the same year, Showa Oil, Shell's distributor in Japan, entered the solar business. This became a significant part of Shell's Japanese business when it consolidated its businesses in that country in 1985 to form Showa Shell Sekiyu K.K.[119]

BP, Europe's other major global oil company, also entered solar energy. In 1981 it formed a solar joint venture with the British engineering company Lucas Industries to develop PV power systems, and it acquired full ownership in the following year. By 1994 it was the second largest European-owned PV manufacturer, after Siemens, and held the third largest world market share. While Siemens dominated with 20 percent of the world market, Solarex held 9.7 percent and BP 9.3 percent. Sanyo, the largest Japanese company, was in fourth place with 7.9 percent.[120] BP was in the forefront of solar development in many countries, opening a panel manufacturing plant in Madrid, Spain, as early as 1983, for example. By 2001, after acquiring Amoco, BP Solar would become the world's second largest PV manufacturer after Sharp. However, both BP and Shell subsequently withdrew from solar energy.

IX CONCLUSIONS

Starting in the late nineteenth century, the idea of getting "power from sunshine" attracted successive generations of entrepreneurial visionaries, including Aubrey Eneas, Frank Shuman, George Keck, Bill Yerkes, Franco Traverso, Tokuji Hayakawa and Kazuo Inamori, who each sought to build viable businesses around using solar power. They were some-times motivated by broad social and environmental agendas to bring electricity to communities that had no access to it, and to provide careful stewardship over the world's resources. A significant number of indi-viduals, including Frank Shuman, Farrington Daniels, Elliot Berman and multiple British colonial officials, believed in the potential of solar energy to bring electricity to the rural poor of developing countries that lacked alternative power sources.

A perennial problem was that solar technologies were not developed sufficiently to compete with conventional fuels, especially as the latter were not priced to incorporate wider environmental costs. The invention of PV cells in the 1950s, which transformed the potential of solar energy, also vastly increased the financing issues as the technology proved both complicated and expensive. In a repeated pattern, public policy interest in solar increased and the business prospects of solar rose whenever the prices of fossil fuels increased, only to decline when those prices subsequently fell.

Solar companies found themselves in a perennial dilemma. Supportive government policies were a perquisite for driving the industry forward. However, solar was rarely the major preoccupation of governments. The industry became prone to boom-and-bust cycles driven by fickle public policies. In the United States, NASA was the key customer during the 1950s and 1960s, but this market was only for exceptional high-quality products. Meanwhile, energy policy as a whole was dominated by policies that favored fossil fuels and nuclear energy. During the late 1970s and 1980s in the wake of increasing oil prices, PURPA and the supportive state government of California finally offered real opportun-ities for solar, but changing ideologies and falling fossil fuel prices meant that this support was not sustained. Subsequently PV roof policies during the 1990s became an important new source of growth for solar energy in Germany.

As multiple small entrepreneurs worldwide discovered, deep pockets were necessary to develop PV technology. As a result, they turned to big firms as well as government subsidies for capital. The electronics and oil companies that entered the solar industry drove major technological developments. Contrary to some conspiracy theorists, these companies, especially those in petroleum, did not invest in solar technology just to block it. As one study observed, "As the hundreds of millions of dollars [the oil companies] invested demonstrate, they remained true believers for far longer than made financial sense."[121] However solar was also only a part of their portfolios. They assembled production and research assets, invested in them and then sold them as circumstances changed. Changes in corporate ownership added to the uncertainties of an industry whose success always seemed to be just around the corner. It was not until the 2000s, and the massive investments in the PV cell production in China, that the situation changed.

NOTES

*   This chapter appeared in an earlier version as Jones, Geoffrey and Loubna Bouamane, "'Power from Sunshine': A Business History of Solar Energy," *Harvard Business School Working Paper*, 12–105 (May 2012), 1–86.
1.   International Energy Agency, *World Energy Outlook*, 1999.
2.   Shuman, "Power from sunshine."
3.   Perlin, "Solar thermal."
4.   Anderson and Chai, "Becquerel."
5.   Jones, *Profits*, 44.
6.   Arellano and Roca-Rosell, "British Engineering."
7.   Madrigal, *Powering*, 84–6.
8.   US Department of Energy, "History of Solar."
9.   Jones, *Profits*, 45.
10. William Adams, cited in Kryza, *Power*, 95.
11. Kryza, *Power*, 103–4.
12. Ibid., 105.
13. Shuman, "Power from sunshine," 291.
14. Jones, *Profits*, 47.
15. Ibid., 69–70.
16. "History of passive solar design," https://www.revolvy.com/main/index.php?s=History%20of%20passive%20solar%20building%20design, accessed January 7, 2018.
17. Boyce, *Keck & Keck*; Barber, *House*, 21–9.
18. Collins and Nash, "Preserving."
19. Ibid.; Mazria, *Passive*.
20. Jones, *Profits*, 71.
21. Denzer, *Solar House*, 296.
22. Ibid., 298. Barber, *House*, 58–9.
23. Denzer, *Solar House*, 298.
24. Koch, *Home*, 71; Barber, *House*, 19–20, 96.
25. Barber, *House*, 142–9; Olgyay and Olgyay, *Design with Climate*; Sheliahovich, "Bioclimatic." The Olgyays, Koch and the other architects were important figures in the history of sustainable architecture in the United States. There were important contemporaries in other countries, including Hassan Fathy, in Egypt.
26. Jones, *Profits*, 73–4.
27. Barber, *House*.
28. Ibid., 206–11.

29. Ibid., 77; Lipartito, "Rethinking." Interview with Russell Ohl by Lillian H. Hoddeson, July 20, 1976, Niels Bohr Library & Archives, American Institute of Physics.
30. Barber, *House*, 188–95.
31. Memo by J.K. Page and P.C. Spensley, World Conference on Solar Energy (November 1955), CO 927/625, National Archives.
32. Daniels, *Farrington Daniels*, 300.
33. Ibid., 302.
34. Schmidt, "Solar prophets."
35. Daniels, *Farrington Daniels*, 336.
36. Memo by J.G. Carr (Department of Energy, UK), "UN Conference on New and Renewable Sources of Supply," July 3, 1981, T 480/27, National Archives.
37. McKibben, "Race."
38. Jones, *Profits*, 77–8.
39. "International Rectifier Corporation, Photovoltaic Conversion of Solar Energy: Present and Future" (n.d.; ca. 1960), AY 4/2482, National Archives.
40. SkySolar, "1912 Baker Electric Car."
41. Jones, *Profits*, 89–90.
42. United Nations Environment Program, "The Prospects for Solar Energy in the Mediterranean Region," November 22, 1976, Peter S. Thacher Environment Collection, Part 1, Box 77, Folder 729, Widener Library, Harvard University. For the UN Environment Program, see also Ivanova, "Designing."
43. Ford Foundation, *Choose*, 313–14.
44. Ibid.; Jones, *Profits*, 111–12.
45. Statement of Denis Hayes, Senior Researcher, World Watch Institute, in US Congress, *Solar Energy*, 106.
46. Statement of Allen Lober, in Long and Garnish, *Solar Energy*, 86.
47. Jones, *Profits*, 327–8.
48. Statements of Wilson Clark and Ron Doctor, in Long and Garnish, *Solar Energy*, 4–20.
49. Jones, *Profits*, 327.
50. Sun, "Funding."
51. Perlin, *From Space*, 54.
52. Sun, "Funding."
53. Jones, *Profits*, 118.
54. Elliot Berman interview, in Johnstone, *Switching*, 49.
55. Perlin, *From Space*, 168–71.
56. Varadi, *Sun*, 38–9.
57. Ibid., 197.
58. Ibid., 249.
59. Sun, "Funding."
60. Parisi, "Technology."
61. Varadi, *Sun*, 249–50; Jones, *Profits*, 120.
62. Quinn, "Maverick."
63. Jones, *Profits*, 120–21.
64. Ibid., 91; Harris, *Wildcatter*, esp. Chapter 8.
65. Beattie, *History*, 149.
66. Jones, *Profits*, 331.
67. Berger, *Charging*, 80–88; Wald, "ARCO"; Johnstone, *Switching*, 82.
68. Madrigal, *Powering*, 117–26; Berger, *Charging*, 24–5; Blum, "Reaching."
69. Madrigal, *Powering*, 30–43; Jones, *Profits*, 333–4.
70. Varadi, *Sun*, 253.
71. Earth Policy Institute, "Climate" webpage.
72. Perlin, *From Space*, 68 n26.
73. Strum and Strum, "American." For the final Carter administration solar budget request (FY 1982), see US Department of Energy, *Secretary's Annual Report*, 11–12, 43.
74. Johnstone, *Switching*, 81.

75. Strum and Strum, "American."
76. Telephone interview with Peter Varadi by Loubna Bouamane, September 7, 2011.
77. Wald, "ARCO."
78. "Mobil Plans to Close Its Solar Energy Program," *New York Times*.
79. Varadi, *Sun*, 250–51.
80. Jones, *Profits*, 334.
81. Sharp, "Sharp History" webpage.
82. Cited in Johnstone, 125–6.
83. Interview with Kazuo Inamori by Geoffrey Jones, Tokyo, May 27, 2010 (hereafter, interview with Inamori).
84. Ibid.
85. Ibid.
86. Ibid.
87. Johnstone, *Switching*, 123.
88. Matsumoto, "Uncertain."
89. Englander, "Japan's."
90. Johnstone, *Switching*, 127.
91. Jäger-Waldau, *Research*.
92. Johnstone, *Switching*, 126–7.
93. Lysen, "Fifty Years."
94. Gadi Kaplan, "Nontraditional sources: a sampler," IEE Spectrum, February 1977, Polaroid Archives, Box M60, Baker Library, Harvard Business School.
95. Jones and Bouamane, "'Power,'" 44.
96. Lagrange, "Photowatt"; Calori and Noel, "Management."
97. Silvi, "Solar Energy."
98. Interview of Franco Traverso, see Ciuffa, "Franco Traverso."
99. European Commission Directorate-General for Energy and European Photovoltaic Industry Association, *Photovolatics in 2010*.
100. Interview with José Abascal by Loubna Bouamane, Seville, June 14, 2011.
101. Arnold, *Windscale*.
102. Sir Harold Roxbee-Cox to Sir Harry Meville (DSIR), May 5 1960, AY 4/2482, National Archives.
103. P.C. Spensley to E. Barlow Wright, May 25, 1960, AY 4/2482, National Archives.
104. P.C. Spensley, Note of Conversation with Admiral Drax, January 23, 1961, AY 4/2482, National Archives.
105. F.C. Tremble, Large Solar Array Development in the U.K., Royal Aircraft Establishment Technical Report 69007, January 1969, DSIR 23/37104, National Archives.
106. Executive Summary by B. Alper, November 17, 1980, AB 94/50, National Archives.
107. Long and Garnish, *Solar Energy*.
108. Energy Technology Support Unit, Atomic Energy Authority, *Strategic Review of the Renewable Energy Technologies: An Economic Assessment*, November 1982, Appendix 7 Solar heating, EC 2/1416, National Archives.
109. Ibid,
110. Griffiths, "Solar Heating."
111. Lauber and Mez, "Three decades."
112. Ibid.
113. Jones, *Profits*, 339.
114. Johnstone, *Switching*, 153.
115. Ibid., 170–71.
116. Ibid., 171–6.
117. Sluyterman, *Keeping Competitive*, Chapter 2.
118. Shell, "1960s to the 1980s" webpage; Solahart, "A brilliant past. An even brighter future" webpage.
119. Solar Frontier, "Profile" webpage.

120. European Commission Directorate-General for Energy and European Photovoltaic Industry Association, *Photovolatics in 2010*.
121. Johnstone, *Switching*, 55.

REFERENCES

Arellano, Nelson and Antoni Roca-Rosell (2013), "British Engineering in Water Desalinization Using Solar Energy in Chile in the Nineteenth Century," *Quipu, Latin American Journal of the History of Science and Technology*, **15**, (2), 163–91.

Anderson, W.W. and Y.G. Chai (1976), "Becquerel Effect Solar Cell," *Energy Conversion*, **15**, (3–4), 1976, 85–94.

Arnold, Lorna (2007), *Windscale 1957. Anatomy of a Nuclear Accident*, New York: Palgrave Macmillan.

Barber, Daniel A. (2016), *A House in the Sun. Modern Architecture and Solar Energy in the Cold War*, Oxford: Oxford University Press.

Beattie, Donald A. (ed.) (1997), *History and Overview of Solar Heat Technologies*, Cambridge, MA: MIT Press.

Berger, John J. (1997) *Charging Ahead: The Business of Renewable Energy and What it Means for America*, New York: Henry Holt.

Berman, Daniel M. (1996), *Who Owns the Sun? People, Politics, and the Struggle for a Solar Economy*, White River Junction, VT: Chelsea Green Publishing Co.

Blum, Ruthie (2008), "Reaching for the Sun," *The Jerusalem Post*, June 12, accessed August 28, 2017 at http://www.jr.co.il/articles/reaching-for-the-sun.txt.

Boyce, Robert (1993), *Keck & Keck: The Poetics of Comfort*, Princeton, NJ: Princeton Architectural Press.

Calori, Roland and Reynood Noel (1986), "Management stratégique dans les industries émergentes à haute technologie," *Revue d'économie industrielle*, **37**, (3), 15–30.

Collins, Judith and Al Nash (2002), "Preserving Yesterday's View of Tomorrow: The Chicago World's Fair Houses," *Cultural Resource Management*, **25**, (5), 27–31.

Ciuffa, Giosetta (n.d.), "Franco Traverso: Silfab, verso la Filiera Integrata del Fotovoltaico," Specchio Economico, accessed August 28, 2017 at http://www.specchioeconomico.com/201003/traverso.html.

Daniels, Olive (1978), *Farrington Daniels: Chemist and Prophet of the Solar Age*, Madison, WI: Daniels.

Denzer, A. (2008), "The Solar House in 1947," in G. Broadbent and C.A. Brebbia (eds.), *Second International Conference on Harmonisation between Architecture and Nature* (Eco-Architecture II conference proceedings), Southampton, UK: WIT Press.

Earth Policy Institute (n.d.), "Climate, energy, and transportation" webpage, accessed August 28, 2017 at www.earth-policy.org/?/data_center/C23.

Englander, Dave (2008), "Japan's wind-power problem," *Green Tech Media*, April 23, accessed August 28, 2017 at www.greentechmedia.com/articles/read/japans-wind-power-problem-828.

European Commission Directorate-General for Energy and European Photovoltaic Industry Association (1996), *Photovolatics in 2010*, Luxembourg: Office for Official Publications of the European Communities.

Ford Foundation (1974), *A Time to Choose: America's Energy Future: Final Report. Energy Policy–United States*, Cambridge, MA: Ballinger Publishing Co.

Griffiths, Gareth (1980), "Solar Heating 'is Not an Economic Investment,'" *Financial Times*, May 14.

Haller, I. and H. Grupp (2009), "Demand by Product Characteristics: Measuring Solar Cell Quality over Time," *Journal of Evolutionary Economics*, **19**, 487–506.

Harris, Kenneth (1987), *The Wildcatter: Portrait of Robert of Anderson*, New York: Weidenfeld and Nicholson.

International Energy Agency (1999), *World Energy Outlook: Looking at Energy Subsidies: Getting Prices Right* (1999 Insights), Paris: IEA Publications. Accessed August 28, 2017 at http://www.worldenergyoutlook.org/media/weowebsite/2008-1994/weo1999.pdf.

Ivanova, Maria (2007), "Designing the United Nations Environment Programme: A story of Compromise and Confrontation," *International Environment Agreements*, **7**, 337–61.

Jäger-Waldau, Arnulf (2008), *PV Status Report 2008: Research, Solar Cell Production and Market Implementation of Photovoltaics* (EUR 23604 EN), European Commission, Directorate-General Joint Research Centre, Institute for Environment and Sustainability, September, Luxembourg: Office for Official Publications of the European Communities. Accessed August 28, 2017 atwww.eurosfaire.prd.fr/7pc/doc/1299661785_lbna23604enc_001.pdf.

Johnstone, Bob (2011), *Switching to Solar: What We can Learn from Germany's Success in Harnessing Clean Energy*, Amherst, NY: Prometheus Books.

Jones, Geoffrey (2017), *Profits and Sustainability: A History of Green Entrepreneurship*, Oxford: Oxford University Press.

Jones, Geoffrey and Loubna Bouamane, "'Power from Sunshine': A Business History of Solar Energy," *Harvard Business School Working Paper*, 12–105 (May 2012), 1–86.

Katz, David (2007), "How I did it: David Katz, CEO, AEE Solar," *Inc.* (as told to Adam Bluestein), September 1, accessed August 28, 2017 at www.inc.com/magazine/20070901/how-i-did-it-david-katz.html.

Koch, Carl (1958), *At Home with Tomorrow*, New York: Rhinehart.

Kryza, Frank T. (2003), *The Power of Light: The Epic Story of Man's Quest to Harness the Sun*, New York: McGraw-Hill.

Lauber, Volkmar and Lutz Mez (2004), "Three Decades of Renewable Electricity Policies in Germany," *Energy and Environment*, **15**, (4), 599–623.

Lagrange, Catherine (2011), "Photowatt, leader français du photovoltaïque, dépose le bilan," Le Point.fr, November 4, accessed August 28, 2017 at www.lepoint.fr/fil-info-reuters/photowatt-leader-francais-du-photovoltaique-depose-le-bilan-04-11-2011-1392748_240.php.

Lipartito, Kenneth (2009), "Rethinking the Invention Factory: Bell Laboratories in Perspective," in Sally H. Clarke, Naomi R. Lamoreaux and Steven W. Usselman (eds.), *The Challenge of Remaining Innovative*, Stanford, CA: Stanford University Press, 132–62.

Long, Geoffrey and J.D. Garnish (1976), *Solar Energy: Its Potential Contribution within the United Kingdom*, London: HMSO.

Lysen, Erik (2006), "Fifty years of solar PV in the Netherlands," September 27, accessed August 28, 2017 at http://docplayer.net/4582865-Fifty-years-of-solar-pv-in-the-netherlands-erik-lysen-utrecht-centre-for-energy-research-uce.html.

Madrigal, Alexis (2011), *Powering the Dream: The History and Promise of Green Technology*, Cambridge MA: Da Capo.

Matsumoto, Miwao (2005), "The Uncertain but Crucial Relationship Between a 'New Energy' Technology and Global Environmental Problems: The Complex Case of the 'Sunshine' Project," *Social Studies of Science*, **35**, (4), 623–51.

Mazria, Edward (1979), *The Passive Solar Energy Book*, Emmaus, PA: Rodale Press.

McKibben, Bill (2017), "The Race to Solar-power Africa," *The New Yorker*, June.

"Mobil Plans to Close Its Solar Energy Program" (1993), *New York Times*, November 5.

Olygyay, Victor and Aladar Olgyay (1963), *Design with Climate: An Approach to Bioclimatic Regionalism*, Princeton, NJ: Princeton University Press.

Perlin, John (n.d.), "Solar thermal," California Solar Center, accessed August 28, 2017 at www.californiasolarcenter.org/history_solarthermal.html.

Perlin, John (1999), *From Space to Earth: The Story of Electricity*, Ann Arbor, MI: Aatec.

Parisi, Anthony J. (1980), "Technology—Elixir for U.S. industry; 1. Apple Computer new technology: An elixir for America's flagging industry; 2. Genentech; 3. Solarex," *New York Times*, September 28, F1.

Quinn, James (1985), "Maverick using new technology: Arco Solar official left to build own photovoltaic cells," *Los Angeles Times*, April 2, accessed August 28, 2017 at http://articles.latimes.com/1985-04-02/business/fi-19489_1_photo voltaic-cells.

Sharp (n.d.), "Sharp history" webpage, accessed August 29, 2017 at http://sharp-world.com/corporate/info/his/h_company/1962/index.html.

Schmidt, Silke (2014), "Solar prophets: A history of UW-Madison's solar energy lab," Wisconsin Energy Unit, December 4, accessed August 28, 2017 at https://energy.wisc.edu/news/solar-prophets-history-uw-madisons-solar-energy-lab.

Shell (n.d.), "1960s to the 1980s" webpage, accessed August 28, 2017 at www.shell.com/about-us/who-we-are/1960s-to-the-1980s.html.

Sheliahovich, Nataliya (n.d.), "Bioclimatic architecture: Brief history and future of the phenomenon," accessed August 28, 2017 at www.elib.grsu.by/katalog/184667-423959.pdf.

Shuman, Frank (1911), "Power from sunshine: A pioneer solar power plant," *Scientific American*, September 30, accessed August 28, 2017 at https://www.scientificamerican.com/article/power-from-sunshine.

Silvi, Cesare (2010), "The Use of Solar Energy in Human Activities Throughout the Centuries," *Annals of Arid Zone* (special issue on renewable energy), **49** (3 September & 4 December), 157–74. Accessed August 28, 2017 at www.gses.it/pub/STEAM_ELECT_SUN_HEAT2.pdf .

SkySolar (n.d.), "1912 Baker electric car," accessed August 28, 2017 at skysolar.co.nz/1912-baker-electric-car.

Sluyterman, Keetie (2007), *Keeping Competitive in Turbulent Markets, 1973–2007*, vol. 3 of *A History of Royal Dutch Shell*, Oxford: Oxford University Press.

Solar Frontier (n.d.), "Profile" webpage, accessed August 28, 2017 at www.solarfrontier.com/eng/company/profile/index.html..

Solahart, (n.d.), "A brilliant past. An even brighter future" webpage, accessed August 28, 2017 at https://solahart.com.au/our-history.

Strum, Harvey and Fred Strum (1983), "American Solar Energy Policy, 1952–1982," *Environmental Review*, **7**, (2), 135–54.

Sun, Shu (n.d.), "Funding Breakthrough Technology: Case summary: Photovoltaics," CBR, Cambridge Integrated Knowledge Centre, and University of Cambridge. Accessed August 28, 2017 at www.cbr.cam.ac.uk/fileadmin/user_upload/centre-for-business-research/downloads/research-projects-output/photovoltaics-case-report.pdf.

US Congress, Committee on Government Operations / Environment, Energy, and Natural Resources Subcommittee (1979), *Solar Energy: Hearings before a Subcommittee of the Committee on Government Operations, House of Representatives, May 12, June 12, 13 and 14, 1978*, Washington DC: US Government Printing Office.

US Department of Energy (1981), *Secretary's Annual Report to Congress*, Vol. II, Washington: US Government Printing Office.

Varadi, Peter F. (2014), *Sun Above the Horizon: Meteoric Rise of the Solar Industry*, Singapore: Pan Stanford Publishing.

U.S. Department of Energy, "History of solar," accessed May 1, 2018 at https://www1.eere.energy.gov/solar/pdfs/solar_timeline.pdf.

Wald, Matthew L. (1989), "ARCO to sell Siemens its solar energy unit," *New York Times*, August 3.

World Solar Photovoltaics Production, 1975–2009, accessed January 8, 2018 at http://www.earth-policy.org/datacenter/pdf/book_wote_energy_solar.pdf.

PRIMARY MATERIALS

Telephone interviews by Loubna Bouamane with José Abascal, June 14, 2011, and Peter Varadi, September 7, 2011; Interview by Geoffrey Jones with Kazuo Inamori, Tokyo May 27, 2010.

National Archives, London.

Niels Bohr Library & Archives, American Institute of Physics, College Park, MD (see www.aip.org/history/ohilist/LINK, accessed August 28, 2017).

Peter S. Thacher Environment Collection, Widener Library, Harvard University, Cambridge, MA.
Polaroid Archives, Baker Library, Harvard Business School, Boston, MA.

4. Financing sustainability*

With Emily Grandjean and Andrew Spadafora

I INTRODUCTION

In March 2009 banking leaders from eleven financial institutions gathered in the Netherlands to form an alliance in support of an alternative financial paradigm. The founding members of the alliance, who collectively managed US $14 billion and provided financial services to seven million customers in almost two dozen countries, were committed to providing an alternative set of values to the perceived failings of those of conventional financial institutions. The three organizations that worked together to found this group, called the Global Alliance for Banking on Values (GABV), included Bangladesh Rehabilitation Assistance Committee (BRAC) Bank in Bangladesh, ShoreBank in Chicago, US, and Triodos Bank in the Netherlands. Membership was restricted to institutions that offered "full banking services" and possessed more than $100 million on their balance sheets. Table 4.1 lists all the founding companies.[1]

The timing of the formation of GABV was not accidental. During the previous decades there had been a remarkable financialization of capitalism. Global financial assets had increased from $56 trillion in 1990 to $206 trillion in 2007.[2] This trend had driven, or at least coincided with, a wave of globalization and a surge of modern economic growth, but the macroeconomic trends had also been lumpy and uneven. There had been a growing number of financial crises, including the Asian financial crisis in 1997 and the collapse of the internet stock market boom in 2000, culminating in the precipitous fall of the subprime housing market in the United States in 2007 which evolved as a global financial crisis. Very large differences in wealth and incomes had opened up in rich countries such as the United States and emerging markets such as China. The degradation of Earth's natural environment, and the perceived risks of

93

Varieties of green business

Table 4.1   Founding members of the GABV, 2009

Institution	Headquarters	Year founded	Institution type	Total assets ($ million)
Alternative Bank Schweiz	Switzerland	1990	Social bank	887
Banco del Éxito (Banex)	Nicaragua	2002	Microfinance	180 (2008)
Banca Popolare Etica	Italy	1999	Social bank	966
BRAC Bank	Bangladesh	2001	Microfinance	1,363
GLS Bank	Germany	1974	Social bank	1,936
Merkur Cooperative Bank	Denmark	1982	Social bank	290
Mibanco	Peru	1998	Microfinance	1,290
New Resource Bank	United States	2006	Social bank	162
ShoreBank	United States	1973	Social bank	2,400 (2008)
Triodos Bank	Netherlands	1980	Social bank	4,279
XacBank	Mongolia	2001	Microfinance	224

Sources: GABV, "Alternative"; GABV, "Banca"; GABV, "Banex"; GABV, "BRAC"; GABV, "GLS"; GABV, "Merkur"; GABV, "Mibanco"; GABV, "New"; GABV, "Triodos"; GABV, "XacBank"; Post and Wilson, "Too Good."

climate change, had also emerged as matters of urgent debate. The drivers of these trends were complex and multi-faceted, but there also emerged a growing consensus among NGOs, environmentalists and others that the conventional financial industry was contributing to making – rather than solving – many of the social and environmental problems that were perceived.[3] There were "reasons to believe," a book on business and sustainability published in 1996 argued, that financial markets "undervalue environmental resources, discount the future, and favor accounting and reporting systems that do not reflect environmental risks and opportunities."[4] The global financial crisis served as a catalyst to create the GABV to formalize links between financial institutions which perceived themselves as offering an alternative to the failed conventional financial system.

This chapter explores the historical origins of the financial institutions which came to form GABV. GABV's members had, the organization website noted, "one thing in common: a shared mission to use finance to deliver sustainable economic, social and environmental development, with a focus on helping individuals fulfil their potential and build stronger communities."[5] Ever since the Brundtland Commission report on *Our Common Future* in 1987, sustainable development had been defined very broadly as achieving economic growth, environmental protection and social equality.[6] It was not surprising, then, that beyond their "shared mission," the banks in GABV looked very different. Triodos, ShoreBank and their equivalents offered savings accounts and made loans and investments.[7] The term "social bank" is used in Table 4.1, but the banks concerned used many other terms beside "social" including ethical, community, sustainable and alternative. While the European social banks were particularly focused on facilitating small businesses pursuing environmental sustainability, the US banks were particularly focused on proving small loans and services to businesses in inner cities, as well as those owned by minority ethnic groups. BRAC and other microfinance institutions (MFIs) were primarily focused on the provision of small-scale financial services to people in emerging markets who lacked access to traditional banking services.[8]

This chapter explores the origins of these different varieties of financial institution, and compares and contrasts their impact and limitations. Social banks are the subject of Section II, while MFIs are discussed in Section III. Section IV concludes.

II THE ADVENT AND DEVELOPMENT OF SOCIAL BANKING

The origin of the concept of social banking can be traced back a long time. As a disproportionate number of the social banks founded after the 1970s were cooperative in structure, the cooperative credit union movement started by Hermann Schulze-Delitzsch and Friedrich Wilhelm Raiffeisen in Germany in the middle of the nineteenth century has been seen by some scholars as a remote ancestor.[9] A far more direct ancestor can be found in the thoughts of Rudolf Steiner, an Austrian philosopher, social reformer and the founder of anthroposophy (a "science of the spirit"), shortly after the end of World War I. He proposed the creation of a "bank-like institution" whose goal would not be to maximize profits, but to support an ecosystem of sustainable enterprises and related educational and cultural institutions.[10] Steiner's views were, and have remained, highly unconventional. In the broadest terms, he offered an alternative view of reality and human history. He argued that human beings lived both on Earth and in the spiritual world, but warned that growing materialism had opened a gap with the spiritual world which needed to be reversed. Anthroposophy was and has continued to be widely considered as esoteric and outlandish. Yet for his followers it offered an explanation of the fundamental drivers of societal, ethical and environmental challenges of modern societies, and a holistic vision of what was needed to overcome them. A distinctive feature of Steiner and his followers was their interest in practical solutions. During World War I and its aftermath, Steiner and those around him developed a new method of children's education, which became the basis for the Waldorf school movement, and sketched guiding principles for organic agriculture and pharmaceuticals made from natural ingredients.[11] The following chapters on organic food and wine will further examine his impact.

Steiner's idea of a "bank-like institution" was not immediately pursued, and his small band of followers focused over the following half-century on education and biodynamic agriculture. During the 1970s, however, Steiner's ideas about finance inspired the founding of the first social bank in modern history, by individuals who believed, as Steiner observed in 1922, that "money is the Spirit at work in the economic organism."[12]

In Germany, the lawyer Wilhelm Ernst Barkhoff and Dr. Gisela Reuther, a tax consultant, founded in 1974 the mutually-owned co-operative Gemeinschaft für Leihen und Schenken (GLS), which translates to "community bank for loans and gifts."[13] Nearly 20 years previously Barkhoff had encountered an anthroposophist trying to finance the building of a new Waldorf school. This set him off on a path of seeking to create an institution whose purpose was not to make money from money, but help finance projects to provide socially useful goods and services.[14] In 1961 Barkhoff and Reuther created a nonprofit trust to financially support more Waldorf schools. In 1974, the government granted this association permission to offer banking services.[15] GLS became Germany's first social bank.

The mission of GLS was based on Steiner's anthroposophical principles, which combined social, cultural and environmental ideals as goals equally worth pursuing.[16] GLS financed biodynamic farming very early on. Barkhoff was so inspired by one group of farmers who wanted to lease an estate and convert it over to biodynamic farming principles that he personally helped to provide the collateral.[17] Over time, GLS's environmental ambitions grew. In 1989, the bank established the first wind power fund in Germany, although it suffered at the outset owing to its investments in the Geowian wind facility which faced high levels of downtime for repairs.[18] In the same year, GLS was a founding member of one of the first formal networks of sustainable banks and investors, the

International Association for Investors in the Social Economy.[19] A sustainable agriculture fund followed in 1992. In 2003, GLS acquired Ökobank, an environmental bank established in Frankfurt in 1988 by environmental activists. Ökobank, which was closely connected to pacifist and green political groups, had branches in Frankfurt and Freiburg at the time of acquisition, but had become enmeshed in financial difficulties. Its acquisition led not only to two new branches for GLS (which had already expanded to Stuttgart and subsequently in 2008 to Berlin and Munich) but also to new product offerings, namely checking accounts, further green investment funds and green construction finance.[20]

Since GLS did not offer interest rates to depositors that were competitive with those of conventional banks, its value proposition was centered on giving its depositors the freedom to choose the sector or sectors in the bank's loan portfolio their money would be used to finance.[21] Lower interest rates – or at least, the perception of diminished financial returns – served as a significant barrier that prevented social banking from growing beyond its niche market. However, GLS's management was not interested in their institution's growth per se, but rather in providing services to support activities it considered promoted sustainability.[22]

In 1974, the same year in which GLS formed, another social bank was established. Based in Britain, Mercury Provident was a "licensed deposit-taking" financial institution.[23] It, too, was founded by followers of Steiner and provided financial support to a number of anthroposophical education and health projects, as well as a variety of other endeavors, including publishing, retirement homes, research in organic agriculture and a women's shoemaking cooperative. As the institution described itself, it looked "for the impulse inspiring the project to sense whether it is altruistic, responds to the urgent needs of the times and works for the future benefit of mankind."[24] Mercury Provident was unique in offering "target accounts" which allowed depositors to select their interest rate (from 0 to 7 percent) and the borrowers to whom their money would be lent. The bank found that their investor clients were often willing to choose the lower interest rates, inspired by the compassionate nature of the projects funded. In the early 1990s, Mercury Provident's portfolio expanded to include a wind farm, organic gardens, recycling facilities and housing cooperatives.[25]

In 1994 Mercury Provident was acquired by Triodos Bank, which had a balance sheet four times larger than that of Mercury Provident.[26] Triodos's capacity increased tenfold with the transformation of Mercury Provident into a locally-based branch of Triodos. By the time of the takeover, Mercury Provident had successfully provided loans to approximately 550 projects.[27] Unfortunately for Mercury Provident's shareholders, at the time of the takeover they were given Triodos stock to replace their original stock, but the terms of the new stock did not fully account for changes in the British/Dutch exchange rate. In 2003 the shareholders had little choice but to accept new terms for their stock, and as a result experienced 16–20 percent reduction in the value of their original investment.[28]

The Dutch-based Triodos Bank was established in 1980, but its founders had been working on concepts since the late 1960s. The founders, a group of like-minded but diverse business professionals – an economist, a professor of tax law, a management consultant and a banker – organized study groups made up of around two dozen social activists in order to collectively investigate the ways in which money and banking could be used to transform society. Inspired by these ideas which were deeply rooted in anthroposophical philosophy, and galvanized by contemporary events such as the May 1968 civil disturbances in Paris, the group worked together to form the Triodos Foundation in 1971. The Foundation provided funds for innovative small businesses, many of whom had struggled to raise funds from conventional sources, including a man who ran a plumbing business out of his van, as well as a woman who ran a bicycle repair shop – an unusual occupation for a woman, at the time.[29]

Although Triodos's statutes committed the bank to upholding anthroposophical principles, the founders were open-minded in their approach. As a Triodos executive later noted, "They wanted it to be as open as possible." Indeed, the founders carefully selected staff members with diverse value systems and who came from a variety of backgrounds, including conventional banking. This early approach to managing Triodos's team became part of the bank's "DNA."[30] 1980, Triodos had secured a banking license and had $600,000 in share capital.[31]

Triodos became a leader in promoting transparency in finance, eventually publishing a corporate magazine that described the activities of its borrowers. Such a magazine was highly unusual in the world of finance at that time, although GLS, too, published announcements about all the projects it funded in a newsletter called *"Bankspiegel."*[32] Following a values-based approach, Triodos routinely took into account long-term outcomes when making business decisions. This reason led to the refusal to be listed on a stock exchange, as Triodos management believed that stock exchanges were biased toward short-term returns. From the start, the bank was solely financed by savings rather than borrowing from other banks or the capital markets.[33] In 1999, Triodos dropped its strict allegiance to anthroposophical principles in order to expand the reach of its portfolio.[34] By then it had played a particularly significant role in supporting the growth of wind energy through the creation of a wind fund which was both financially successful and played a significant role in helping to grow wind turbine start-ups in Denmark, Germany and the Netherlands.[35]

A number of other social banks with roots in anthroposophy emerged elsewhere in Europe. Merkur Andelskasse (Merkur Cooperative Bank) was founded in Aalborg, Denmark in 1982 by a small collective of approximately 15 people inspired by GLS's example and interested in experimenting with new methods of saving and lending. They were also motivated by anthroposophical concepts regarding the optimal functioning of society, and they saw their initiative as a way to support educational, environmental and cultural initiatives, while promoting the dignity of all individuals, particularly members of disadvantaged groups. The individuals involved in the beginning were not actually interested in establishing a fully-fledged bank; they simply wanted a means of using their savings to help each other fund innovative projects. However, just a few years later, the European Community decided to harmonize banking policy across its member countries. This meant that credit unions, mutual organizations and other association-based financial institutions would begin to be governed by banking laws. In Denmark, government officials decided that savings and loan associations such as Merkur would become cooperative banks, as part of a grandfathering scheme that allowed these associations to bypass the minimum capital requirement traditionally required of banks.[36]

In its infancy, Merkur was operated solely as a labor of love by its volunteers, but over time it became more systematically organized. The bank conducted its record-keeping by hand until it was able to find a data center that could record its transactions.[37] In 1985, following a merger with another independent finance project, Merkur received a banking license and opened an office in Aalborg. By 1992 it had established another office in Copenhagen.[38] As the bank developed, Merkur did not necessarily seek to limit its growth, so long as the growth happened "organically," through the accumulation of deposits rather than growing by means of capital markets. As Merkur's CEO Lars Pehrson later observed, the bank's growth did not indicate that it was becoming any less sustainable in its profile, rather, "When we grow, it's because we have a strong profile."[39] By 2009, Merkur reported serving over 2,600 lending clients and 13,000 deposit clients, as well as a total of $290 million of total assets.[40]

Merkur was able to provide support for two "sister associations" in Scandinavia: Ekobanken, which was founded in Sweden in 1996, and Cultura Bank, which was founded a year later in Norway. Ekobanken was a cooperative bank that supported ventures seeking to promote "higher ecological, social, cultural, and economic sustainability."[41] The bank invested in a wide range of projects, including renewable energy, organic agriculture, schools for individuals with special needs, and sustainable housing, and it published information about its financial activities in its magazine *Goda Affärer* ("good business").[42] In the decade after its foundation, Ekobanken achieved a balance sheet growth of 15 to 20 percent each year.[43] By the end of 2008, Ekobanken had $50 million on its balance sheet.[44] Cultura Bank, another anthroposophical bank inspired by GLS, was originally structured as a cooperative but became a licensed savings bank in 1996. Much like Ekobanken, it sought to have a positive impact on the environment, culture and society, and it counted organic agriculture, education and healthcare projects among the prominent items in its loan portfolio.[45] By 2009, it held $65 million in assets.[46] For Ekobanken and Cultura Bank, the growing complexities of banking regulation made the process of acquiring formal banking status much harder than in the case of Merkur.[47]

One European social bank that emerged separately from the anthroposophical movement was the Ecology Building Society (EBS). The EBS was a mutual savings bank located in Yorkshire, Britain, and was founded in 1981 by a group of ten people who each contributed about $1,000 to meet the minimum capital requirement. Leading the group was David Pedley, an attorney who had encountered difficulty in obtaining a mortgage on a property with antique fittings he refused to modernize. As an EBS employee later noted, after gathering the support of nine other people, Pedley was able to "cut through all the red tape" involved in setting up a building society. Having managed to become a legal entity, the EBS allowed its members to bypass restrictions on home mortgages often imposed by traditional banks.[48] Many of the EBS's founding members were inspired by the back-to-the-land and self-sufficiency movements, which led them to offer loans in atypical situations. As Gus Smith, who worked as Director at EBS later reflected, "We were prepared to lend on very run-down properties. I mean, ruins ... And also, we were prepared – which other societies certainly weren't – to lend piecemeal."[49] The EBS would lend funds to people interested in repairing certain parts of their properties, and then lend them additional sums in the future to pursue other repair projects. Smith noted,

These people had a mission, they had a vision, they wanted to improve [their properties], they wanted a different kind of life, they were prepared to work for it, and they weren't going to default on their payments. And, certainly, in the early years, we had no problems of that nature.[50]

Though the organization operated on a small scale, the EBS played a significant role in promoting the self-build real estate market within Britain.[51]

At the time of its founding, the EBS was regulated by the Registrar of Friendly Societies. However with the Building Societies Act of 1986, the Building Societies Commission became the new regulatory authority.[52] Smith saw himself as "mildly adversarial" to regulatory officials, who he felt had been steeped for too long in conventional finance and needed to be educated about more sustainable financial practices. During the EBS's annual review, Smith later recalled, "I can remember them asking me point blank, why are you so risk-averse? Why don't you take more risks? And I said, because we don't believe in it! That is not our way of doing things."[53] Indeed, the EBS did not lend high-interest rate mortgages since it seemed unlikely to them that the property market would be able to maintain its high growth indefinitely, and the organization did not believe it was ethical to give out loans to people who could not afford them.[54]

EBS was also careful to avoid lending to people who wanted to buy properties for dishonorable ends. Before the housing market crash, there was a surge of interest in "buy-to-let" properties, which property owners would acquire in order to rent out the units. In some cases, property owners would buy run-down buildings and then rent them to others without having first fixed up the properties. In order to prevent this from happening, EBS offered a "buy-to-renovate-to-let" option to prospective new property owners. Under the terms of the loan contract, properties had to meet certain standards before they could be let, and renovations had to comply with ecological principles.[55]

EBS was rather unusual in the financial sector for its lack of interest in mainstream business strategy. "We aren't absolutely wedded to our existence as an institution ... We exist to put ourselves out of business," observed Paul Ellis, the Chief Executive Officer of EBS.[56] Regardless of this, EBS still sought out ways to grow in order to apportion its costs over a broader pool of assets.[57] EBS was also conscious of ethical practices as it related to the compensation of its own employees, and the organization decided that its CEO's salary would be limited to an amount no more than five times that of the lowest-paid full-time employee. Adding further to its list of unconventional methods, in 1987 the Board of Directors of the EBS decided to redesign its annual general meeting in order to promote greater participation. It named the event "Ecology Day," and it was free to EBS's membership. Participants spent the first half of the day discussing formal matters, while the latter half of the day was a festival, complete with circle dancing, food and crafts. Attendance was massive at these annual events, and Ecology Day helped promote a heightened sense of community among its members.[58]

EBS was less successful in appealing to individuals outside of its immediate community. Its employees encountered great difficulty in persuading people to care about transparency in finance or other issues of sustainability. As Ellis noted,

> I think ethical finance is a kind of not understood aspect of ethical consumerism. You know, we'll all quite readily go and buy organic vegetables or whatever, maybe buy fairly traded textiles … I suppose there's always been a kind of view that money's kind of neutral, people don't understand the links between various transactions. So we quite often get people come into us who say, "Oh, we'd like to bank with you. I get 5% on my ISA from the Halifax, do you match that?" "Well, no … ! Have you ever thought about how they manage to pay you 5%?"[59]

Over time EBS came to view itself less as an advocacy organization than an "enabling mechanism" or platform for its members – of which there were approximately 10,000 in 2007 – to spark broader debate among the public.[60] By 2009, EBS possessed nearly $152 million in assets and reported profits of $555,000, which was an increase of about $40,000 in 2008, despite the dire circumstances of the global financial crisis.[61]

Within the US, a pioneering social bank called ShoreBank was founded in Chicago in 1973. The origins of this venture lay with a group of professional bankers who worked for a local community bank. They included Ronald Grzywinski, the bank's president, as well as Milton Davis, Jim Fletcher and Mary Houghton. This group had launched an urban development division which offered loans to minority-owned small businesses. In 1973 they acquired a small bank, South Shore National Bank, which threatened to leave Chicago's South Side as its white residents were fleeing the area, and formed a bank holding company under a recent regulation which permitted such a company to invest in community development if it was focused on people with low and middle incomes.[62] Through its loans, ShoreBank encouraged residential and retail development in impoverished urban areas of Chicago, and it promoted environmental causes. The business model rested on making small loans to people with poor credit histories, and it took a decade for the banking business to become profitable. By 2000 ShoreBank had accumulated $1 billion in loans in its portfolio. By then it had expanded to other US cities, including Michigan and Cleveland, helped create a bank to finance environmental businesses in Portland, Oregon, and even opened small-business loan programs in Eastern Europe.[63]

The new century brought expansion and collapse. By 2008 Shore-Bank's balance sheet showed approximately $2.4 billion in assets.[64] It accumulated a significant number of risky loans and had launched an aggressive expansion campaign. This was a weak situation to enter the global financial crisis. The crisis hit lower-income individuals – Shore-Bank's primary pool of clients – especially hard, leading the bank to flounder. These factors, in combination with other factors related to its management, contributed to the bank's failure. Although several financial instructions, including Goldman Sachs and Citigroup, attempted to bail out the bank, ShoreBank was closed in 2010, the year after it cofounded GABV.[65]

Another social bank was created in the United States in San Francisco in 2006. Peter Lin, with three coorganizers, founded New Resource Bank. Liu was an international senior banker with a strong interest in renewable energy who, in the early 2000s, was inspired to create New Resource Bank after seeing the market potential for an environmentally focused bank while working for the California state treasurer's office and a couple of pension funds.[66] In order to realize his vision, Liu recruited three others to help establish the bank: Peter Blom, CEO of Triodos Bank; Mark Finser, President and CEO of the anthroposophical US-based nonprofit RSF Social Finance; and Bob Epstein, the founder of the US-based nonprofit Environmental Entrepreneurs. Amid growing concern in the US for environmental causes catalyzed by, among many factors, the Al Gore film *An Inconvenient Truth*, and increasing awareness of energy insecurity, the group of four successfully raised $24.7 million to found New Resource Bank.[67]

In creating the bank, the founders decided to follow the model of a standard community bank with an environmentally oriented profile, since a more conventional banking structure catering to a niche industry was more vulnerable to risk and invited increased regulatory oversight.[68] As Liu later noted, New Resource Bank was set up to be "a community of people that together can create resources that will empower members of their community to do great things."[69] However, adopting the model of a community bank led to a situation where the founders lacked clarity on their overall strategy. The bank offered a "solar home equity financing" loan, as well as solar certificates of deposit used to fund solar projects in the state.[70] However, a significant proportion – 65 to 88 percent each year – of the bank's projected three-year loan portfolio was dedicated to real estate loans that were not sustainability-oriented in nature. Although the founders expected the real estate loans to help the bank grow quickly, these loans, in combination with an overall aggressive growth strategy, led the bank into crisis when the housing market collapsed in 2007. In the wake of the crisis, New Resource Bank's management team, investors and directors agreed to pursue their mission of sustainability with greater clarity and focus, as well as a longer-term horizon for achieving financial goals.[71]

With the exception of ShoreBank and New Resource Bank, then, social banking grew primarily as a European phenomenon, with northwest Europe as its center. This geographical pattern reflected, in part, the far greater influence of anthroposophy in Europe than in the United States, and also Europe's greater engagement with environmental concerns; European countries had taken the lead in passing proactive environmental legislation by the late twentieth century while the environment became heavily politicized in the US. The period also saw the organic food industry and renewable energy rapidly scale in Europe, especially in Denmark, Germany and Switzerland. This meant more green businesses to fund, and more individuals willing to accept below-market interest rates in the interests of doing good. In contrast, in the US the challenges faced by minorities and inhabitants of inner cities in fund-raising resulted in those issues being the major concern in the US banks. Everywhere, however, the values-based approach to lending and the dependence on savings for funding limited growth. By the end of 2009, social banking remained a niche within the global banking sector, with the total assets of seven of the largest social banks estimated at approximately $11 billion (see Table 4.1). ShoreBank's subsequent demise also demonstrated the risks of scaling for this form of financial institution.

III THE DEVELOPMENT OF MICROFINANCE

In contrast with social banking, microfinance involved providing loans, financial accounts and insurance to the very poor in the emerging world. Yet social banks were involved in facilitating the activities of MFIs. Triodos Bank entered microfinance in 1994 through a South African bank, and over the following decade established a number of investment funds in support of microfinance along with NGOs. The Fair Share Fund launched in 2002 was one of the very few funds in Europe that enabled individuals to invest in microfinance.[72] Equally the different focuses of the two types of institutions was indicative of the broadness, even vagueness, of the concept of sustainability. Social banks, at least in Europe, were focused on renewable energy, organic agriculture and education. In contrast, MFIs were focused on poverty alleviation. There was also a difference in scale. According to a survey by the World Bank, in 1995 over 75 percent of the sample microfinance loan volume was disbursed in Asia, while 20 percent was disbursed in Latin America and 3 percent in Africa.[73] By the end of 2008, microfinance had over $50 billion in assets in emerging markets, which was far larger than the assets of social banks (Table 4.2).

Table 4.2   Microfinance in emerging markets, 2008

Region	Number of MFIs	Number of borrowers (millions)	Assets ($ million)	Equity ($ million)
Africa (sub-Saharan)	250	6.1	4,663	1,086
East Asia and Pacific	157	12.4	10,142	857
Eastern Europe and Central Asia	233	2.5	11,164	1,640
Latin America	323	11.6	17,845	2,969
Middle East and North Africa	53	2.3	1,374	473
South Asia	204	35.4	5,158	912
Total	1,220	70.4	50,347	7,937

Source: MicroFinance Information eXchange, "Selected."

In Bali, Indonesia, I Gusti Made Oka and Sri Adnyani Oka – husband and wife newlyweds – were among the pioneers of microfinance in the mid-1950s, when they recognized and helped fulfill their friends' needs for small, short-term loans. After profitably accepting deposits and disbursing loans to members of their community, all the while earning the respect and trust of their clients, in 1968 the Okas opened Bank Pasar Umum (BPU) which specialized in offering monthly interest payments to its depositors, as well as one-month loans. Since the Okas lacked a professional office, their employees traveled to clients' homes for appointments. By 1970, BPU had accumulated nearly $40,000 in profits. That same year, the Okas used these profits, plus an additional $13,200 loan from another bank, to open Bank Dagang Bali (BDB), a licensed, full-service bank with 30 employees in Denpasar. BDB grew quickly, and even acquired a car to use as a mobile bank. Between 1975 and 1995, its net profits grew exponentially from $14,458 to $1,228,320, benefiting from, but also providing assistance to, Indonesia's booming economy as the country developed rapidly during that timeframe.[74]

By 1983, the state-owned Bank Rakyat Indonesia (BRI), the country's oldest bank and one of its largest, began to follow BGB's example. BRI began to reform Indonesia's local banking system, called the unit desa, in order to shape it into a self-sustaining network of micro-banking institutions offering profitable microfinance services. Aided by these significant changes to the banking system, between the mid-1970s and the mid-1990s Indonesia's poverty rate plummeted from 40 percent to 11 percent.[75]

Mohammed Yunus, who was later called the "Father of Microfinance," pioneered the development of microfinance and an influential lending model in Bangladesh. Yunus was inspired to found Grameen Bank, named after the Bengali word for "rural," after conducting field research in an impoverished village near a university where he was teaching. While experimenting with a variety of methods to alleviate the villagers from poverty, Yunus found that small loans were a particularly effective tool.[76] In 1976, Yunus started a banking project that operated on principles in stark contrast with those traditionally followed by conventional banks. He later commented:

> My strategy was: Whatever conventional banks did, I did the opposite. If banks lent to the rich, I lent to the poor. If banks lent to men, I lent to women. If banks made large loans, I made small loans. If banks required collateral, my loans were collateral-free. If banks required a lot of paperwork, my bank was illiterate-friendly. If the client had to go to the bank, my bank went to the village.[77]

Yunus envisioned microfinance as a way to help the poor gain critical access to capital in order to pursue entrepreneurial ventures that would give them the opportunity and confidence to become financially independent. In order to make his strategy work, Yunus carefully developed a method called the "Grameen Group Lending Model" for lending money that promoted compliance with the terms of the loans. Following this model, five individuals – restricted to women who were not family members – voluntarily self-organized a lending circle based on mutual trust, transparency and accountability. After the five borrowers participated in a financial education training session, two individuals were granted loans. Once the loans were repaid, additional loans of increasing size were extended to other members of the group. The groups met on a weekly basis in order to repay the loans and cultivate a stronger sense of community. To further strengthen accountability within the group, if a single member failed to pay back a loan, the entire group would become ineligible for loans.[78] In 1983, after years of appealing to the government to pass a law that would allow for Grameen Bank's unique form of banking, Yunus's request was finally fulfilled. Established as a commercial banking entity, the Grameen Bank opened its doors and subsequently its lending model – which demonstrated extraordinarily high loan repayment rates – became the model by which other MFIs around the world operated over the following decades.[79]

By the late 1990s Grameen Bank had over two million borrowers, 95 per cent of whom were women, representing a total of between $30 million and $40 million in loans per month. It reported repayment rates of 98 per cent. It also reported a modest level of profits, $1.5 million, between 1985 and 1996, although a study which adjusted for provision for loan losses came up with losses of nearly $18 million over this period.[80]

In the mid-1970s when Yunus first began experimenting with microfinance, an organization called Accion, which was founded in Venezuela by University of California, Berkeley law student Joseph Blatchford in 1961, also began experimenting with microfinance. Blatchford had been motivated to found Accion after discovering the profound state of economic and social turmoil throughout Latin America.[81] In 1973, an Accion team in Brazil began testing the feasibility of issuing loans to small businesses in Recife, a city in northeast Brazil. After four years, the project had proven to be a success.[82] The manager of the microfinance project later reflected on the ways in which his team was able to create a sense of legitimacy for impoverished individuals struggling to expand their businesses: "We came up with the name 'microenterprise' to get the banking world to start thinking about these little economic activities as serious enterprises and it stuck. It worked with the bankers and it gave the micro-entrepreneurs status that they never had before."[83]

In the 1980s and 1990s, Accion expanded its microfinance operations to 14 countries in Latin America. Just as had been the case in Bangladesh, repayment rates among their borrowers were extraordinarily high, at 97 percent. Accion grew rapidly; the amount of money it disbursed as loans in aggregate across Latin America increased twentyfold between 1989 and 1995. However, its reach was still relatively small, as it calculated that its loans had impacted just 2 percent of its potential client base. In order to scale up, in 1992 it helped found BancoSol in Bolivia, a bank for the poor which later became one of the founding members of GABV.[84]

In 1991, Accion established a pilot program in Brooklyn, New York in order to provide financial assistance to impoverished individuals in the US, where economic inequality was becoming increasingly pronounced.[85] In the US, microfinance developed somewhat differently, as the complexity of financial markets in these areas required borrowers to possess a higher level of financial management skills. As a result, MFIs needed to provide a more robust suite of services to borrowers, including education and training in order to help microenterprise owners navigate multi-layered regulatory requirements that individuals in emerging markets were often able to avoid by operating in informal sectors.[86] According to Accion, within Texas alone the $42 million in loans that it disbursed between 1994 and 2005 resulted in the creation of 982 jobs and $78 million in economic activity. Accion's US network as a whole experienced substantial growth, disbursing $180 million in loans to 20,000 individuals by 2007.[87]

In 2000 and 2005, Accion also expanded to sub-Saharan Africa and India, and experimented with various poverty-alleviation methods tailored to local needs, such as credit scoring. In order to advance its mission around the world, Accion pursued partnerships with diverse stakeholders such as regulators, universities and technology companies in order to develop and share ideas that promoted financial inclusion.[88]

One NGO with a strong social mission – the Bangladesh-based nonprofit BRAC – played a major role in promoting microfinance. Founded in 1972 in the wake of Bangladesh's independence from Pakistan, BRAC was given remarkable leeway for nearly a decade in pursuing its poverty-alleviation goals, as the new Bangladeshi government was too weak to offer its own resources. BRAC quickly developed a strong reputation among donors and charitable organizations such as Oxfam for delivering on its goals, which later helped the organization raise funds in other parts of the world. In 1974, BRAC introduced a microfinance program with a holistic approach to alleviating poverty.[89] As BRAC's founder Sir Fazle Hasan Abed later noted,

> We looked at poverty from many different angles. It is not just income, or opportunities, or agricultural productivity, or health alone, or lack of education. All kinds of things constitute poverty. It's a multidimensional syndrome which causes people to be less productive, to be less efficient, to be miserable.[90]

Following this holistic view of poverty, the organization offered its microfinance clients a broad range of services, including education programs, healthcare and legal assistance.[91] In the beginning, the program only disbursed loans to groups, rather than individuals – a less risky form of lending. The program was successful, and eventually was expanded to other countries as BRAC grew, including Sierra Leone, Uganda and Myanmar. As Sir Abed observed later, "Microfinance has had tremendous impact in getting the poorest people access to money. Not everybody has done well, but many people have done well."[92]

Microfinance also met with success in certain countries within Africa, including in Kenya where half the population lived below the poverty line.[93] Dr. Elizabeth Mary Okelo, who pioneered microfinance for women in Kenya, entered the finance industry shortly after completing her undergraduate education in Uganda in the mid-1960s. After successfully persuading finance company recruiters to consider her candidacy despite their policy of not hiring women, Okelo went to work at Barclays Bank in Britain, and eventually transferred to a branch in Kenya. In 1977, Okelo became Kenya's first female bank manager. The UN Decade for Women had begun the year before, and since Kenya had signed the UN statute, Okelo and other activists in Kenya began pressuring the government to grant greater freedoms to women in Kenya. At the time, women were unable to secure loans without a male guarantor or collateral – which few women could offer. With the help of Michaela Walsh, who had co-founded Women's World Banking, a global nonprofit organization that assists MFIs around the world, as well as with the help of activists recruited and organized by Walsh, Okelo was able to reach an agreement with Barclays Bank of Kenya. Barclays, along with Women's World Banking and Okelo's newly-established organization Kenya Women Finance Trust, signed an accord that permitted women in Kenya to obtain loans without collateral. Okelo later noted, "This was a game-changer in banking."[94]

Kenya Women Finance Trust was formally registered in 1982 and established as an NGO affiliate of Women's World Banking. The organizing team was made up of individuals with professional experience in law or banking. Fortunately, at the time of its founding the managing director of Barclays Bank of Kenya was progressive – he allowed Okelo to run the organization from within the Barclays Bank office and attend conferences related to women's empowerment. Starting with a membership base of 100 women, the organization grew immensely over the following decades.[95] By 1998, it had lent more than $3.3 million to approximately 16,000 women since its founding, and in 2009 alone the organization lent $172 million.[96]

Kenya was fertile ground for other pioneering microfinance organizations, including K-Rep, which was founded in 1984 as an organization that provided grants and other forms of assistance to NGOs working to promote small and micro business development. In 1989, the organization transformed its strategy into one of providing loans rather than grants to NGOs, and it initiated a microfinance project. Ten years later, K-Rep established K-Rep Bank as the first commercially-licensed MFI, with headquarters in Nairobi.[97] K-Rep Bank became Kenya's largest microfinance bank, following the Grameen model of group lending, and in 2005 provided approximately $34 million in loans to 69,000 individuals. It faced significant challenges as it grew, including competition from similar organizations such as Kenya Women Finance Trust, as well as the difficulty of offering financial products and services that met the varying needs of its clients. K-Rep's client base differed widely in terms of the types of loan each individual needed, as well as in individual level of poverty.[98]

For a time there was an enormous optimism about the transformational potential of microfinance. Academic studies pointed to income gains resulting from the use of micro loans. A major survey of the economics literature in 1999 identified up to 10 million households receiving microfinance funds. Jonathan Morduch, focusing especially on evidence from Bolivia, Bangladesh and Indonesia, pointed to evidence that "poor households are being given hope and the possibility to improve their lives through their own labor," although he noted that most programs needed to be subsidized through grants and indirectly through soft terms on loans from donors.[99] In 2005 the UN launched the "International Year of Microcredit" in order to galvanize further public support for the sector.[100] In 2006, Yunus and the Grameen Bank were awarded the Nobel Peace Prize for their efforts to create economic and social development.

By then the earlier enthusiasm about microfinance was beginning to wane. There were stories of exploitative interest rates being charged and general malpractice. Mexico provided one example. Ricardo Salinas Pliego, a leading businessman, founded Banco Azteca in 2002.[101] As Salinas later recounted, "Our proposal was to create a bank for the base of the pyramid; it was a bank that promoted social integration, providing access to the financial system to all of those who did not have access."[102] Six years after it was founded, Banco Azteca disbursed on average 12,000 loans each day.[103] However, a high-profile article published in the US magazine *Newsweek* in 2007 reported that the bank disbursed loans to individuals who did not fully understand the terms, and that Banco Azteca's average annual percentage rate (APR) charged on loans was a rapacious 110%.[104] Salinas later defended the bank's strategy:

> What these false promoters of the well-being of the neediest people don't realize is that a $300 loan has to have a very high interest rate because of

fixed costs. My cost to execute a $300 loan is the same as the cost for a $3,000 loan. It is the same cost to authorize, manage, and collect a $3,000, or a $30,000, or a $3,000,000 loan; it is all the same. The cost related to the principal is greater so the rate has to be higher.[105]

Insofar as the numbers were accurate, the observation suggested that microfinance could only operate without subsidies if it charged usurious interest rates which would make borrowers highly indebted.

While many MFIs were committed to social and ethical principles, including those who joined GABV, Banco Azteca was not alone in charging high interest, or otherwise engaging in bad practices.[106] The year after the foundation of GABV, Nicaragua-based Banex collapsed following malpractice of employees.[107] A 2009 study by the Consultative Group to Assist the Poor (CGAP) – an international organization housed at the World Bank – reported that international microfinance investment funds were swelling with cash from investors primarily concerned with profit maximization rather than social objectives. However, CGAP also found that the high interest rates charged by microfinance banks such as Banco Azteca were outliers; less than 1 percent of borrowers paid interest rates as high as 85 percent. Yet it also reported that the returns on equity for the most profitable quintile of global microfinance loans in a recent year was higher than 34 percent. The ethics of profiting from the poor were grey.[108] Academic researchers using new methodologies, in particular randomly offering loans to some people and not others, showed disappointing evidence of the impact of microfinance on key welfare indicators such as education.[109] Yunus himself was forced to resign from Grameen Bank by the Bangladesh government in 2011, apparently for political reasons but amid lurid allegations of his ethical behavior and managerial competence.[110] In the same year he founded a nonprofit venture fund designed to finance social businesses worldwide.[111]

While the microfinance sector achieved remarkable growth, in some cases this came at the cost of its original social objectives. By then the limited impact of microfinance overall on poverty reduction and improving other social indicators was also becoming apparent.[112]

IV CONCLUSION

This chapter has examined a set of institutions designed to finance people and businesses in the interests of achieving greater social and environmental sustainability.

Triodos's support of renewable energy in Europe, the EBS's promotion of the self-build real estate market, BRAC's assistance to millions of very poor people in Bangladesh and elsewhere – and many other examples – were significant achievements. They signaled the potential of sustainable-type financial institutions to achieve different outcomes to conventional finance.

Yet the challenges of financing sustainability emerge clearly from the historical evidence. The scale of social banks depended on the willingness of savers to invest in them, yet as the chief executive of the EBS observed, ethical consumers appeared more excited about buying organic vegetables than in using their money to finance sustainable businesses. Social banks were also primarily facilitators, dependent on the availability of appropriate projects to invest in. As the experience of ShoreBank showed, rapid scaling could bring an institution in this sector down as it involved unconventional risks. Microfinance achieved greater scale than social banking, but because the lending model was not intrinsically tied to strong socially-oriented principles, the concept was abused by conventional banking institutions in exploitative ways. Over time it became apparent that microfinance had failed, at least as yet, to live up to early hopes that it could both transform the lives of the poor and be profitable.

The institutions which came to form GABV were united in wanting to pursue alternative and sustainable strategies to conventional financial institutions, but it was striking that the nature of those strategies varied so greatly. Social banks were largely a European phenomenon, often inspired by anthroposophy, and heavily invested in supporting organic agriculture, renewable energy and Waldorf schools. MFIs reimagined impoverished individuals in emerging markets as creditworthy individuals who could use small loans to gain financial independence. A commitment to greater transparency among social banks, and some MFIs, was perhaps the strongest common theme. This was indicative of the lack of consensus of what alternative, ethical, social or sustainable really meant, in more than general terms. This vagueness was not an ideal basis for challenging and replacing the long-established norms of the conventional financial industry.

In the new century, and especially after the global financial crisis, there was a heightened awareness both of the risks of the giant conventional financial system, and the opportunities to exercise a positive impact on the environment and society through impact investing and other strategies. Steiner's initial insight about the benefits of creating a new type of "bank-like institution" was as relevant as ever. The challenge lay, as the experience of social banking and microfinance demonstrated, in defining the real meaning of sustainability and finding a way to scale truly alternative financial institutions which could radically change the world for the better.

NOTES

* We would like to thank Ai Hisano for comments on an earlier version of this chapter.
1. Benedikter, *Social*, 46.
2. McKinsey & Co, "Financial," 2.
3. Jones, *Profits*, 270–72.
4. Schmidheiny and Zorraquín, *Financing*, 4, cited in Jones, *Profits*, 270.
5. GABV, "About."
6. World Commission, *Common Future*.
7. Weber and Remer, "Social," 2.
8. Karlan and Goldberg, "Microfinance," 20.
9. Milano, "Social Banking," 24–7.
10. Lindenberg, *Rudolf*, 698–701.
11. Jones, *Profits*, 31–8; Lachman, *Rudolf Steiner*; Amrine, "Discovering."
12. Steiner, "Lecture IV."
13. Barkhoff and Partner mbB, "Kanzleigeschichte."
14. Jones, *Profits*, 274–5.
15. GLS Treuhand, "Chronologie."
16. GLS Bank, "English"; Jones, *Profits*, 274.
17. Ibid., 139.
18. Ibid., 66.
19. "Geschichte," https://www.gls.de/privatkunden/ueber-die-gls-bank/geschichte/.
20. Schneeweiss, "GLS Bank," 109; Milano, "Social Banking," 32.
21. Ibid., 10–11.
22. Dohmen, *Good*, 26.
23. Osmond, "Work," 107.
24. Ibid.
25. Bibby, "Ethical"; Lynch, "Ethical," 20.
26. Gosling, "Ethical"; Jones, *Profits*, 276.
27. Allen, "Triodos."
28. Bibby, "Heart."
29. Triodos Bank, "An Overview"; Käufer, "Banking"; interview with Thomas Steiner (Head of Corporate Communication), and James Niven (Head of Public Affairs) by Andrew Spadafora, Zeist, November 4, 2013 (hereafter interview with Steiner and Niven).
30. Triodos Bank, "An Overview"; interview with Steiner and Niven.
31. Jones, *Profits*, 276.
32. Schneeweiss, "GLS Bank," 109; Dohmen, *Good Bank*, 11.
33. Henderson, Isaacs and Kaufer, "Triodos Bank," 4.
34. Interview with Steiner and Niven; Dossa and Kaufer, "Triodos Bank," 2.
35. Henderson, Issacs and Kaufer, "Triodis Bank," 8.
36. Interview with Lars Pehrson (CEO, Merkur Andelskasse) by Andrew Spadafora, Copenhagen, October 30, 2013 (hereafter interview with Pehrson); Global Alliance for Banking on Values, "Merkur."
37. Interview with Pehrson.
38. GABV, "Merkur."
39. Interview with Pehrson.
40. GABV, "Merkur."
41. Ekobanken, "About."
42. Ibid.; Ekobanken, "Ekobanken's."
43. Goldstein, "Banking."

44. Weber and Remer, "Social," 5.
45. FEBEA, "Cultura."
46. GABV, "Cultura."
47. GABV, "Ekobanken."
48. All conversions into US dollars use exchange rate in the respective year.
49. Interview with Paul Ellis (Chief Executive), Gus Smith (former Director), Jim Walker (former Director), Pam Waring (Finance Director and Secretary) and Tony Weekes (former Director), by Andrew Spadafora, Silsden, November 8, 2013 (hereafter interview with Ellis, Smith, Walker, Waring and Weekes).
50. Ibid.
51. Ibid.
52. National Archives, "Building."
53. Interview with Ellis, Smith, Walker, Waring and Weekes.
54. Ibid.
55. Ibid.
56. Ibid.
57. Ibid.
58. Ibid.
59. Ibid.
60. Ibid.; GABV, "Ecology."
61. Ecology Building Society, "Annual," 20.
62. Post and Wilson, "Too Good."
63. Ibid.; Greising, "Recession."
64. Ibid.
65. Ibid.
66. Johnson, "Banking."
67. Marquis and Almandoz, "New," 1–6. The bank was acquired by Amalgamated Bank in 2018.
68. Gronewold, "Finance."
69. Baedeker, "New Resource Bank."
70. Gronewold, "Finance."
71. Marquis and Almandoz, "New," 1–6.
72. Dossa and Kaufer, "Triodis Bank," 4–5.
73. World Bank, "A Worldwide," 20.
74. Robinson, *The Microfinance*, 147–51.
75. Seibel and Ozaki, "Restructuring," vii; Robinson, *The Microfinance*, xxi.
76. Yunus, "Banker," vii–viii.
77. Hawser, "Features."
78. Grameen Research, Inc., "Grameen Methodology."
79. Yunus, "Creating," 48.
80. Morduch, "The Microfinance," 1575–6, 1589–90.
81. Accion, "1960s."
82. Accion, "1970s."
83. Ibid.
84. Accion, "1980s–1990s."
85. Accion, "1990s."
86. Bernanke, "Microfinance"; Assanie and Virmani, "Incubating," 4.
87. Bernanke, "Microfinance."
88. Accion, "2000."
89. BRAC, "Microfinance."
90. Interview with Sir Fazle Hasan Abed, interviewed by Tarun Khanna, April 24, 2014, Creating Emerging Markets Project, Baker Library Historical Collections, Harvard Business School, http://www.hbs.edu/creating-emerging-markets (hereafter interview with Abed).
91. BRAC, "Microfinance."

92. Interview with Abed.
93. Karugu and Kanyagia, "K-Rep," 2.
94. Interview with Dr. Elizabeth Mary Okelo, interviewed by Henry McGee, February 27, 2015, Creating Emerging Markets Project, Baker Library Historical Collections, Harvard Business School, http://www.hbs.edu/creating-emerging-markets.
95. Ibid., 29–30; Walsh, *Founding*, 96–7.
96. The Nation, "Bank"; Michira, "Women's."
97. Sidian Bank, "History"; Ali, "The Regulatory," 124.
98. Karugu and Kanyagia, "K-Rep," 2.
99. Morduch, "Microfinance."
100. United Nations, "UN."
101. Forbes, "#124 Ricardo."
102. Interview with Ricardo Salinas Pliego, interviewed by Regina García Cuéllar, May 31, 2013, Creating Emerging Markets Project, Baker Library Historical Collections, Harvard Business School, http://www.hbs.edu/creating-emerging-markets (hereafter interview with Pliego).
103. Forbes, "#124 Ricardo."
104. Epstein and Smith, "The Ugly."
105. Interview with Pliego.
106. Cull, Demirgüç-Kunt, and Morduch, "Microfinance."
107. "A Tribunales."
108. Rosenberg et al., "The New."
109. Banerjee et al., "Miracle."
110. Burke, "Microfinance."
111. Yunus Social Business, http://www.yunussb.com/about/.
112. Kristof, "The Role."

REFERENCES

"A Tribunales por estafa y fraude directivos del extinto Banco del Éxito," accessed January 18, 2018 at www.lavozdelsandinismo.com/nicaragua/2011-01-26/a-tribunales-por-estafa-y-fraude-directivos-del-extinto-banco-del-exito.

Accion (n.d.), "1960s: Accion's early days," accessed October 20, 2017 at www.accion.org/content/1960s-accions-early-days.

Accion (n.d.), "1970s: Microlending begins," accessed October 20, 2017 at www.accion.org/content/1970s-microlending-begins.

Accion (n.d.), "1980s–1990s: Expanding opportunity – building a model," accessed November 4, 2017 at www.accion.org/content/1980s–1990s-expanding-opportunity–building-model.

Accion (n.d.), "1990s: Bringing microfinance home – the U.S. initiative," accessed November 4, 2017 at www.accion.org/content/1990s-bringing-microfinance-home-us-initiative.

Accion (n.d.), "2000: New millennium, new horizons," accessed November 4, 2017 at www.accion.org/content/2000-new-millennium-new-horizons.

Accion (2009), "Microfinance leader awarded prestigious IDB Prize for Latin American development," accessed November 4, 2017 atwww.accion.org/content/microfinance-leader-awarded-prestigious-idb-prize-latin-american-development.

Ali, Abd Elrahman Elzahi Saaid (2015), "The Regulatory and Supervision Framework of Microfinance in Kenya," *International Journal of Social*

Science Studies, **3**, (5), 123–30. Accessed November 3, 2017 at www.redfame. com/journal/index.php/ijsss/article/viewFile/1004/939.

Allen, Caroline (1995), "Triodos Bank, Mercury Provident Merge in New Bank," *Reuters News*, July 3.

Amrine, Frederick (2011), "Discovering a genius: Rudolf Steiner at 150," accessed January 2, 2018 at http://www.rudolfsteiner.org/fileadmin/vision-in-action/being-human-2011-01-Amrine-Discovering.pdf.

Assanie, Laila and Raghav Virmani (2006), "Incubating Microfinance: The Texas Border Experience," Federal Reserve Bank of Dallas, Southwest Economy, September/October, 3–7.

Baedeker, Rob (2007), "New Resource Bank has amazing customer service and lets you do good with your checking account," accessed December 2, 2017 at www.sfgate.com/business/article/New-Resource-Bank-has-amazing-customer-service-2486747.php.

Barba, Robert and Joe Adler (2010), "Deal shows ShoreBank was savvy to the end," *American Banker*, August 24.

Banerjee, Abhijit, Esther Duflo, Rachel Glennerster and Cynthia Kinnan (2015), "The Miracle of Microfinance? Evidence from a Randomized Evaluation," *American Economic Journal: Applied Economics*, **7**, (1), 22–53.

Barkhoff and Partner mbB (n.d.), "Kanzleigeschichte," accessed November 18, 2017 at www.barkhoff-partner.de/index.php?id=8.

Benedikter, Roland (2011), "European Answers to the Financial Crisis: Social Banking and Social Finance," *Spice Digest*, Spring.

Benedikter, Roland (2011), *Social Banking and Social Finance: Answers to the Economic Crisis*, New York: Springer.

Benedikter, Roland (2012), "Social banking and social finance: Building stones towards a sustainable post-crisis financial system?" *European Financial Review*. Accessed November 20, 2017 at www.europeanfinancialreview.com/ ?p=2027.

Bernanke, Ben S. (2007), "Microfinance in the United States," Board of Governors of the Federal Reserve System, accessed November 20, 2017 at www.federalreserve.gov/newsevents/speech/bernanke20071106a.htm.

Bibby, Andrew (1993), "Ethical bank updates its homespun style," *The Independent*, June 5, accessed September 29, 2017 at www.independent.co.uk/news/business/ethical-bank-updates-its-homespun-style-1489941.html.

Bibby, Andrew (1994), "Heart of gold, feet of clay?" *The Guardian*, March 27, accessed October 25, 2017 at www.theguardian.com/money/2004/mar/28/ethicalmoney.observercashsection.

BRAC (n.d.), "Microfinance programme," accessed October 20, 2017 at www.brac.net/microfinance?view=page.

Burke, Jason (2011), "Microfinance guru Muhammad Yunus faces removal from Grameen Bank," *The Guardian*, February 21, accessed January 17, 2018 at www.theguardian.com/world/2011/feb/21/muhammad-yunus-microfinance-grameen-bank-bangladesh.

Copestake, James, Susan Johnson, Mateo Cabello, Ruth Goodwin-Groen, Robin Gravesteijn, Julie Humberstone, Max Nino-Zarazua and Matthew Titus (2016), "Towards a Plural History of Microfinance," *Canadian Journal of Development Studies / Revue canadienne d'études du développement*, **37**, (3), 279–97.

Cozarenco, Anastasia (2015), "Microfinance Institutions and Banks in Europe: The Story to Date," No 15-027, Working Papers CEB, ULB – Université Libre de Bruxelles. Accessed November 20, 2017 at www.responsiblefinance forum.org/wp-content/uploads/microfinance_in_europe_31.pdf.

Cull, Robert, Asli Demirgüç-Kunt and Jonathan Morduch (2009), "Microfinance Meets the Market," *Journal of Economic Perspectives*, **23**, (1), 167–92.

De Clerck, Frans (2009), "Ethical Banking," in Laszlo Zsolnai, Zsolt Boda and Laszlo Fekete (eds.), *Ethical Prospects: Economy, Society and Environment*, Berlin: Springer Science & Business Media, 209–28.

Dohmen, Caspar (2011), *Good bank: Das modell der GLS Bank*, Freiburg: Orange Press.

Dossa, Zahir and Katrin Kaufer(2015), "Triodos Bank: Measuring Sustainability Performance," *International Institute for Management Development Case IMD792* (September 11).

Douthwaite, Richard (n.d.), "How a bank can transform a neighborhood," accessed November 4, 2017 at www.feasta.org/documents/shortcircuit/index. html?sc4/shorebank.html.

Ecology Building Society (2010), "Annual Report 2009," archived webpage www.ecology.co.uk/pdf/about/2009-annual-report.pdf (June 12, 2012), accessed October 31, 2017 at web.archive.org.

Ekobanken (n.d.), "About Ekobanken," accessed November 17, 2017 at www. ekobanken.se/en/about-ekobanken/.

Ekobanken (n.d.), "Ekobanken's unique transparency," accessed November 17, 2017 at www.ekobanken.se/en/.

Epstein, Keith and Geri Smith (2007), "The Ugly Side of Micro-lending," *Bloomberg Businessweek*, December 24.

European Commission, "A European initiative for the development of micro-credit in support of growth and employment," accessed November 20, 2017 at eur-lex.europa.eu/legal-content/EN/TXT/PDF/?uri=CELEX:52007DC0708R (01)&from=EN.

FEBEA (n.d.), "Cultura Bank," accessed November 17, 2017 at www.febea.org/ en/febea/members/cultura-bank.

Forbes (2009), "#124 Ricardo Salinas Pliego & family," accessed October 3, 2017 at www.forbes.com/lists/2009/10/billionaires-2009-richest-people_Ricardo-Salinas-Pliego-family_U8K0.html.

Global Alliance for Banking on Values (GABV) (2017), "About," accessed September 27, 2017 at www.gabv.org/about-us.

GABV (n.d.), "GLS Bank," accessed September 29, 2017 at www.gabv.org/ members/gls-bank.

GABV(n.d.), "Alternative Bank Schweiz AG: Key figures," archived webpage www.gabv.org (June 6, 2012), accessed October 28, 2017 at web.archive.org.

GABV(n.d.), "Banca Popolare Etica: Key figures," archived webpage www.gabv. org (June 18, 2012), accessed October 28, 2017 at web.archive.org.

GABV(n.d.), "Banex: Key figures," archived webpage www.gabv.org (January 12, 2010), accessed October 28, 2017 at web.archive.org.

GABV(n.d.), "BRAC Bank: Key figures," archived webpage www.gabv.org (July 1, 2012), accessed October 28, 2017 at web.archive.org.

GABV (n.d.), "Cultura Bank: Key figures," archived webpage www.gabv.org (June 8, 2013), accessed November 2, 2017 at web.archive.org.

GABV (n.d.), "Ecology Building Society," accessed October 31, 2017 at www.gabv.org/members/ecology-building-society.

GABV (n.d.), "Ekobanken," accessed November 3, 2017 at www.gabv.org/members/ekobanken.

GABV (n.d.), "GLS Bank: Key figures," archived webpage www.gabv.org (June 17, 2012), accessed October 28, 2017 at web.archive.org.

GABV(n.d.), "Merkur Cooperative Bank," archived webpage www.gabv.org (February 12, 2010), accessed October 28, 2017 at web.archive.org.

GABV (n.d.), "Merkur Cooperative Bank: Key figures," archived webpage www.gabv.org (June 15, 2012), accessed October 28, 2017 at web.archive.org.

GABV (n.d.), "Mibanco, Banca de la Microempresa: Key figures," archived webpage www.gabv.org (June 17, 2012), accessed October 28, 2017 at web.archive.org.

GABV (n.d.), "New Resource Bank: Key figures," archived webpage www.gabv.org (May 15, 2012), accessed October 28, 2017 at web.archive.org.

GABV (n.d.), "Triodos Bank: Key figures," archived webpage www.gabv.org (June 17, 2012), accessed October 28, 2017 at web.archive.org.

GABV (n.d.), "XacBank: Key figures," archived webpage www.gabv.org (May 15, 2012), accessed October 28, 2017 at web.archive.org.

GLS Bank, "Geschichte," accessed January 8, 2018 at https://www.gls.de/privatkunden/ueber-die-gls-bank/geschichte.

GLS Bank (n.d.), "English portrait," accessed September 28, 2017 at www.gls.de/privatkunden/english-portrait/.

GLS Treuhand (n.d.), "Chronologie," accessed November 18, 2017 at www.gls-treuhand.de/media/pdfs/Chronologie.pdf.

Goldstein, Ritt (2009), "Banking, the Swedish model," *Christian Science Monitor*, June 22, accessed November 17, 2017 at www.csmonitor.com/World/Europe/2009/0622/p06s16-woeu.html.

Gosling, Paul (1994), "Ethical banks to merge," *The Independent*, January 30, accessed September 29, 2017 at www.independent.co.uk/news/business/ethical-banks-to-merge-1410422.html.

Grameen Research, Inc. (n.d.), "Grameen Group lending model," accessed October 18, 2017 at www.grameenresearch.org/grameen-group-lending-model/.

Grameen Research, Inc. (n.d.), "Grameen methodology," accessed October 18, 2017 at www.grameenresearch.org/grameen-methodology-2/.

Greising, David (2010), "Recession played a part, but ShoreBank wounded itself, too," *The New York Times*, May 22, accessed November 4, 2017 at www.nytimes.com/2010/05/23/business/23cncshorebank.html.

Gronewold, Nathanial (2009), "Finance: 'Green' Banks Sprout from Ruins of Economic crisis," *Greenwire*, April 6.

Hawser, Anita (2007), "Features: Big banks eye micro credit," *Global Finance*, June 1, accessed October 18, 2017 at www.gfmag.com/magazine/june-2007/features-big-banks-eye-micro-market.

Henderson, Rebecca, Kate Isaacs and Katrin Kaufer, "Triodis Bank: Conscious Money in Action," *Harvard Business School Case 9-313-109* (revised June 20, 2013).

Jeucken, Marcel (2001), *Sustainable Finance and Banking: The Financial Sector and the Future of the Planet*, Sterling and London: Earthscan.

Johnson, Jim (2007), "Banking on a Different Kind of Green," *Waste & Recycling News*, September 3.

Jones, Geoffrey (2017), *Profits and Sustainability: A History of Green Entrepreneurship*, Oxford: Oxford University Press.

Karl, Marlene (2015), "Are ethical and social banks less risky? Evidence from a new dataset," Deutsches Institut für Wirtschaftsforschung, accessed October 5, 2017 at www.diw.de/documents/publikationen/73/diw_01.c.508003.de/dp1484.pdf.

Karlan, Dean and Nathanael Goldberg (2011), "Microfinance Evaluation Strategies: Notes on Methodology and Findings," in Beatriz Armendáriz and Marc Labie (eds.), *The Handbook of Microfinance*, Hackensack and London: World Scientific, 17–58.

Karugu, Winifred N. and Diane Nduta Kanyagia (2008), "K-Rep Bank: Alleviating poverty through micro-finance," *UN Development Programme: Growing Inclusive Markets*, accessed November 4, 2017 at www.africa-platform.org/sites/default/files/resources/kenya_krep_bank_2008.pdf.

Käufer, Katrin (2011), "Banking as if society mattered: The case of Triodos Bank," accessed September 31, 2017 at colab.mit.edu/sites/default/files/Banking_as_if_Society_Mattered.pdf.

Kristof, Nicholas (2009), "The role of microfinance," *The New York Times*, accessed November 4, 2017 at kristof.blogs.nytimes.com/2009/12/28/the-role-of-microfinance/?_r=0.

Lachman, Gary (2007), *Rudolf Steiner: An Introduction to His Life and Work*, New York: Penguin.

Lewis, Alan and Craig MacKenzie (2000), "Morals, Money, Ethical Investing and Economic Psychology," *Human Relations*, **53**, (2), 179–91.

Lewis, Alan and Paul Webley (1994), "Social and Ethical Investing," in Alan Lewis and Karl-Erik Wärneryd (eds.), *Ethics and Economic Affairs*, London: Routledge, 171–82.

Lindenberg, Christoph (1997), *Rudolf Steiner: Eine Biographie, Vol. 2: 1915–1925*, Stuttgart: Verlag Freies Geistesleben, 698–701.

Lynch, James J. (1991), *Ethical Banking: Surviving in an Age of Default*, New York: Springer.

MacKenzie, Craig and Alan Lewis (1999), "Morals and Markets: The Case for Ethical Investing," *Business Ethics Quarterly*, **9**, (3), 439–52.

McKinsey & Company (2013), "Financial globalization: Retreat or reset?" McKinsey Global Institute, accessed January 16, 2018 at https://www.mckinsey.com/global-themes/employment-and-growth/financial-globalization.

Marquis, Christopher and Juan Almandoz (2013), "New Resource Bank: In pursuit of green," *Harvard Business School Case 9-412-060* (revised May 21, 2013).

Michira, Moses (2010), "Women's finance group trains small business owners," *All Africa Global Media*, June 29.

MicroFinance Information eXchange (2009), "Selected microfinance indicators – 2007: Updated on December 12, 2008," accessed November 20, 2017 at www.themix.org/sites/default/files/publications/At%20a%20Glance%20-%20 MFI%20Indicators_0.pdf.

Milano, Riccardo (2011), "Social Banking: A Brief History," in Olaf Weber and Sven Remer (eds.), *Social Banks and the Future of Sustainable Finance*, London: Routledge, 15–47.

Morduch, Jonathan (1999), "The Microfinance Promise," *Journal of Economic Literature*, **37**, (4), 1569–614.

National Archives (n.d.), "Building Societies Act 1986," accessed October 3, 2017 at www.legislation.gov.uk/ukpga/1986/53/contents.

Nilsson, Jonas (2009), "Segmenting Socially-Responsible Mutual Fund Investors: The influence of Financial Return and Social Responsibility," *The International Journal of Bank Marketing*, **27**, (1), 5–31.

Osmond, John (1986), *Work in the Future: Alternatives to Unemployment*, London: Thorsons Publishing Group.

Post, James E. and Fiona S. Wilson (2011), "Too Good to Fail," *Stanford Social Innovation Review*, accessed October 27, 2017 at www.ssir.org/articles/entry/ too_good_to_fail.

Robinson, Marguerite S. (2002), *The Microfinance Revolution: Lessons from Indonesia*, Washington, DC: World Bank Publications.

Rosenberg, Richard, Adrian Gonzalez and Sushma Narain (2009), "The new moneylenders: Are the poor being exploited by high microcredit interest rates?" Consultative Group to Assist the Poor, accessed November 19, 2017 at www.cgap.org/sites/default/files/CGAP-Occasional-Paper-The-New-Money lenders-Are-the-Poor-Being-Exploited-by-High-Microcredit-Interest-Rates-Feb-2009.pdf.

Schmidheiny, Stephan and Federico Zorraquín (1996), *Financing Change: The Financial Community, Eco-Efficiency, and Sustainable Development*, Cambridge, MA: MIT Press.

Schneeweiss, Eva (2012), "GLS Bank: Successfully Sustainable," in Heiko Spitzeck, Michael Pirson and Claus Dierksmeier (eds.), *Banking with Integrity: The Winners of the Financial Crisis?* London: Palgrave Macmillan, 107–14.

Seibel, Hans Dieter and Mayumi Ozaki (2009), "Restructuring of state-owned financial institutions: Lessons from Bank Rakyat Indonesia," *Asian Development Bank*, accessed October 31, 2017 at www.adb.org/sites/default/files/ publication/27527/financial-institutions.pdf .

Sidian Bank (n.d.), "History," accessed November 2, 2017 at www.sidianbank. co.ke/about-us/history.

Steiner, Rudolf (1922), "Lecture IV," accessed September 29, 2017 at wn.rsarchive. org/Lectures/GA340/English/RSP1972/19220727p01.html.

The Nation (1998), "Bank lent women Sh200m," *Africa News Online*, December 4.

Triodos Bank (n.d.), "An overview of our history," accessed September 31, 2017 at www.triodos.com/en/about-triodos-bank/who-we-are/history/.

United Nations (2004), "UN launches International Year of Microcredit 2005," accessed November 20, 2017 at www.un.org/press/en/2004/dev2492.doc.htm.

Walsh, Michaela (2012), *Founding a Movement: Women's World Banking, 1975–1990*, New York: Cosimo, Inc.

Weber, Olaf and Sven Remer (2011), "Social Banking: Introduction," in Olaf Weber and Sven Remer, *Social Banks and the Future of Sustainable Finance*, Abington, UK: Taylor & Francis, 1–14.

World Bank (n.d.), "A worldwide inventory of microfinance institutions," Sustainable Banking with the Poor Project, accessed September 27, 2017 at www.microfinancegateway.org/sites/default/files/mfg-en-paper-sustainable-banking-with-the-poor-a-worldwide-inventory-of-microfinance-institutions-2001.pdf.

World Commission on Environment and Development (1987), *Our Common Future*, Oxford: Oxford University Press.

WWF (2009), "Blueprint Germany: A strategy for a climate safe 2050," accessed November 20, 2017 at www.wwf.de/fileadmin/fm-wwf/Publikationen-PDF/blueprint_germany_wwf.pdf.

Yunus, Muhammad (2010), *Banker to the Poor: Micro-lending and the Battle against World Poverty*, New York: PublicAffairs.

Yunus, Muhammad (2007), *Creating a World Without Poverty: Social Business and the Future of Capitalism*, New York: PublicAffairs.

Yunus, Muhammad, "Social Business," accessed January 11 2018 at http://www.yunussb.com/about.

PRIMARY MATERIALS

Interview by Andrew Spadafora with Paul Ellis, Gus Smith, Jim Walker, Pam Waring and Tony Weekes, Silsden, November 8, 2013.

Interview by Andrew Spadafora with Lars Pehrson, Copenhagen, October 30, 2013.

Interview by Andrew Spadafora with Thomas Steiner and James Niven, Zeist, November 4, 2013.

Creating Emerging Markets (CEM) project, Baker Library Historical Collections, Harvard Business School, http://www.hbs.edu/businesshistory/emerging-markets. Interview by Tarun Khanna with Sir Fazle Hasan Abed, April 24, 2014; interview by Henry McGee with Dr. Elizabeth Mary Okelo, February 27, 2015; interview by Regina García Cuéllar with Ricardo Salinas Pliego, May 31, 2013.

5. Organic food and national image: The paradox of New Zealand*

With Simon Mowatt

I INTRODUCTION

This chapter turns to the growth of the organic food industry. In particular, it explores why organic food production and consumption grew in some countries much more than others. The focus is on the case of New Zealand, where organic food made limited progress, in contrast to a number of quite similar European countries, especially Denmark.

Before the nineteenth century, there was nothing but organic agriculture and food. This changed with the growth of industrial farming and the application of chemical fertilizers. Rising agricultural productivity fed urban populations but also raised concerns about the human health consequences of applying chemicals to food. The result was the slow emergence of a movement that came much later, known as organic agriculture. The first experiments with composting, green manuring and mulching without chemicals and pesticides was in Germany in the late nineteenth century. During 1924 Rudolf Steiner, the founder of anthroposophy, delivered a set of lectures that became the basis for biodynamic agriculture, the first systematic exposition of the principles of organic farming. The trademark Demeter was introduced in 1928 as a way to distinguish biodynamic products from others. In the English-speaking world, early organic farming proponents included Franklin H. King, an American agricultural professor, who traveled throughout China, Korea and Japan before 1914, and Albert Howard, a British colonial official in interwar India. Howard's foundational book, *An Agricultural Testament*, published in 1940, became a textbook for organic farming in the English-speaking world.[1]

Yet, the organic farming movement remained a niche for decades longer. Few farmers were interested in growing organic food, and few consumers were interested in eating it. If they were interested, there were no retailers to buy it from, and only very slowly were these voids filled.

The creation of distribution channels was a lengthy and challenging process, not least because it involved making the case that organic food was a relevant, useful concept. In the United States, Walnut Acres, a Pennsylvania farm and mail order natural foods company, started in 1946 with a 100-acre farm; the first harvest came from six old apple trees on the farm. A mail order business selling the products of the farm followed.[2]

Organic food gained momentum after standards and certification were developed beyond the Demeter trademark. In 1967 the Soil Association, a British organic advocacy group formed in 1946, published its first set of organic standards. Biodynamists created the International Federation of Organic Agriculture Movements (IFOAM) in 1972, which began developing international standards in the late 1970s.[3]

Starting in the 1980s, and more so in the 1990s, organic food began to transition from the marginal to the mainstream. However, the growth of the organic food market was not evenly spread. As Table 5.1 shows, per capita expenditure on organic food consumption varied widely. For example, in 1997, New Zealand's per capita consumption (in international dollars)[4] was low compared to all the other countries, and very low compared to countries such as Denmark and Switzerland. This proved to be an ongoing phenomenon. Table 5.1 includes data on per capita consumption of organic food for the same countries in 1997 and 2014. New Zealand remained ranked very low compared to almost all the countries on the list, except for Japan.

The marked contrast between the organic industries of Denmark and New Zealand attracted particular attention by contemporaries. Of similar size, both countries have more than two-thirds of their land under cultivation, and both have well-developed dairy sectors that are primarily for export.[5] The dairy industry in both countries was organized as cooperatives. Historically, too, the dairy and pork industries of both countries were competitors in price-sensitive Britain, at least until Britain's 1973 entry into the EU (then known as the European Economic Community) made it more challenging for New Zealand products to enter that market.

The low level of per capita organic food consumption is also curious because New Zealand has a strong environmentally friendly image stretching back to the development of Victorian-era tourism, which associated the country with its pristine environment. New Zealand's first national park, Tongariro, was established only five years after the 1872 establishment of the world's first park, Yellowstone in the United States.

Varieties of green business

Table 5.1   Organic food markets in New Zealand and selected countries, 1997 and 2014

Country	Population (millions)	GDP per capita, PPP* (intl.$**)[a]	Organic market size (US$ millions)	Market share organic (% total food sales)	Per capita spent on organic food (intl.$)	Per capita spent on organic food (intl.$)[b]
	1997	1997	1997	1997	1997	2014
New Zealand	4	17 890	22	0.1	6	25
Germany	82	24 130	1 800	1.2	22	124
United Kingdom	59	23 590	450	0.4	8	44
Switzerland	7	32 360	350	2.0	49	279
Denmark	5	25 360	300	2.5	60	217
Sweden	9	24 220	110	0.6	13	141
United States	266	31 620	4 000	1.6	15	102
Japan	125	24 960	1 700	1.0	14	11

Notes: Conversion rate US $1 = 0.7520 Euro.
* PPP = purchasing power parity.
** Intl.$ = international dollars.

Sources: [a]Data from World Bank, http://data.worldbank.org/indicator/NY.GDP.PCAP.PP. CD; [b]Data from Willer and Lernoud, *World*. Other data adapted from Thompson, "International," 664, Table 1; Willer and Yussefi, *Ökologische*; Campbell and Fairweather, "Development," 5.

The national park system helped create the image of New Zealand as a natural and sportsman's paradise, with early proselytizers such as Zane Grey writing on both the country's natural beauty and excellent angling.[6] In 1901 the country became the first in the world to establish a government department devoted to tourism: the Department of Tourist and Health Resorts took ownership of some of the country's principal natural attractions, such as the natural hot springs in Rotorua and Hanmer.[7]

New Zealand invested in its clean image throughout the twentieth century. A study published in 2011 argued that the image of the country as "clean and green" had been "naturalised into the collective psyche."[8] In 1999 the national marketing agency, Tourism New Zealand, launched a campaign titled "100% Pure New Zealand," which promoted a uniform message across tourist markets and became an enduring global tourism brand with its emphasis on an unspoiled landscape.[9] The tourism minister at that time opined that "the 100% Pure New Zealand brand has positioned New Zealand on the world stage in terms of its environmental standards."[10] The monetary value of the brand image was well understood; after all, the Organisation for Economic Cooperation and Development (OECD) reported in 1996 that "the image of a 'green and clean' country helps with the export of meat, wool, timber and fish, and attracts foreign tourists."[11] In 2000 the New Zealand Ministry of the Environment assessed that approximately NZ$530 million was earned annually from tourism, and that approximately NZ$938 million annually went into the economy in general. The country's largest exporter, the dairy cooperative Fonterra, estimated in 2000 that the value of the "clean and green" image was worth between NZ$18,000 and NZ$49,000 to each farmer per annum.[12]

A final reason why the slow development of the organic food market in New Zealand is curious is that the country was active in the early development of organic agriculture; this is covered in the next section. Section III looks at the structure of New Zealand agriculture, policy shifts and the stunted growth of organic farming. Section IV discusses the limited development of the retail market, and Section V concludes with closing thoughts.

II ORIGINS OF ORGANIC AGRICULTURE IN NEW ZEALAND

By the time Steiner founded the biodynamic movement, New Zealand was already highly integrated into European, primarily British, food production systems. Following the introduction of refrigeration in the 1880s, meat – and from the turn of the century, dairy – emerged as major export sectors competing on the British market.[13] These sectors developed following the conversion of much of the native landscape to pasture and the introduction of grasslands following colonization, a process that was effectively complete by 1901. The re-creation of the landscape reinforced the idea of New Zealand as a bounteous Eden, as it keyed into the moral ethos of pastoral "improvement" equated with virtue and godliness.[14] Star and Brooking have argued that rather than simply reflect a core–periphery pattern of development, initially the intensification of agriculture was partly driven by New Zealand farmers, many of whom organized in networks of cooperatives and purposefully engaged in experimenting with chemical fertilizers and new seed strains to serve export markets.[15]

Nevertheless, by the mid-1920s, the increased use of phosphates was being driven primarily by the government's Department of Scientific and Industrial Research, working closely with its London counterparts, to drive higher productivity for export markets.[16] By 1921 New Zealand already earned 93 percent of its export income from grass-related products, with a firmly established "productionist" ethos based on export quantity and an ever-increasing dependence on phosphate and other chemicals to increase output; this dependency persists to the present day.[17] In marked contrast to this commodity-driven approach, at this time Danish dairy imports were attempting to compete by differentiation through the creation of strong brands, such as Lurbrand, which were gradually extended to other products (such as bacon) as a strategy to create a long-term national quality image in export markets.[18]

Before the 1980s, the development of organic agriculture in New Zealand broadly paralleled that found elsewhere, which was a reaction to the intensification of farming. Between the two world wars, several New Zealanders were active participants in the international movement that sought to develop biodynamic farming. Members of the New Zealand Anthroposophical Society were early correspondents with Steiner's followers, and members visited the biodynamic movement headquarters in Dornach, Switzerland, in 1930 to learn techniques and obtain seeds. Numbering 30 members in 1939, the group renamed themselves the Rudolf Steiner Biological Dynamic Association for Soil and Crop Improvement, and grew to a national membership of 200 by 1945, when they became the Biodynamic Farmers and Gardening Association.[19]

During the postwar years, local groups in New Zealand continued to develop local associations affiliated with their international counterparts. The Humic Compost Club was formed following the principles of the Soil Association in 1941, and eventually was renamed the NZ Organic Compost Society in 1953, and then the New Zealand Soil Association in 1970, with periodic reciprocal visits between organizations.[20] The Bio-dynamic Farmers and Gardening Association experienced declining interest, with membership at a low of 112 members in 1962. Although 1958 had witnessed the first commercial order of 145 sacks of organically grown wheat in the country, only a handful of farmers were members of the association, with most remaining members simply being interested in the principles rather than practice of biodynamic agriculture. However, there was a subsequent revival of interest, and by 1985 the Bio-Dynamic Association counted 540 members.[21] Meanwhile, the New Zealand

organic community continued to be involved in the international movement. There was a New Zealand representative on the board of IFOAM
from its foundation until 1999.[22]

Interest in organic farming in New Zealand received a new stimulus
after successful farm conversations, subject of the popular *Country
Calendar* television program in 1981, attracted new food producers.[23]
The Biodynamic Farmers and Gardening Association began the process
of registering New Zealand for the Demeter certification trademark in
1978, which was completed in 1986.[24] A local BioGro standard was
established in 1982 by the New Zealand Biological Producers Council,
which was created as an independent body formed by the Soil Association, the Biodynamic Farmers and Gardening Association, and the
Henry Doubleday Association to help develop the organic market.[25] This
standard, which was established without any input from New Zealand
policy makers,[26] was accredited by IFOAM in 1985.[27] Members from the
organization addressed attendees at a 1998 conference, hosted by Lincoln
College, a long-established agricultural college located in the Canterbury
region (the IFOAM World Congress had been held there in 1994). There
was also a new influx of enthusiasm from European emigrants to New
Zealand starting in the 1970s. North Canterbury, which benefited from
the skills brought by these recent immigrants, along with its rooted local
organic farming tradition, developed the strongest capabilities in organic
production, formalized around Lincoln College.[28]

Organic production remained small, as it did elsewhere, until the
1980s. In 1990 the value of the organic food domestic market in New
Zealand was merely NZ$1.1 million, with only NZ$100,000 in exports.[29]
At the same time, the large conventional agricultural sector was focused
on exports and willing to use how many pesticides and chemicals it
needed to maximize output. In the 1970s, for example, the substantial
New Zealand kiwi fruit industry applied between 12 and 17 applications
of pesticides as compared to three in California, the next most intensive
sprayer of that fruit in the world.[30]

III AGRIBUSINESS AND POLICY

During the 1980s, there were significant shifts in agricultural policy in
New Zealand. Previously, government-mandated Producer Boards struc-
tured conventional agriculture. These boards served key export markets,
especially Britain, which took nearly three-quarters of all New Zealand's
agricultural exports before the 1970s.[31] This regime changed after 1984,
when the neoliberal Labour Government of David Lange launched a

radical program of deregulation, which was far ahead of other developed countries. The Producer Board system was dismantled and subsidies scrapped.[32] From the mid-1980s onward, government policies firmly pitched New Zealand agricultural producers into the world market without government support, as Table 5.2 demonstrates.

Table 5.2   Percentage producer support estimates for selected OECD countries

	1983	1986–88	1988–2000	2000
Australia	–	9	6	6
EU	–	44	40	38
Japan	–	63	63	64
New Zealand	34	1	1	1
Switzerland	–	73	71	71
United States	–	25	23	22
OECD	–	39	35	34

Note: OECD figures start in 1986.

Sources: 1983 data from Vitalis, "Domestic reform." All other data adapted from OECD, *Agricultural policies*, 16.

The government pulled back its role to providing research and advisory services, which included exploring the potential of the organic sector, especially in the light of an apparent growth in the European market for organic food. Conscious that the history of much of New Zealand's food exports had been driven by a focus on production rather than quality, the government was very much aware that it needed to focus on quality in order to contest the most lucrative European markets in the future, especially with key rivals such as Denmark. The Ministry of Agriculture and Food carried out a survey of organic production in the country in 1987.[33] There were also research visits to examine developments in organic agriculture abroad. A program was established to examine how organic agriculture could add to food exports. As part of this initiative, New Zealand produced a report in 1988 on organic viticulture in Europe that identified environmental pressures and especially scandals on the use of diethylene glycol in Italian and Austrian wine, which stimulated the growth of organic wine production.[34]

The now-deregulated private sector showed little initial interest in such government reports on the potential for organic exports. It was not until 1992 that Zespri, formerly the New Zealand Kiwifruit Marketing Board, began to encourage kiwi fruit producers to move toward organic production, and in particular to embrace integrated farming and pest management systems under a "kiwi-green" banner, which met the requirements of European retailers seeking to promote "green" products while also allowing the majority of producers to continue using chemical pesticides. These and other initiatives resulted in organic agricultural exports reaching NZ$35 million by 1998, mostly kiwi fruit, apples and processed vegetables.[35] However, neither policy makers nor agribusiness were enthusiastic to provide financial support for conventional farmers who wanted to transition to organic. In 2000 the Primary Production Select Committee Organic Working Group, the first coordinated attempt to bring the government and the private sector together on the issue, concluded that it should be left to market forces to influence whether farmers switched production to organic.[36]

In a conservative and oligopolistic environment, market forces provided little incentive for radical change. The total amount of land under organic cultivation was modest by 1999 compared to the selected European countries (Table 5.3). It was still modest 15 years later, even though it had expanded its share of total agricultural land.

Table 5.3   Organic farming in New Zealand and selected countries, 1999 and 2014

Country	Organic hectares	Organic % total agricultural land	Organic % total agricultural land
	1999	1999	2014
New Zealand	11 500	0.07	0.9
Germany	452 279	2.64	6.4
Britain	240 000	1.20	3.3
Switzerland	84 124	7.80	12.2
Denmark	146 685	6.00	6.4
Sweden	155 674	5.50	16.3
United States	900 000	0.02	0.6
Japan	5 083	0.9	0.3

Sources: Willer and Yussefi, *Ökologische*; Willer and Lernoud, *World*.

Large food producers such as Wattie Frozen Food Ltd. (acquired by US-based H.J. Heinz Co. Ltd. in 1992) experimented with organic production for export markets. The firm started to export BioGro-certified vegetables to Japan and Europe in 1991, although the latter was vulnerable to shifting Japanese import regulations, while export constraints on the supply side affected vegetables such as peas.[37] There was little momentum outside of this. In 1994 80 percent of New Zealand organic exports were from Heinz-Watties and Zespri-affiliated farmers.[38] These two groups dominated the export trade, and even though growth accelerated from a low base (Table 5.4), it was still insignificant at 0.6 percent of agricultural exports in 2000, and consistently failed to reach forecast levels.[39]

Table 5.4   Food exports in New Zealand, 1991–2000 (NZ $million)

	1991	1992	1993	1994	1995	1996	1997	1998	1999	2000
Certified organic	0.1	–	–	6	–	12	20	28	35	60
Total dairy produce exports	2,420	2,814	3,179	3,379	4,376	4,625	4,085	4,376	4,625	4,778
Meat	2,588	3,002	3,057	2,874	2,903	2,828	2,730	2,903	2,828	3,376
Vegetables	196	262	246	314	336	390	272	336	390	366
Fruit, nuts and cereals	792	905	781	772	909	1,064	782	909	1,064	978
Total nonorganic	5,996	6,983	7,264	7,339	8,524	8,907	7,869	8,524	8,907	9,498

Sources: Organic Producers Export Group, "NZ organic"; Parliamentary Commissioner for the Environment, *Clean*; Grice et al., *State*, 14; Statistics New Zealand.

Insofar as there was interest in the organic market, it focused on exports. Heinz-Watties withdrew its limited organic lines from supermarkets in 1997, a move that struggling market gardeners considered damaging to the possibility of gaining supermarket interest in the sector and restricting them to "alternative" consumers.[40] There had already been a decrease in the number of BioGro-certified small farmers between 1994 and 1997, because in the 1980s many ecologically driven producers who had experimented with peri-urban lifestyle farms had left the industry.[41]

In the absence of incentives in the system, conventional farmers in New Zealand focused on key buyers, which had emerged as large retailer groups in Europe. In 1997 a coalition of British retailers, working together as the Euro-Retailer Produce Working Group (EUREP), established an independent umbrella standard, called EurepGap, which covered a broad range of agricultural practices; this was ISO/IEC Guide 65.[42] This was not, in itself, an organic standard, yet agricultural producers shifted their attention to satisfying its requirements. Zespri became one of the first organizations to pass EurepGap's most stringent audit. The state-owned enterprise AgriQuality offered its Certenz standard in 2000, which was firmly and successfully aimed at achieving ISO/IEC Guide 65 to service export markets without ideological components.[43] This certification standard offered pragmatists a route to market outside of the organic system, which lacked clarity for producers because the government was still considering whether to adopt BioGro, Demeter or Certenz as the national standard despite recognition that this indecision was harming exports and hindering market entry for small producers.[44]

Both the limited entrance of large firms into organics and the creation of standards caused deep suspicion among small organic farmers who held strong ideological views. Conversely, managers in conventional firms looked askance at hippie-style small organic producers.[45] The BioGro standard required that person, property and product all follow organic philosophies, but after the entry of agribusiness, some committed certifiers concentrated on product certification, hoping that "progressive conversion" would follow as opportunists and pragmatists became swayed by ideological argument.[46] "The progressive mainstreaming of organic production," complained one report in 1998, had "been achieved only with the loss of much of the broader organic vision."[47]

These debates remained marginal to the majority in New Zealand food production, such as the dairy industry – which represented the country's largest export sector and remained uninterested in organic agriculture. In some countries, dairy farmers took the lead in promoting organic milk and working with their governments and others to create standards. This was the case in Sweden, where the organic KRAV-labeled milk developed a large market after it was adopted by Arla, the country's largest dairy.[48] In Denmark, a process of consolidation of dairy cooperatives began in 1970 with the formation of Mejeriselskabet Danmark (MD). By 1999 the successor company, MD Foods, controlled 90 percent of milk production in the country, and it drove an expansion of organic milk that came to represent 20 percent of the milk sold in Denmark. This growth was greatly assisted by state-backed organic standards. In 1989 lobbying by organic farmers, the Danish consumer cooperative Fællesforeningen for Danmarks Brugsforeninger (FDP) and others led to the Danish government establishing a Danish Organic Food Council. At the council, all the stakeholders met regularly to discuss issues and were the first to officially label for organic products. The red "Ø" label, which showed that a product was state-certified organic, became a significant force in establishing the credibility of organic products.[49]

There was no equivalent of these developments in New Zealand. The New Zealand Dairy Board merged with the two largest New Zealand dairy cooperatives to represent 96 percent of the industry. It formed Fonterra in 2001, which was highly equivocal about organic certification.[50] Dominant agricultural incumbents, notably Fonterra and its relationship with both large-scale dairy farms and small producers, acted to maintain organic production as nonmainstream. As organic farming grew in scale elsewhere, especially in Europe, there were few incentives to make the investment needed to catch up in the category, especially as some direct competitors, including the Danish dairy sector, benefited from subsidies.[51] In 2001, more than two-thirds of New Zealand organic production were fruits and vegetables, with grains and dairy products making up the remainder.[52]

The lack of government engagement with organic agriculture, including not creating an equivalent to the Danish red "Ø" label, and the reluctance of the dairy industry to invest in organic, were evidently major factors in the slower growth of organic agriculture in New Zealand. The explanation for this lack of enthusiasm is less clear. A 1998 study of the limited growth of the organic sector hypothesized that some parties "considered that New Zealand's much vaunted 'clean green' image must therefore be defended from products that might look a little too green and thereby call into question the food safety attributes of conventional products. This has been a major reason for some industries refusing to foster organic development."[53] A study in a marketing journal in 1997 had already suggested that the country's clean and green image made it less receptive to environmental issues.[54] This issue is considered further below.

IV   CREATING A CONSUMER MARKET

The small growth of the domestic New Zealand organic food market reflected, in part, major constraints in both retailing and wholesaling. In a global perspective, the creation of a substantial market for organic foods from the late twentieth century came as a result of purposeful business strategies. The most important was the creation of a retail infrastructure that made buying organic food both possible and desirable. This happened in two distinctive ways: with either natural foods stores or conventional supermarkets playing key roles in market creation (Table 5.5).

Table 5.5   Distribution of retail sales of organic food in selected countries, 1998 (%)

	Multiple retailers	Other supermarkets/ greengrocers	Farmers markets/ direct sales	Natural food shops	Other
Denmark	75	5	5	15	0
Sweden	80	5	5	10	0
Britain	65	10	20	5	0
Germany	45	10	10	35	0
United States	31	0	0	62	7

Source: Adopted from Thompson, "International," 664, Table 1.

In the United States, the key driver of the organic food market was the growth of some small natural foods stores into large retail chains. By 2000 a single company, Whole Foods Market, held one-third of the $6 billion US organic food market. There was a parallel development in Germany, with the growth of the biodynamic foods retailer Alnatura and the organic wholesaler Rapunzel.[55]

In much of the rest of Europe, conventional retailers drove the market. This was the case in Denmark, which by the turn of the twenty-first century had the highest per capita consumption of organic food. In 1982 the Danish consumer cooperative FDP, which was a large retailer, began selling organic carrots produced by a radical community of intellectuals and students. The cooperative, owned by its members, felt their radical experiment was a response to the worries of their members about pesticides, whose use had grown rapidly in postwar Denmark. In 1987 the FDP also began selling organic milk. In a culture in which drinking milk is widespread, this was a significant step. Although organic milk was sold at a premium to conventional milk, it was, in absolute terms, not significantly expensive for many consumers, reducing one potential obstacle to purchase. This allowed organic milk to became an entry point for Danish organic consumers.[56] The red "Ø" label, established in 1989, further enhanced consumer trust in organic food.[57] Four years later, the

FDP's Super Brugsen chain store lowered the retail price of organic food products by up to 40 percent and decided to sell organic products throughout the nation, not only in the capital city of Copenhagen. The reduced prices drove up sales of organic milk by nearly 500 percent over the following years,[58] and the Danish market was deemed to have reached early maturity by 1993.[59] By 2000 the FDP stocked 800 organic products,[60] and other large supermarkets accounted for around three-quarters of the sales of organic food; this represented approximately 2.5 percent of the total Danish food market by the late 1990s.[61] By 1998 75 percent of organic foods in Denmark, and 80 percent in Sweden, were purchased from multiple retail chains.[62]

The growth of organic products was more subdued in Britain; nevertheless, conventional supermarkets were key factors in the growth of the organic market. The largest supermarket chains began stocking fresh organic fruits and vegetables: Safeway began in 1981, followed by Asda in 1986 and Sainsbury's in 1987. During the 1990s, the outbreak of, and publicity given to, "mad cow disease" (or bovine spongiform encephalopathy, BSE), caused by the use of byproducts from diseased animals in animal feed, facilitated the greater mainstreaming of organic products. This, and other food scares, diminished consumer confidence in conventional farming.[63] In addition to retailers embracing organics as a way to restore confidence in the food supply chain, they increasingly adopted it as part of their differentiation strategy. Supermarkets, including Marks & Spencer and Sainsbury's, moved directly into product development[64] and provided funding for organic research.[65]

In New Zealand, neither the Danish–British nor the US–German models for expanding the organic market occurred. Supermarkets in New Zealand were extremely concentrated; for example, by 2001, only two supermarket groups – Food Stuffs and the Australian-owned Progressive – controlled 100 percent of the supermarket sector.[66] They engaged mainly in price-based competition and displayed little interest in organic products. During the 1980s and most of the 1990s, supermarket buyers argued that there would not be sufficient continuity of supply or guarantee of quality standards.[67] At the end of the decade, both supermarket groups began to offer a handful of products, but these were "ghettoized" with separate display area for organic wholesalers and manufacturers, and promotions were limited to conventional products.[68] One estimate is that supermarkets accounted for just over one-quarter of organic food sales in 2000.[69]

The most sustained efforts to develop an organic food market came from entrepreneurs who, as elsewhere, were typically motivated by ideological concerns and typically possessed minimal capital or conventional retail experience. Frequently, they were influenced by experiences abroad when they encountered organic foods or concepts, but as a group they found it unexpectedly challenging to develop the market in New Zealand.

The first ventures were local and sometimes transient. Among the first was Piko Wholefoods, established in 1979 in the Canterbury region of New Zealand's South Island. It was an outlet for a local Whole Food Producers Co-operative and set up by seven of its members. The group had a strong ideological commitment to local issues and little desire to serve beyond its local community. It was very much a local producer-seller, with no ambitions to expand further, although it has proved a long-lasting venture: it still operated in 2018.[70]

In 1980 the first retail store opened on the North Island: Harvest Wholefoods was founded in Grey Lynn, an Auckland suburb.[71] Harvest was started by Elizabeth "Lippy" Chalmers, her husband Rick, and his brother Greg (although his actual name is Stephen), with a loan from Lippy's mother. The family was motivated by both personal factors and international experience. Although the Chalmers family had an interest in environmentalism after reading *Silent Spring*,[72] originally published in 1962, the initial business impulse came because Lippy and Rick's young son, Daniel, suffered from dairy intolerance and eczema. The family recognized an opportunity for the supply of suitable foods after an alternative doctor persuaded them of the benefits of dietary change.[73] Unlike general health shops, the family stocked a limited range of vegetables, nuts, raisins and seeds, as well as flour they ground themselves, and refused to sell vitamins, minerals or dairy products. They used links to producers' cooperatives to source eggs from free-range chickens and to buy organic whole wheat and rye for baking. Greg had recently returned from working in a macrobiotic restaurant in London, and originally was keen to establish the first such outlet in New Zealand. Around this time, one of his friends also returned from London and set up Kiaora Naturals, a macrobiotic import and wholesale business in West Auckland, and added a retail element by designating part of a warehouse as East West Wholefoods.[74] Harvest Wholefoods became Greg's main customer when he started to produce around 300 kilos a week of nigari tofu for sale in the store, and he decided not to open a restaurant. The tofu he made became the turning point that set Harvest Wholefoods on an even keel.[75] The same story could be told about many such ventures in Europe and the United States at this time.[76]

The tofu business was consolidated into Harvest Soyfoods, and word of mouth quickly attracted strong sales from national health shops, cafes and restaurants, and the family capitalized on this demand in 1981 by producing tofu for customers outside of Harvest Wholefoods, although the product was unpackaged and unbranded.[77] Early customers were "Indonesians, vegetarians, people switching from dairy to soy on the advice of naturopathic doctors, and spiritual seekers such as Hare Krishna and Divine Light people," all communities with which the Chalmers had strong links.[78] There were shifts in ownership and strategy. Harvest Wholefoods was sold to Lippy's sister, and the Chalmers invested the capital in importing new Japanese production equipment and larger premises to produce tofu.[79] In 1983, after Greg decided to leave the business, they sold Harvest Soyfoods to Paul and Trevor Johnston,[80] who renamed the business Bean Supreme. They retained the Chalmers on staff for the first year because they had paid the Chalmers 50 percent up front and the remaining amount twelve months later. At the end of that time, the Chalmers promised not to produce tofu for ten years. Bean Supreme grew rapidly, driven by increasing Asian immigration and the growing demand for tofu; it was increasingly no longer seen as only a health product but also as calcium sulfate, an inorganic compound, which was often used as a coagulant (something the Chalmers were opposed to).[81]

Sensing an opportunity to sell organic tofu, the Chalmers asked Bean Supreme to produce it for their new retail venture, East West Organics, which they had founded after three years in a commercial cleaning business that made a profit but failed to satisfy their environmental ambitions.[82] Bean Supreme was concentrating on growing the mass market for tofu and working toward supermarket distribution for their brand, so the Johnsons declined the invitation. In 1986 the Chalmers once again set up their own manufacturing facility, this time called The Organic Soy Company.[83] In 1988 Kaiora Natural began to supply BioGro-certified organic soybeans to The Organic Soy Company, enabling East West Organics to retail the only certified organic product in the country.[84]

The Chalmers's decision to invest in organics had been motived by personal factors. So too was the creation in 1984 of Ceres Wholefoods, named after the Roman goddess of the harvest, which opened in Ellerslie, Auckland as New Zealand's first fully organic food shop. The store grew from a fresh produce stall at the fair held at the Michael Park School, a Waldorf school that employed Steiner's educational philosophy. Juliet Lamont had returned from living in Germany with an interest in Steiner's principles, and was motivated by the desire to feed her children, who attended the school, in line with biodynamic principles. Lamont formed a local organic vegetable production cooperative with small farmers, initially to offer organic food. With the assistance of a friend and with a small investment of NZ$1,000 raised by ten people, Lamont established the cooperative into a small store. She was active with Demeter and BioGro, and developed connections with retailers and growers. The Biodynamic Association was keen to develop consistent practices and brand awareness through retailers, and worked to inform and train retail staff.[85]

In 1986 Ceres Wholefoods merged with a bookstore managed by Rodnie Whitlock; it specialized in anthroposophical books, including those on biodynamic agriculture. Lamont and Whitlock were explicit in their mission, stating, "We believed in what we were doing. The ethical side was paramount to us," and they also understood the daunting challenges they faced. "We had an idea," Lamont noted, "and that was all." The biggest challenge was simply that the consumers were not there. "People were not looking for organic food," so Lamont and Whitlock believed that they needed to make the case and create a market. Their strategy was to attract one consumer at a time, educating and convincing them why they should pay more for organic food. They further believed that if they did this successfully, eventually a growing demand would facilitate a growing supply, and with it a decrease in prices.[86] By 1993 Lamont had returned to a teaching career, and Ceres was advertised in the *Organic Growers Directory* as "specialists in biodynamic products with the Demeter trademark," offering dairy products, grains, Weleda skincare products and books by Rudolf Steiner and his followers.[87] Although the store itself did not remain long in the retail market (discussed below), it had a large impact on the development of the supply of organic goods through its wholesale arm.

An interest in alternative food production and wider social engagement ideals also propeled Jim Kebbell and Marion Wood in 1991 to establish Commonsense Organics, in Wellington.[88] Kebbell, who had trained as a Catholic priest and worked on international development projects, and Wood, who had also worked in social development projects, had been converted to organic production following Wood's mother's long-term interest in ecological matters. She had been a member of the Henry Doubleday Society, understood the need to reform agriculture after reading Rachael Carson's *Silent Spring* and insisted that a 12-acre block of land acquired in 1975 be farmed organically. Wood and Kebbell worked with five other families to develop organic produce for sale. They were joined by Marinus La Rooij, an emigrant from the Netherlands, who had worked in the biodynamic movement in Europe and was involved with the development of the BioGro standard. In 1983 he helped them become the fifteenth producer to be certified. La Rooij had ambitions to develop organic production on a commercial scale and grow the market.[89]

In 1991 Wood and Kebbell saw an opportunity to integrate forward into retail, which they thought would support organic production. In particular, their vision was to set up an alternative to supermarket grocery stores so as to attract new customers to the market. They saw the presentation of existing organic foods by food cooperatives as often off-putting, sometimes intentionally so in order to differentiate organic foods from mainstream foods. Their first shop, Commonsense Organics, was opened with the support of a loan from the National Bank, delayed rent payments from a sympathetic landlord, and an investment of NZ$10,000 from Wood, Kebbell and two others. This investment was made possible by the investors not taking any salary and Wood working full-time elsewhere. The retail store embraced mainstream display ideas, following the example of Whole Foods Market in the United States, and customer service also aspired to supermarket standards rather than the amateur approach they considered food cooperatives offered. The business broke even in 1995. By 2006 Commonsense had grown to a regional chain of 4 stores and 89 staff members.[90]

The signs that organic sales might take off, as seen happening elsewhere, also attracted a handful of conventional entrepreneurs, such as Ivor Miller, a South African pharmacist who had relocated to Auckland. He thought that the New Zealand market might respond to a large-scale organic retailer comparable to the Huckleberry Farms retail chain he had observed on a visit to Hawaii. Miller perceived that organic retailers such as East West Organics and Harvest Wholefoods were undercapitalized and thus unable to grow the market. Miller obtained permission to use the Huckleberry Farms name in New Zealand.[91] Working with his wife Delise, and daughter Nadine, Miller opened his first store in Auckland in 1993. He soon discovered that there was much less consumer interest than in Hawaii, and that it was difficult to secure adequate supplies. In an attempt to establish scale in 2002, the company entered into a 50:50 joint venture with Hardy's Healthy Living, a national chain of health stores. However, this worked out badly, as did a franchising arrangement to license Huckleberry's in South Korea in 2005.[92]

There was also a slow development of organic wholesaling, the lack of which had initially seriously handicapped the growth of the market. The firm of Fresh Direct was a first mover. The origins of this firm can be traced back to Edward Turner, a British emigrant, who founded Turners and Growers in 1897. After incorporation in 1921, the firm grew to become the major player in the import, auction and distribution of fruit in

New Zealand. In 1951 the firm established Fruit Distributors Ltd., a national organization of wholesale merchants that became the dominant importer of fruit into New Zealand for 40 years, with the monopoly of all imported citrus, pineapples and bananas. The Chinese gooseberry, which was unpopular with American consumers because of Cold War tensions, was formally renamed the kiwi fruit in 1959 by Edward's son, Harvey. The Turner family retained control of the company until 1994, when the Guinness Peat Group (an investment holding company now known as the Peats Group) purchased 42 percent of Turners and Growers Ltd. In 1993, Edward's great-grandsons, Jeffrey and Peter Turner decided to leave the firm and set up their own wholesaling business, Fresh Direct, which they established in 1995.[93]

With a strong understanding of the New Zealand market, the brothers sought to differentiate their business, and they identified an opportunity after a visit to California, during which time they were as impressed by the market potential of organic foods as were the New Zealand government researchers. With the insight that New Zealand lacked organic wholesalers similar to those encountered at Californian trade fairs, the brothers were the first to see this as an opportunity to serve the domestic rather than the export market, where the emergent retail and manufacturing firms were dealing direct with small suppliers. Although the Turners approached organic wholesale initially only as a commercial proposition, they realized that in order to fully exploit the market, they needed to employ managers who were knowledgeable and passionate about the segment; thus, they created the Purefresh Organic division in 1997. The new managers found pragmatic farmers who were seeking a premium for organic products but were often conservative and "one spray away" from leaving the sector if price conditions deteriorated. This is what happened to many small suppliers for Heinz-Watties when prices were renegotiated after difficulty in convincing supermarkets buyers to stock organic products.[94]

Ceres Wholefoods also evolved from a retail store into a national wholesaler to other parties, such as East West Organics and Commonsense Organics, and experienced strong growth. By the mid-1990s, Ceres had begun to supply organic rice milk to supermarkets, which gave the firm the experience and confidence of dealing directly with the supermarkets, for which they originally supplied only canned produce. As with Fresh Direct, Ceres found that its offerings were often segregated to an organic section that was not promoted. However, with a gradual increase in supplies, sales for Ceres grew at an annual rate of more than 20 percent in the 1990s. In 2001, Ceres became the first BioGro-certified organic distributor in New Zealand.[95]

By the early 2000s, then, major New Zealand cities had retail stores that sold organic food and a distribution structure to serve them. However, this did not lead to a major expansion of the market because there remained a constraint on the supply side. It was estimated in 2007 that over two-fifths of organic food sold in New Zealand was imported. This remained a vicious cycle in that the inability of both the natural food stores and the supermarkets to grow the organic market provided limited incentives for New Zealand farmers to switch their production.[96]

There also appeared to be considerable consumer resistance to buy organic food, a theme that was constantly stressed by those interviewed on this subject. They offered a number of potential explanations. The most obvious is that organic food products in every country are almost always sold at premium price compared to conventional products, which is a price-sensitive constraint to consumers.[97] While living standards in 1950s New Zealand were among the highest in the world, thereafter a prolonged period of slow growth resulted in the country's real per capita income falling behind other developed countries;[98] see Table 5.1 for the scale of the gap by 1997. There is a plausible argument that New Zealand consumers simply had less disposable income to spend on organic foods, although Table 5.1 also makes it evident that crude per capita income figures are a poor indicator of levels of per capita organic food consumption at a national level. In 1997, for example, Sweden's per capita income was just a little less than Denmark's, but its per capita spending on organic food was only one-fifth of that of Denmark. The Danish example makes it clear that large firms (if not small stores) had some discretion over price levels. The single biggest factor in the growth of the Danish organic market was the large price cut by the FDP in 1993, which sharply reduced the premium for organic products.[99] There was no equivalent move by the large supermarkets in New Zealand.

There is a consensus in the literature that the "willingness to pay" for organic food is influenced by factors other than price. These include trust in the certification system and the quality of the food, as well as, sometimes, the brand names.[100] Two common themes stand out. The first includes concerns for the natural environment, especially because natural pesticides have a lower water contamination impact than chemical pesticides, and are less harmful to wildlife. The second is the perceived health and nutritional advantages of organic food.[101] Typical early-entry consumers for organic foods were better educated than other consumers, and often included pregnant women or mothers concerned about the health of their children.[102] However, cross-cultural studies have shown that the emphasis given to particular values varied between countries. A study of why German consumers were more willing to buy organic food than their British counterparts, for example, found common consumer attitudes in the two countries on food safety and healthiness, but that British consumers did not link eating organic food with wider concerns about the natural environment, while their German counterparts did.[103]

As already implied by the lack of enthusiasm of the New Zealand government to support organic agriculture, it might well be that New Zealanders as a whole were either less concerned about environmental dangers than some of their counterparts elsewhere, or – as in the British case – did not strongly associate eating organic with saving the planet. As New Zealand historian James Belich has argued, this might reflect the cultural legacy of colonization, with the country sharing with other English-speaking settler economies a common heritage based on the dispossession of indigenous peoples, extensive agriculture and low population density.[104] This might have resulted in a value set based on privileging eating a lot of food as cheaply as possible, with little concern for environmental impact. Such a broad generalization would need to be qualified by evidence from the United States, where individuals, such as Jerome Rodale, and some states, including California and Colorado, count as global pioneers in organic food. Certainly, however, New Zealand's history is different to Denmark's; the latter faced an ecological catastrophe in the middle of the eighteenth century that heightened environmental sensitivities for future generations.[105]

In the case of New Zealand, unwillingness to pay seems to have been driven by the country's green and clean image. This appears to have sharply reduced interest in the health benefits of organic food, as there was a widespread perception that the existing food chain was safe. This was reflected in the scarcity of intensive production methods accepted in Europe, such as battery farming, and in the prevalence of grazing-based dairy farming and absence of food scares such as BSE. New Zealand is well endowed with land and a small population. It has no nuclear energy, and is far removed from fallout from nuclear disasters in other countries, such as Three Mile Island in the United States and Chernobyl in Soviet Ukraine, in 1979 and 1986 respectively; and low levels of industrialization means no acid rain.[106] "Consumers think everything grown in New Zealand is clean and green," two executives of Purefesh Organics noted, "so what's the point [of buying organic], and that's a major reason why we are only 1 percent [of the grocery market] compared to Europe or the States."[107]

As organic food retailers started businesses, they repeatedly encountered this problem, to their great frustration. "The perception was that we were green," noted Lamont and Whitlock, "[but] we were not."[108] There was indeed plentiful evidence that the perception was not based on reality. During the late 1980s, the Ministry of Agriculture and Fisheries reports described the "green paradise" reputation as "somewhat un-deserved."[109] A critical review by the British-based *New Scientist*, entitled "New Zealand's Poisoned Paradise," was published in 1993.[110] In 1996 the country was criticized by the OECD for being the only member without an ongoing statutory commitment to regularly reporting on the state of its environment.[111] Desmaris has described the "100% pure New Zealand" slogan as highly problematic as it set both an "unrealistic environmental bar to reach and sustain for the country" and set New Zealand up for scrutiny and disappointment.[112] Rudzitis and Bird sug-gested that "New Zealand's green image is overinflated, a form of 'greenwash,' given the actual conditions and recent environmental poli-tics."[113] It also erected a barrier to businesses, including for organic foods, because even as organic producers claimed to improve the environment, that claim appeared irrelevant. In a large survey conducted in 2002, more than two-thirds of New Zealanders either agreed or strongly agreed that the country was "clean and green"; 9.2 percent strongly agreed, 57 percent agreed and 17.6 percent neither agreed nor disagreed.[114] For entrepreneurs in organic retailing, an imagined green-ness emerged as a powerful obstacle to market development that was challenging to overcome, not least as it would have involved making the case that the country's huge agricultural business produced food that was less healthy and wholesome than organic products.

V CONCLUSIONS

This chapter has explored the apparent puzzle why both the organic food market and organic agricultural output remained subdued in New Zealand even as it expanded elsewhere between the 1970s and 2000s. The country was an early mover in organic movements, and during the 1980s both the government and businesses were aware of global trends and market opportunities. However the oligopolistic conventional retail sector subse-quently invested little to develop the market, while small organics retailers struggled to scale their businesses. The large agricultural export sector developed a two-tier system that marginalized the organic produc-tion sector to the premium domestic and export markets. While some large-scale exporters, such as Zespri, moved toward some organic pro-duction, the leading business in dairy products, Fonterra, did not. The government failed to establish a clear, nationally accepted standard for certification or to provide subsidies to promote organic farming.

It is always speculative to determine why something did not happen, but a number of explanations stand out. As in Denmark, New Zealand's dairy industry and retail food sector are highly concentrated. In Denmark, this concentrated structure fostered a strong momentum in favor of promoting organic food. In New Zealand, the structure worked the opposite way. There was no attempt by the dairy industry or the supermarkets to allocate their powerful resources to facilitate a shift in farmer or consumer perceptions.

Policy makers and consumers evidently did not prioritize the promotion of organic food, and neither did the managers running oligopolistic businesses. This may have reflected the country's historical legacy, as well as the economic stagnation and falling incomes that beset New Zealand in the second half of the twentieth century. However, this chapter has also pointed to the national perception of New Zealand as a clean and green country as an underlying structural obstacle. This was a competitive advantage for the country's agricultural exports as a whole, as well as for tourism, at least in the short-term, but a stumbling block for the organic sector. On the one hand, the development of an organic agriculture sector threatened to undermine the brand value of New Zealand's conventional agriculture, which rested heavily on the country's image. On the other hand, retailers encountered resistance from consumers who were confident of their existing food sources and natural environment.

Imagined greenness proved an extremely difficult exogenous factor for entrepreneurs seeking to build the organic market. In essence, they needed to convince consumers living in a country with far more grazing cows and sheep than people, and whose government had long run marketing campaigns that it was a natural paradise, that they should pay a price premium to buy food that they claimed was healthier and more environmentally friendly. In effect, and quite differently from the situation in Denmark, or in post-BSE Britain, New Zealand proponents of organic food and agriculture needed to change the self-image of the country, and change it in a negative way. It was, and has remained, a formidable entrepreneurial challenge.

NOTES

* This chapter appeared in an earlier version as Jones, Geoffrey and Simon Mowatt (2016), "National Image as a Competitive Disadvantage: The Case of the New Zealand organic food industry," *Business History*, **58**, (8), 1262–88.
1. Jones, *Profits*, 24–38.
2. Ibid., 61; O'Sullivan, *American Organic*, 121–3.
3. Jones, *Profits*, 235–7.

4. The US international dollar is also known as the Geary–Khamis dollar; it is used to compare the values of international currencies.
5. Squires et al., "Level"; Christensen and Saunders, *Economic*, vii, 32; Saunders et al., *Organic Farming*.
6. See Grey, *Tales*.
7. Tourism New Zealand, *100 Years Pure Progress*.
8. Egoz, "Clean," 63; Insch, "Conceptualisation," 286.
9. Desmarais, "Caught"; Tourism New Zealand, "Pure"; Bell, "100% Pure," 346; Connell et al., "Towards"; Insch, "Conceptualisation," 286; Morgan et al., "New Zealand," 348.
10. Milne, "Initiative."
11. Organisation for Economic Cooperation and Development, *Environmental*, 2.
12. Ibid.; True, "Country," 205.
13. By 1910, the leading exports from New Zealand in sterling were wool (£8.3 million), meat (£4 million), gold (£1.9 million), dairy (£1.8 million) and cheese (£1.2 million); see Hunter, "Commodity," 286, Table 1.
14. Pawson and Brooking, "Empires," 101–3.
15. Star and Brooking, "Department."
16. By 1901 the "greatest estate of all" – Maori land – had been largely settled by settler communities; see Star and Brooking, "Department," 192. Pawson and Brooking, in "Empires," outline that this followed the purchase of Maori lands by the Crown and after the 1840 signing of the Treaty of Waitangi, which gave Maori equal rights. Networks of cooperatives were central to meat and dairy exports, and in 1911 one-third of dairy exports were through cooperatives, see Hunter, "Commodity," 288–9. However, Star and Brooking concede to the argument made by Belich that following World War I, there had been a process of "re-colonisation" in which connections reinforced previous colonial relationships; see Belich, *Replenishing*; Star and Brooking, "Department."
17. The equivalent figures for other former colonies such as Australia (and Argentina and Uruguay) at the time were similar but none had such a large proportion of land mass under intensive cultivation as New Zealand. Phosphate consumption increased from 25,000 tons in 1900 to 400,000 tons in 1925, and, following World War II, New Zealand quickly and enthusiastically adopted the significant use of agrochemicals and pesticides such as DDT and 2,4,5-T, becoming one of the largest per capita users of the chemical worldwide until production ceased in 1987. It was noted that New Zealand producers saw no possibility of overproduction with ready access to British consumers, and felt little need to consider diversification or adding value through marketing. Pawson and Brooking, "Empires," 98, 103–5.
18. Higgins and Mordhorst, "Reputation."
19. G.B. Winkfield ("Winkey"), who lived in Keri Keri, had connections to the Westfield Freezing Works, and following his return from visiting Dornach, he developed a local network of famers and orchardists; see Shirley Wall (Compiler), "History of the Bio-Dynamic Association," *Bio-Dynamic Newsletter*, Winter 1987, 7–11, Organic Food Co-op Records (OFCR), 97-246-5/03, Alexander Turnbull Library (ATL), New Zealand National Archives (hereafter, Wall, "History," OFCR, ATL); Lockeretz, *Organic Farming*.
20. Jones and Mowatt, "National," 6.
21. Wall, "History," OFCR, ATL.
22. Campbell and Liepins, "Naming," 29.
23. Dairy farm conversions, managed by farmers such as Tom Stevens and John and Norrie Pearce, were particularly influential; see Wall, "History," 8, OFCR, ATL.
24. Ibid., 9.
25. New Zealand Biological Producers Council, "Networking with Similar Organisations," 1993, 1, OFCR, 97-246-5/02, ATL; see also Doris Zuur, "Alternative Viticulture in Europe: Integrated Organic and Bio-Dynamic Production," 1988, 54–5, Ministry of Agriculture and Fisheries (MAF), W5415 17243, Box 70, ATL (hereafter, Zuur, "Alternative").
26. Campbell and Liepins, "Naming," 29.

27. International Federation of Organic Agriculture Movements (IFOAM), "Circular."
28. Campbell and Fairweather noted that this region developed capacity starting with the establishment in 1977 by Bob Crowder of the Biological Husbandry Unit at Lincoln College, which offered courses on organic production. This led to the establishment of organic gardening as a course at Christchurch Polytechnic. Campbell and Fairweather, "Development," 11. These institutions served as a bridge between organic agriculture and commercial agriculturalists when larger agribusiness firms, such as Heinz-Watties, became interested in the market in the 1990s. Coombes and Campbell noted the importance of European immigrants with experience in organics as important in stimulating the organic community market garden culture in the Nelson region, but also noted that many left the industry after only a few years. Coombes and Campbell, "Recent," 7.
29. Campbell and Fairweather, "Development," 5.
30. McKenna and Campbell, "Not Easy," 14.
31. Until Britain joined the European Common Market in 1971, it accounted for 70 percent of New Zealand's agricultural exports. True, "Country," 202.
32. Vitalis, "Domestic Reform," 16. For a review of this transformation in and its effects on the New Zealand market, see McKenna and Campbell, "Not Easy."
33. Zuur, "Alternative." 54. Also see Campbell et al., "Auditing Sustainability."
34. Zuur, "Alternative," MAF, ATL. See also Engelhard Boehncke and Inkan Boehncke, "Report on the Activities of Prof. Dr. Engelhard Boehncke, and Dipl. Ing. Inkan Boehncke as MAF Technology Fellows of Organic Animal Production from February 11 to March 2, 1991," International Bureau of Animal Affairs, Germany, MAF, W5415 17243, Box 70, ATL. See also J.A. Springett, "Overseas Travel Report: Report on Visits to USA, France, UK and West Germany, 30 May–16 July 1990, Organic Farming and Sustainable Agriculture," Overseas Travel Report for the Head Office, Information Bureau, 1990, MAF, W5415 17243, Box 77, ATL (hereafter, Springett, "Overseas").
35. McKenna and Campbell, "Not Easy," 14.
36. Campbell and Fairweather, "Development," 42.
37. Campbell et al., "Auditing Sustainability," 160; Campbell and Fairweather, "Development," 13.
38. Saunders et al., *Organic Farming*, section 1.3.1.
39. The value of agricultural exports in the year ending March 2000 was NZ$10,064 million, representing 41 percent of the nation's exports. Saunders et al., *Food Market*, 10, 21.
40. Coombes and Campbell, "Recent," 12.
41. Campbell and Fairweather, "Development," 5–9; Egoz, "Clean."
42. This standard was broadened to GlobalGap in 2007. Campbell et al., "Global Retailer Politics"; Campbell et al., "Auditing Sustainability."
43. "Organics: A New Face in Agriculture. The Report of the Primary Production Committee on its Inquiry into Organic Agriculture in New Zealand," 5, Draft 1 as of February 22, 2001, MAF, PP 4/2/3 INQ/ORG/D1 W5190 16127, ATL (hereafter, "Organics," MAF, ATL). Campbell and Fitzgerald, and Campbell et al. review the two-tier system and cite a large range of studies on the evolution and dynamics of the system. In particular, they focus on the impact on the organic export market of EurepGap. Campbell and Fitzgerald, "Food Exports"; Campbell et al., "Global Retailer Politics"; Campbell et al., "Auditing Sustainability," 167–8. AgriQuality was a department within the Ministry of Agriculture and Fisheries until it was separated into a state-owned enterprise in 1998.
44. No official standard was adopted. See "Certification Issues," MAF, W5190, 16127, ATL. In 2000 Bio-Gro had 700 members, Demeter had 100 and AgriQual had 66. See "Organics: A New Face in Agriculture," 5, MAF ATL (PP 4/2/3 INQ/ORG/ D1 W5190 16127), 59.
45. Cowperthwaite, "Certenz," 29; Campbell and Liepins, "Naming"; Coombes and Campbell, "Dependent"; Cambell and Fairweather, "Development," 10, 35; interview by Geoffrey Jones and Simon Mowatt with Chris Morrison, founder, Phoenix Organics, Auckland, January 25, 2012 (hereafter, Morrison interview).

46. There is evidence that this did happen to some extent. Campbell and Fairweather, "Development," 10, 35.
47. Ibid., 38–9.
48. Broberg, "Labelling," 833. The stimulus provided by mainstream retail led to Arla increasing the producer premium paid to dairy farms by 15 percent, further stimulating farm conversion. Christensen and Saunders, *Economic*, 10.
49. Torjusen et al., *European*, 49–50.
50. "Organics," 6, MAF, ATL.
51. Ibid., 7.
52. Willer and Yusseffi, *Ökologische*.
53. Campbell and Fairweather, "Development," 39.
54. MacKay, "Playing," 28–32.
55. Jones, *Profits*, 182–4.
56. Interview by Geoffrey Jones with Karsten Korting and Thomas Roland, FDP Managers, Copenhagen, May 22, 2012 (hereafter, Korting and Roland interview).
57. Swiss Import Promotion Programme, *Organic*, 97.
58. Korting and Roland interview.
59. Hamm and Michelsen, "Organic."
60. Squires et al., "Level," 393.
61. Food and Agriculture Organization, *World*.
62. Thompson, "International," 665, Table 3.
63. For a review of the pattern of food scares in Europe, see Knowles and Moody, "European Food."
64. Cox and colleagues demonstrated that in Britain the shift to higher value-added foods, such as chilled ready-to-eat meals, was part of the competitive strategy supermarkets employed to differentiate themselves; they offered unique foods and own-brand food, and coordinated complex supplier networks; see Cox et al., "Firm."
65. In his New Zealand government report, Springett noted the role of Marks & Spencer and Sainsbury's in stocking certified products as contrasting with competitors that were willing to stock uncertified products with "little regard for anything but a high premium." Springett also noted that the British Organic Farmers and the Organic Growers Association petitioned Sainsbury's to provide funding, and Sainsbury's had recently funded a joint "Sainsbury's – Food from Britain" national survey and feasibility study for organic livestock production in Britain. See Springett, "Overseas," 2, 11, MAF, 77ATL.
66. Commerce Commission (2001), "Decision no. 348," Section 86; Rotherham, "Dream."
67. In the early adoption of organics into Britain supermarkets, buyers made the same arguments. Mr. Segger, the managing director of Organic Farm Foods, in Lampeter, Wales, said that he was forced to approach the company chairmen and their wives directly in order to obtain contracts with Tesco, Sainsbury's and Marks & Spencer, and recommended New Zealand producers employ the same tactic. See Springett, "Overseas," 26, MAF, ATL.
68. Interview by Geoffrey Jones and Simon Mowatt with Jeffrey Turner and Ana Aloma, original general managers of Purefresh Organic, and with Robert Quinn, trading manager of Purefresh Organic, Auckland, January 21, 2012 (hereafter, Turner, Aloma and Quinn interview).
69. Campbell and Ritchie, *Organic*, 4, 6–8.
70. Campbell, *Recent Developments*, 31–2; Campbell and Fairweather, "Development," 11.
71. The address at 403 Richmond Road, Grey Lynn, was in an area of Auckland in decline and with a large Polynesian population. In 2018 the store still traded from the same location and under the same name (also incorporating 405 Richmond Road), although Harvest Wholefoods is now part of the Huckleberry Farms group, and Grey Lynn is highly gentrified, with some of the highest house prices in the country. The original store was New Zealand's first whole foods and natural foods store as well as the first macrobiotic retail store. It had been the location of the Ranfurly Cooperative Store, which claimed to sell organic produce but in fact did not. Interview by Geoffrey Jones and

Simon Mowatt with Elizabeth Chalmers, founder, Chalmers Organics, and founder, Harvest Wholefoods, Auckland, January 26, 2012 (hereafter, Chalmers interview).

72. On the influence of Carson on the revival of environmentalism in the 1960s, see Jones, *Profits*, 86.
73. Describing themselves as "60s hippie children," the family first approached the doctor after running out of hydrocortisone cream. As vegetarians, they initially found the doctor's recommended elimination diet difficult because they found few vegetarian foods produced without sugars, and so realized there could be a need for alternative health foods. Chalmers interview.
74. The location was 374 West Coast Road, Glen Eden.
75. Chalmers interview.
76. Dobrow, *Natural*, Chapters 2 and 3.
77. They produced the tofu using simple, homemade equipment in a small back room, and they learned the process by referring to *The Book of Tofu*, by William Shurtleff and Akiko Aoyagi.
78. Letter from Martha Wagner, July 24, 1981, cited in Shurtleff and Aoyagi, *Tempeh*.
79. Chalmers interview.
80. Greg and his partner had a baby, and his partner wanted to leave Auckland. The Johnsons had also traveled in the United States and become interested in vegetarianism and the health movement, and products such as tofu and soymilk. The Johnsons diversified into other areas related to health and well-being. Chalmers interview. See also Chapple, "Soybeans."
81. The Immigration Act (1987) created a change in policy, leading to a rapid increase in immigrants from Asian countries rather than the "traditional" sources of immigration such as Britain. Between 1987 and 1991, immigration from "nontraditional sources," largely China and Hong Kong, increased from 7.3 percent to 16.8 percent. See Bedford et al., "Globalisation."
82. Chalmers interview.
83. Bean Supreme grew at around 18 percent per annum from 1986 to 2002 to a revenue of NZ$3 million. Chapple, "Soybeans." The Johnsons later sold the Bean Supreme brand to Sanatorium, one of New Zealand's largest branded food manufacturers. Shurtleff and Aoyagi, *Tempeh*. The Chalmers sold East West Organics in 1998 to concentrate on the development of Chalmers Organics. Chalmers interview.
84. Shurtleff and Aoyagi, *Tempeh*.
85. Bio-Dynamic Association, "To Outlets for Demeter Products," letter dated February 20, 1992, OFCR, 97-246-3/03, ATL.
86. Interviews by Geoffrey Jones and Simon Mowatt with Noel Josephson and Rodnie Whitlock, founders, Ceres Organics, Auckland, January 26, 2012 (hereafter, Josephson and Whitlock interview).
87. New Zealand Biological Producers Council, *Organic Growers Directory*, back page, OFCR, 97-246-1/08, ATL.
88. Interviews by Geoffrey Jones and Simon Mowatt with Marion Woods and Jim Kebbell, founders, Commonsense Organics, Wellington, January 30 2012 (hereafter, Woods and Kebbell interview).
89. Vincent, "Organic," 152.
90. Commonsense Organics internal report, *Walking the Talk: Sustainability Report 2006*, 1–13.
91. There was no contract or other business relationship between the businesses other than a goodwill undertaking to allow Miller to use the name in New Zealand. Interview by Geoffrey Jones and Simon Mowatt with David Spalter, general manager, Huckleberry Farms, and family member of founder, Auckland, January 24, 2012 (hereafter, Spalter interview).
92. David Spalter, husband to Nadine, took over the permanent management of the stores in 2002 on her pregnancy. Spalter interview.

93. McClure, "Turner, Harvey"; Stead, *One Hundred.* See also New Zealand History, "Chinese gooseberry."
94. Turner, Aloma and Quinn interview.
95. Ceres Enterprises, "From Humble Beginnings."
96. Grice et al., *State.*
97. After a visit to various retailers in the United States and Europe in 1990, Springett wrote in a New Zealand government report the following typical example in a health store in Boulder, Colorado: "Ginger, organic $6.99/lb, Ginger conventional, $2.39/lb; Carrots certified organic 69c/lb, conventional 29c/lb and Lemons certified organic 89c each, conventional 29c each"; Springett, "Overseas," 11, MAF, ATL. In a later report, Springett also compared produce in Sainsbury's and Marks & Spencer, finding: "Beans organic 85p/lb, conventional 59p/lb; cabbage organic 65p/lb, conventional 32p/lb; bread organic 55p, similar conventional 50p"; see J.A. Springett, "Summary: Report on Visits," 97-246-5/02, ATL.
98. Greasley and Oxley, "Outside."
99. Wier et al., "Consumer," 261.
100. Krystalis and Chryssohoidis, "Consumers."
101. Hughner et al., "Who."
102. Torjusen et al., *European.*
103. Baker et al., "Mapping."
104. Belich, *Replenishing.*
105. Kjærgaard, *Danish.*
106. Morrison interview.
107. Turner, Aloma and Quinn interview.
108. Ibid.; Josephson and Whitlock interview; Morrison interview.
109. Springett, "Overseas," 51, MAT, ATL.
110. True, "Country," 206.
111. Parliamentary Commissioner for the Environment, *Clean,* 6; McKenna and Campbell, "Not Easy."
112. Desmarais, "Caught."
113. Rudzitis and Bird, "Myth," 18. Rudzitis and Bird also review arguments that government proposals in 2010–11 for open-cast mining on conservation lands had the potential to undermine the 100 percent brand; Morrow and Mowatt review arguments that the 100 percent brand is risky without clearer government support to protect the environment. Morrow and Mowatt, "Implementation."
114. Hughey et al., *Perceptions,* 7, Table 2.

REFERENCES

Baker, Susan, Keith E. Thompson, Julia Engelken and Karen Huntley (2004), "Mapping the Values Driving Organic Food Choice: Germany vs the UK," *European Journal of Marketing,* **38,** (8), 995–1012.

Bedford, Richard, Charlotte Bedford, Elsie Ho and Jacqueline Lidgard (2002), "The Globalisation of International Migration in New Zealand: Contribution to a Debate," *New Zealand Population Review,* **28,** 69–97.

Belich, James (2009), *Replenishing the Earth: The Settler Revolution and the Rise of the Anglo-World, 1783–1939,* Oxford: Oxford University Press.

Bell, Claudia (2008), "100% Pure New Zealand: Branding for Back-packers," *Journal of Vacation Marketing,* **14,** 345–55.

Broberg, Oskar (2010), "Labelling the Good: Alternative Visions and Organic Branding in Sweden in the Late Twentieth Century," *Enterprise & Society*, **11**, 811–38.

Campbell, Hugh (1996), *Recent Developments in Organic Food Production in New Zealand: Part 1: Organic Food Exporting in Canterbury*, Dunedin, New Zealand: University of Otago.

Campbell, Hugh, Carmen McLeod and Christopher Rosin (2006), "'Auditing Sustainability': The Impact of EurepGap in New Zealand," in Georgina Holt and Matthew Reed (eds.), *Sociological Perspectives of Organic Agriculture: From Pioneer to Policy*, Wallingford, UK: CABI International, Chapter 10.

Campbell, Hugh, Carmen McLeod and Christopher Rosin (2007), "Global Retailer Politics and the Quality Shift in New Zealand Horticulture," in M.R. Butcher, J.T.S. Walker and S.M. Zydenbos (eds.), *Future Challenges in Crop Protection: Repositioning New Zealand's Primary Industries for the Future*, Christchurch, New Zealand: Plant Protection Society, 11–27.

Campbell, Hugh and John Fairweather (1998, September), *The Development of Organic Horticultural Exports in New Zealand*, Research Report No. 238, Canterbury, New Zealand: Agribusiness and Economics Research Unit, Lincoln University.

Campbell, Hugh and Margaret Ritchie (2002, June), *The Organic Food Market in New Zealand: 2002*, Research Report Number 1, Dunedin, New Zealand: Centre for the Study of Agriculture, Food and Environment, University of Otago.

Campbell, Hugh and Ruth Fitzgerald (2000), "New Zealand's Food Exports in the 21st Century: Whither the Green Option?" *Proceedings of the New Zealand Society of Animal Production*, **60**, 72–7.

Campbell, Hugh and Ruth Liepins (2002), "Naming Organics: Understanding Organic Standards in New Zealand as a discursive Field," *Sociologia Ruralis*, **41**, 21–39.

Ceres Enterprises (2018), "From humble beginnings. The founding of Ceres," accessed January 15, 2018 at https://www.ceres.co.nz/our-story.

Chapple, Irene (2002), "Soybeans bring happiness after years of hard yakka," *New Zealand Herald*, June 21.

Christensen, Vivi and Caroline Saunders (2003), *Economic Analysis of Issues Concerning Dairy Farming*, Research Report No. 257, Canterbury, New Zealand: Agribusiness and Economics Research Unit, Lincoln University.

Commerce Commission (2001), "Decision no. 438: Decision pursuant to the Commerce Act 1986 in the matter of an application for a clearance by Progressive Enterprise Ltd and Woolworths (New Zealand) Ltd.," public version, accessed January 15, 2018 at http://www.comcom.govt.nz/business-competition/mergers-and-acquisitions/clearances/clearances-register/detail/354.

Connell, Joanne, Stephen Page and Tim Bentley (2009), "Towards Sustainable Tourism Planning in New Zealand: Monitoring Local Government Planning under the Resource Management Act," *Tourism Management*, **30**, 867–77.

Coombes, Brad and Hugh Campbell (1998), "Dependent Reproduction of Alternative Modes of Agriculture: Organic Farming in New Zealand," *European Journal for Rural Sociology*, **38**, 127–45.

Coombes, Brad and Hugh Campbell (1998), "Recent Developments in Organic Food Production in New Zealand: Part 4: The Expansion of Organic Food Production in Nelson and Golden Bay," *Studies in Rural Sustainability Research Report*, **5**, University of Otago.

Cowperthwaite, Valerie (2000), "Certenz: Threat to Organics?" *Soil and Health*, **59**, (4), 29–30.

Cox, Howard, Simon Mowatt and Martha Prevezer (2002), "The Firm in the Information Age: Organizational Responses to Technological Change in the Processed Foods Sector," *Industrial and Corporate Change*, **11**, 135–58.

Daugbjerg, Carsten and Darren Halpen (2008), "Governing Growth in Organic Farming: The Evolving Capacities of Organic Groups in the United Kingdom and Denmark," paper presented at the 58th PSA Annual Conference, April 1–3. Accessed June 23, 2017 at http:orgprints.org/13951.

Desmarais, Fabrice (2015), "Caught in an Inconvenient Nation-Branding Promise: The Problematic '100% pure New Zealand' Slogan," *Interdisciplinary Environmental Review*, **16**, 1–16.

Dobrow, Joe (2014*), Natural Prophets: From Health Foods to Whole Foods: How the Pioneers of the Industry Changed the Way We Eat and Reshaped American Business*, New York: Rodale.

Egoz, Shelley (2000), "Clean and Green but Messy: The Contested Landscape of New Zealand's Organic Farms," *Oral History*, **28**, 63–74.

Grey, Zane (1926), *Tales of the Angler's Eldorado*, London: Hodder & Stoughton.

Food and Agriculture Organization of the United Nations (2001), *World Markets for Organic Fruit and Vegetables: Opportunities for Developing Countries in the Production and Export of Organic Horticultural Products*, Ede, Netherlands: FAO. Accessed April 30, 2012 at http://www.fao.org.ezp-prod1.hul.harvard.edu/DOCREP/004/Y1669E/y1669e00.htm.

Greasley, David and Les Oxley (1999), "Outside the Club: New Zealand's Economic Growth, 1870–1993," *International Review of Applied Economics*, **14**, (2), 173–92.

Grice, Janet, Mark Cooper, Hugh Campbell and Jon Manhire (2007), *The State of the Organic Sector in New Zealand, 2007*, Dunedin, New Zealand: Centre for the Study of Agriculture, Food and Environment, University of Otago.

Hamm, Ulrich and Johannes Michelsen (1996), "Organic Agriculture in a Market Economy: Perspectives from Germany and Denmark," in T. Østergaard (ed.), *Fundamentals of Organic Agriculture: Proceedings from the 11th IFOAM International Scientific Conference*, Copenhagen: Tholey-Theley.

Higgins, David and Mads Mordhorst (2008), "Reputation and Export Performance: Danish Butter Exports and the British Market, c.1880–c.1914," *Business History*, **50**, 185–204.

Hughey, Kenneth, Geoffrey Kerr and Ross Cullen (2002), *Perceptions of the State of the Environment: The 2002 Survey of Public Attitudes, Preferences and Perceptions of the New Zealand Environment*, Canterbury, New Zealand: Lincoln University, Educational Solutions Ltd.

Hughner, Renée Shaw, Pierre McDonagh, Andrea Prothero, Clifford J. Shultz II and Julie Stanton (2007), "Who are Organic Food Consumers?" *Journal of Consumer Behaviour*, **6**, 1–17.

Hunter, Ian (2005), "Commodity Chains and Networks in Emerging Markets: New Zealand, 1880–1910," *Business History Review*, **79**, 275–304.

Insch, Andrea (2011), "Conceptualisation and Anatomy of Green Destination Brands," *International Journal of Culture, Tourism and Hospitality Research*, **5**, 282–90.

International Federation of Organic Agriculture Movements (IFOAM) (1985), "Circular Letter to all Voting Members from the Board of Directors Concerning the IFOAM Technical Committee," May 15, 97-246-1/08, ATL.

Jones, Geoffrey (2017), *Profits and Sustainability: A History of Green Entrepreneurship*, Oxford: Oxford University Press.

Jones, Geoffrey and Simon Mowatt (2016), "National Image as a Competitive Disadvantage: The Case of the New Zealand Organic Food Industry," *Business History*, **58**, (8), 1262–88.

Kjærgaard, Thorkild (1994), *The Danish Revolution, 1500–1800: An Eco-historical Interpretation*, Cambridge: Cambridge University Press.

Knowles, Tim and Richard Moody (2007), "European Food Scares and Their Impact on EU Food Policy," *British Food Journal*, **109**, 43–67.

Krystalis, Athanasios and George Chryssohoidis (2005), "Consumers' Willingness to Pay for Organic Food: Factors that Affect it and Variation per Organic Product Type," *British Food Journal*, **107** (5), 320–43.

Lockeretz, William (ed.) (2007), *Organic Farming: An International History*, Trowbridge, UK: Cromwell Press.

McClure, Margaret (1998), "Turner, Harvey," *Te Ara—the Encyclopaedia of New Zealand*, accessed June 23, 2017 at https://teara.govt.nz/en/biographies/4t31/ turner-harvey. First published in *Dictionary of New Zealand Biography*, **4**.

MacKay, Jo (1997), "Playing with Green?" *Marketing Magazine*, **16**, (2), (March), 28–32.

McKenna, Megan and Hugh Campbell (2003), "It's Not Easy Being Green: The Development of 'Food Safety' Practices in New Zealand's Apple Industry," *International Journal of Sociology of Agriculture and Food*, **10**, 45–55.

Milne, Amy (2008), "Initiative will help attract tourists," *Southland Times*, May 28, 7.

Morgan Nigel, Annette Pritchard and Rachel Piggott (2002), "New Zealand, 100% Pure: The Creation of a Powerful Niche Destination Brand," *Journal of Brand Management*, **9**, 335–54.

Morrow, Jeremy and Simon Mowatt (2015), "The Implementation of Authentic Sustainable Strategies: i-SITE Middle Managers, Employees and the Delivery of 100% Pure New Zealand," *Business Strategy and the Environment*, **24**, 656–66.

New Zealand History (n.d.), "Chinese gooseberry," accessed January 15, 2018 at http://www.nzhistory.net.nz/the-chinese-gooseberry-becomes-the-kiwifruit.

O'Sullivan, Robin (2015), *American Organic: A Cultural History of Farming, Gardening, Shopping and Eating*, Lawrence, KS: University of Kansas Press.

Organisation for Economic Cooperation and Development (2001), *Agricultural Policies in OECD Countries: Monitoring and Evaluation*, Paris: OECD.

Organisation for Economic Cooperation and Development (1996), *Environmental Performance Reviews: New Zealand*, Paris: OECD. Accessed January 15, 2018 at https://www.oecd.org/environment/country-reviews/find-a-review.htm.

Organic Producers Export Group (various years), "NZ organic exports," accessed January 15, 2018 at http://www.organictradenz.com.

Parliamentary Commissioner for the Environment (2007), *How Clean is New Zealand? Measuring and Reporting on the Health of our Environment*, Wellington: Parliamentary Commissioner for the Environment. Accessed January 8, 2014 at http://www.pce.parliament.nz/publications/all-publications/how-clean-is-new-zealand-measuring-and-reporting-on-the-health-of-our-environment.

Pawson, Eric and Tom Brooking (2008), "Empires of Grass: Towards an Environmental History of New Zealand Agriculture," *British Review of New Zealand Studies*, **17**, 95–114.

Rotherham, Fiona (2002), "The Dream Deal," *Unlimited*, 40–46.

Rudzitis, Gundars and Kenton Bird (2011), "The Myth and Reality of Sustainable New Zealand: Mining in a Pristine Land," *Environment*, **53**, 16–28.

Saunders, Caroline, Gareth Allison and Anita Wreford (2004, October), *Food Market and Trade Risks*, Wellington: Parliamentary Commissioner for the Environment.

Saunders, Caroline, Jon Manhire, Hugh Campbell and John Fairweather (1997, June), *Organic Farming in New Zealand: An Evaluation of the Current and Future Prospects Including an Assessment of Research Needs*, Canterbury, New Zealand: Department of Economics and Marketing, Lincoln University

Shurtleff, William and Akiko Aoyagi (2011), *History of Tempeh and Tempeh Products (1815–2011): Extensively Annotated Bibliography and Sourcebook*, Lafayette, CA: Soyinfo. Centre. Accessed January 15, 2018 at http://www.soyinfocenter.com/pdf/148/Temp.pdf.

Swiss Import Promotion Programme (2011), *The organic market in Europe*, accessed January 15, 2018 at http://orgprints.org/18347/1/kilcher-etal-2011-sippo.pdf.

Squires, Lisa, Biljana Juric and Bettina Cornwell (2001), "Level of Market Development and Intensity of Organic Food Consumption: Cross-cultural Study of Danish and New Zealand Consumers," *Journal of Consumer Marketing*, **18**, 392–409.

Star, Paul and Tom Brooking (2007), "The Department of Agriculture and Pasture Improvement, 1892–1914," *New Zealand Geographer*, **63**, 192–201.

Statistics New Zealand, Interactive online database. Table: Key Statistics Table 7.04 – Value of principal exports (excluding re-exports) – SH (Annual–Jun) 1991–2000. Accessed January 15, 2018 at http://archive.stats.govt.nz.

Stead, Ken (1997), *One Hundred I'm Bid: A Centennial History of Turners & Growers*, Auckland: Kestrel Publishers.

Thompson, Gary (2000), "International Consumer Demand for Organic Foods," *HortTechnology*, **10**, (4), 663–74.

Torjusen, Hanne, Lotte Sangstad, Katherine O'Doherty Jensen and Unni Kjaernes (2004), *European Consumers' Conceptions of Organic Food: A Review of Available Research*, Oslo: National Institute for Consumer Research.

Tourism New Zealand (2001), *100 Years Pure Progress: 1901–2001, Tourism New Zealand, One Hundred Years of Tourism*, Wellington: New Zealand Tourism.

Tourism New Zealand (2009), *Pure as: Celebrating 10 years of 100% pure New Zealand*, accessed June 20, 2017 at http://www.tourismnewzealand.com/media/1544/pure-as-celebrating-10-years-of-100-pure-new-zealand.pdf.

True, Jaqui (2005), "Country before Money? Economic Globalization and National Identity in New Zealand," in Eric Helleiner and Andreas Pickel (eds.), *Economic Nationalism in a Globalizing World*, New York: Cornell University Press, 202–20.

Vincent, Priya (ed.) (2006), *Organic Roots: Inspiration from the Founders of the Modern Organic Farming Movement*, Self-published: Lulu.com.

Vitalis, Vangelis (2008), "Case Study 2: Domestic Reform, Trade, Innovation and Growth in New Zealand's Agricultural Sector," OECD Trade Policy Working Paper No. 74.

Wier, Mette, Lars Gaarn Hansen, Laura Moerch Andersen and Katrin Millock (2003), "Consumer Preferences for Organic Foods," in Organisation for Economic Cooperation and Development (ed.), *Organic Agriculture: Sustainability, Markets and Policies*, Oxford: CABI Publishing.

Willer, Helga and Julia Lernoud (eds.) (2015), *The World of Organic Agriculture: Statistics and Emerging Trends 2015*, Frick and Bonn: Research Institute of Organic Agriculture and International Federation of Organic Agriculture Movements.

Willer, Helga and Minou Yussefi (2001), *Ökologische Agrarkultur Weltweit–Statistiken und Perspektiven*, Bonn: IFOAM.

PRIMARY MATERIALS

Interviews by Geoffrey Jones and Simon Mowatt with Elizabeth Chalmers, Auckland, January 26, 2012; Noel Josephson and Rodnie Whitlock, Auckland, January 26, 2012; Chris Morrison, Auckland, January 25, 2012; David Spalter, Auckland, 24 January, 2012; Jeffrey Turner, Ana Aloma and Robert Quinn, Auckland, January 21, 2012; Marion Woods and Jim Kebbell, Wellington, January 30, 2012.

Interview by Geoffrey Jones with Karsten Korting and Thomas Roland (Fælles-foreningen for Danmarks Brugsforeninger, FDP), Copenhagen, May 22, 2012.

New Zealand National Archives, Alexander Turnbull Library, Wellington, New Zealand:

Bio Dynamic Farming and Gardening Association

Ministry of Agriculture and Fisheries (MAF)

New Zealand Biological Producers Council

Organic Food Co-op Records (OFCR).

6. Creating the market for organic wine: Sulfites, certification and green values

With Emily Grandjean

I INTRODUCTION

This chapter explores why the creation of the market for organic wine has proved so challenging and contested. Organic wine producers and retailers found it tough to persuade consumers to buy their wines as the category developed from the 1970s. Conventional wine producers were especially reluctant to switch to organic methods. Developing a common set of standards for organic wine proved problematic. These are familiar issues in the emergence of new categories: the development of common norms, agreed definitions, clear boundaries and cognitive legitimacy are frequently contested processes.[1] In organic wine, they proved especially contested, and hard to resolve.

The wine industry is ancient. Although Eastern Europe, the Middle East and Asia have a long tradition of winemaking, by the nineteenth century it was France, Italy, Spain and Portugal that had become the recognized prestigious home of the wine industry, called the "Old World." It was during this era that Europe acquired its modern form of small family vineyards, cooperative wineries and regional appellations.[2] Europe still accounted for 96 percent of the value of global wine exports in the 1980s, but thereafter wine exports from long-established producers beyond Europe – particularly the United States, Australia, New Zealand, Chile, Argentina and South Africa – built international reputations. Wine producers from these countries invested heavily in new technologies and marketing, benefited from cheaper land and better climates for wine growing, and created larger companies. A distinction was made within the industry between Old World wines, which drew on long-established traditions of winemaking in distinctive local soils and climates in Europe, and New World wines, where science and the role of the winemaker were emphasized.[3]

All wines were organic until the nineteenth century, when chemical fertilizers were introduced into agricultural farming techniques.[4] The use of pesticides expanded from the 1940s.[5] Sulfur dioxide, also called "sulfites," began to be added to wine in the late nineteenth century, following the emergence of the petrochemical industry. Technological advances in chemical delivery systems, such as the sulfur-based Campden tablet, in the early twentieth century also contributed to the growing use of sulfites.[6] Sulfites were used for several purposes throughout the winemaking process; they killed unwanted bacteria, prevented spoilage by bacteria, inhibited the process of oxidation and served as a stabilizer in bottles of wine.[7]

As Section II explains, the search for a way back from using chemicals and additives was belated. It was not until the 1970s that organic wine started to be produced on a significant – albeit tiny – scale in Europe and the United States. However, for multiple reasons the organic wine market gained little traction, despite the efforts both of the pioneering winemakers discussed in Section II and the wine retailers discussed in Section III. Adding to the challenge was that wines made using unconventional methods acquired multiple names, including "organic," "biodynamic" and "natural."[8]

Multiple certification schemes also developed, as discussed in Section IV. This contributed to a situation where, although it is clear that the organic wine market has remained quite small, there has been uncertainty regarding its actual size. The estimates of the size of organic vineyard acreage and the organic wine market shown in Table 6.1, therefore, should be treated with caution. They are derived from multiple sources, which differ in their methodologies; some sources report certified organic only; biodynamic is sometimes included and sometimes not; and some numbers may include non-certified organic, including "natural" wine. Insofar as these numbers are reliable, it would appear that organic wine has achieved, after four decades of effort, only a small fraction of the global wine market.[9] However there are huge differences between countries. The market for organic wine is far larger in Sweden, a country with 9 million inhabitants, than in the United States, with 326 million. Sweden's per capita wine consumption was (in 2017) two and a half times greater than that of the United States, yet still the different size of organic wine markets is a striking testament to the uneven spread of organic wine consumption.[10]

Table 6.1   Global "organic wine" market, 2003–17

Country	Area of organic vineyards, 2003–04 (hectares)	Area of organic vineyards, 2011–13 (hectares)	Organic grape area as % of total grape area, 2015 (%)	Value of exports of organic wine, 2011–16 (US$ million)	Organic wine market sales, 2011–17 (US$ million)
United States	7 875	11 400	2.9	–	200
France	16 400	65 000	9	–	715
Italy	31 170	57 000	11.9	146	73
Spain	14 900	81 000	10.2	–	34
Britain	–	–	17.7	–	130
Denmark	–	–	–	–	13
Germany	2 500	7 000	8.1	–	245
Sweden	–	–	–	–	330
World	88 000	256 000	4.7	–	3 405

Note: Data sources come from a single year within the year range included in the column title. Not all vineyards/grapes grown are used for the production of wine.

Sources: Beverage Trade Network, "Let's"; Brandl, "Organic"; Brodt et al., "Market"; CBI, "CBI Trends"; Duren, "Spain"; Millésime Bio, "Overview"; Millésime Bio, "Press"; interview with Neil Palmer; Pekic, "Italian"; Pink, "The Sustainable"; Systembolaget, "2017 Launch Plan"; Willer and Lernoud, "The World"; Willer and Yussefi, "The World"; Winemonitor, "Press Release"; Woolf, "How Big."

As Section V notes, the slow growth of the organic wine industry as a whole stood in contrast to organic tea, which experienced relatively unfettered growth from the 1990s. Section VI shows that organic wine finally began to get some traction in the twenty-first century, but primarily in northwest Europe and in a handful of cosmopolitan global cities.

Throughout the chapter, the term "organic" is used broadly to describe wine that is produced largely without the use of synthetic fertilizers or pesticides,[11] although organic certification schemes typically involved many other, more subtle requirements, including restrictions on sulfites.

II THE EARLY ORGANIC WINE INDUSTRY

Though the modern organic wine industry remained small in scale for decades, its geographic spread was impressive even in the 1970s when the industry first achieved significant scale. During that decade pioneers of organic wine emerged around the world, largely united in their effort to keep food products safe from synthetic chemicals and to act as stewards of the environment for future generations. A number of others were motivated by a desire to let nature run its course during the winemaking process, in order to let a wine's *terroir* – the flavor and aroma associated with the climate and soil conditions in which grapes are grown, as well as the sociohistorical traditions employed throughout the winemaking process – express itself more vividly and to create the "purest" wine possible. In pursuit of these goals, winemakers encountered a number of obstacles within their vineyards and wineries, and wine retailers encountered a different set of challenges in the marketplace. These challenges will be the main focus of this section.

In Germany, the production of organic wine started to take root by the early 1950s. Germany had a long history of concern for natural food and healing products evidenced in the natural food stores known as Reform Houses since the 1880s.[12] However, the early organic winemakers were hardly applauded. In the village of Mettenheim in the German state of Rhineland-Palatinate, Otto-Heinrich Sander began implementing organic principles on his family-owned estate in order to reduce topsoil erosion and avoid monoculture. He was belittled for his efforts.[13] Sander persisted in his approach, and eventually the winery became certified organic, including as biodynamic by Demeter.[14] Unfortunately, the derision Sander faced in the 1950s would be echoed in the experiences of organic winemakers in Germany and around the world for decades to come, as the principles of organic farming spread and, little by little, entered the mainstream.

In France, efforts to promote organic farming began in the late 1950s.[15] However organic winemaking would not get underway for a further two decades. Pierre Frick was among the pioneering organic viticulturists who started in Alsace, a northeastern region of France bordered by the Rhine. Frick grew up in a family that was mindful of the environment and worked to live in harmony with nature. Over time, Frick developed a "stronger consciousness" on his own, and engaged with the ideas of Rudolf Steiner. When Frick took over his parents' vineyard in 1976, there were only two other organic viticulturists in Alsace.

The decision to follow biodynamic methods was "a matter of conscience," Frick later remarked. "What drives us, me, is the struggle to keep human life on this planet by preserving our environment." He added, "Humans for a long time were merely trying to survive in their environment; now we control it, we are overpowering it through science." For Frick, this philosophy compelled him toward activism. He and other biodynamic farmers who called themselves "reapers," banded together to destroy crops that did not comply with regional French organic or biodynamic standards while claiming to do so.[16] Frick's dedication to environmental stewardship transcended the economics of his business. As he later remarked, "When you have strong beliefs, you should follow them regardless of financial considerations."[17]

A different but related trend also arose around that time: one in which winemakers and retailers alike sought a more "pure" expression of nature in a glass of wine. Many of these winemakers were influenced by the writings of the French postwar scientist and *négociant* (wine merchant) Jules Chauvet who had become critical of excessive use of additives in wine.[18] Like Chauvet, some of these winemakers worked in Beaujolais and included Guy Bréton, Jean Foillard, Marcel Lapierre and Jean-Paul Thévenet.

The group, which the celebrated American organic wine importer Kermit Lynch would later call the "Gang of Four," was led by Lapierre, who had begun experimenting with no-sulfite-added winemaking in 1978.[19] In the early 1980s, he adopted organic winemaking methods soon after a friend introduced him to Chauvet.[20] Along with the other members of the Gang of Four, Lapierre advocated returning to traditional winemaking methods, based on Chauvet's earlier work, which avoided the use of synthetic herbicides and pesticides, minimized the use of additives, and rejected chaptalization,[21] among other winemaking practices.[22] Members of the Gang of Four were motivated to adopt organic methods by their desire to make wines that expressed *terroir*, untainted by the flavor of additives or synthetic chemicals.[23]

During the 1970s, interest in creating and consuming wines with clear *terroir* surged due in part to growing support for regionalism and the environment. According to Demossier, the concept of *terroir* was bolstered by the French certification system of *appellation d'origine contrôlée* (AOC) originally established in 1935 which sought to legitimize claims of regional flavor and quality characteristics while strengthening the economic power of local elites. The ideology of *terroir* and the AOC system were also driven by an interest in combating the rising trend of uniformity and industrialization in the global wine market. Through the concept of *terroir*, winemakers were able to make claims about their craftsmanship using region-specific knowledge gleaned from local experts or older family generations. They were also able to claim the role of mediator and even translator of nature in the production of wine. However, the validity of such claims was sometimes tenuous, as some winemakers claimed differences in *terroir* even when discussing adjacent plots of land. For their part, some organic and biodynamic winemakers made claims about the longstanding "natural" dimensions of their methods and the *terroir* of their products, despite the fact that many vineyards in France were subject to numerous and significant human interventions over the course of many centuries. Nevertheless, *terroir* emerged as an important environmental and sociohistorical attribute of wine actively sought by winemakers and consumers alike, and it had a strong influence on property values, as well as the reputation and price of wine.[24] However, the use of organic methods to create wine that expressed *terroir* often came at a cost.

As organic winemakers like Frick and the Gang of Four discovered, making wine using organic methods was often more challenging in both the vineyard and winery. Organic methods usually required a great deal more manual labor, since they did not allow for the use of synthetic chemicals to prevent fungi, weeds or insects from damaging their crops. While many organic viticulturists experienced higher operational costs associated with an increased use of labor, some claimed that their costs rose only during the first few years of organic winemaking and subsequently fell once they developed expertise in organic methods.[25] Studies in Australia, Germany and New Zealand demonstrated great variability in production costs due to vineyard conditions and management practices, although in many cases the costs of organic farming were higher.[26] Biodynamic wine-growing was especially labor-intensive. The avoidance of chemicals was only part of the process. Following Steiner's belief that the universe was interconnected, planting and other activities were coordinated with the movements of celestial bodies such as the moon and the planets. Nine special compost preparations made with natural ingredients were used as fertilizer. They were put into cow horns, buried in the soil, and then dug up and the contents distributed throughout the vineyard.

The extra effort and financial burden associated with organic winemaking were major threats to the emergent category's growth, as many winemakers preferred the convenience of conventional methods, as well as the lower costs. As a result, organic wine made slow progress, even in the major wine-producing countries. A rare exception in Italy was the estate of Badia a Coltibuono (meaning "Abbey of the Good Harvest") in Tuscany, which had started by selling bottles of Chianti Classico Riserva in 1957. In 1985, Coltibuono's new winemaker Roberto Stucchi Prinetti began converting the estate to organic farming after studying biodynamic agriculture, and seeing the growing organic movement in California. Stucchi Prinetti was motivated to convert the estate for a variety of reasons: "Environmental awareness, health of the workers, health of the soil, wine quality, [and] long term cost effectiveness. I could summarize as long-term sustainability."[27] By 2000 alcoholic beverages made up nearly 5 percent of the conventional food market in Italy, but they made up only 0.5 percent of the organic food market.[28]

Spain came to grow more organic wine, even if Spanish consumers did not drink it. Although Spain was located within the Old World, the history of its wine industry was far from linear because of political and economic upheavals, including the Spanish Civil War and tight restrictions on foreign investments under Francisco Franco's dictatorship. From 1970, the country's wine industry began to modernize, and winemakers started to place greater emphasis on quality over quantity, aided by regulations on provenance in viticulture.[29] A forerunner of organic winemaking in Spain was Josep Maria Albet i Noya, who in the late 1970s began converting his vineyard to organic and biodynamic methods after a Dutch company contacted him in search of a Spanish organic wine producer. After taking a course on biodynamic methods from a former Swedish Minister of Agriculture, Albet i Noya successfully made and sold organic wine, becoming convinced – as his counterparts in other countries had – of the benefits associated with organic viticulture.[30] Other wineries in Spain, including Bodegas Robles and Bodegas Torres, followed suit.[31] However, as indicated by Table 6.1, Spanish organic wines found their markets outside the country. By the mid-2010s Spain had become the world's largest organic wine producer, producing some 27 percent of the world total, but Spanish consumers only accounted for 1 percent of organic wine consumption. In contrast, France produced 22 percent of the world's organic wine, and French consumers drank 21 percent of that total.[32]

Organic winemaking also started in Britain. Unlike Italy and Spain, the country had only a very small wine-growing industry. The pioneering organic viticulturist Roy Cook founded an organic vineyard called Sedlescombe in East Sussex.[33] It was the first vineyard of its kind in Britain. Cook had experience as an organic gardener, and at the time was living in a caravan on 10 acres of land seeking to live self-sufficiently while earning some income teaching English as a foreign language. The land was south-facing and sheltered by a hill, and Cook initially considered growing tomatoes before he learned of English wines being served in a nearby restaurant. The first vines were planted in 1979, and the first harvest was three years later. At the time, English wine was close to being a laughing stock, and Cook's adoption of organic agricultural methods "raised eyebrows even further."[34] The production of organic wine faced particular challenges. A British-based Master of Wine (M.W.), Andy Howard, noted, "To produce organic in the UK is a particular challenge because of weather issues ... The cooler, wetter climates are more difficult for making organic wines. [France, Italy, and Spain are] warmer, drier ... you've got more possibilities of switching over to organic because you probably need to do less anyway."[35] In 1987, however, Sedlescombe's reputation was secured when another M.W. wrote in the leading London evening newspaper that the vineyard's wines were "some of the most delicious English wines I have ever tasted."[36]

In the New World, the state of California was historically the dominant area of wine production in the United States.[37] California emerged at the center of countercultural movements of the 1960s, during which time a small number of pioneers of organic farming began their work in the state.[38] The counterculture era was associated with a shift in consumer food preferences toward organic, vegetarian and macrobiotic foods.[39] However this provided no real incentive to organic winemaking. Although many "hippies" reacted to the spirit-drinking cultures of their parents by starting to drink wine, they did not favor the low-quality sweet wines which California had become famous for, but rather imported French wines.[40]

Organic winegrowing was slow to make an appearance in California, even as the region shifted to growing better wine than in the past. Tony Coturri, an organic winemaker located in Sonoma county, was one pioneer who helped shape the early organic wine industry within California. In 1979, Coturri and other members of his family established Coturri Winery in Glen Ellen, a village in the southern tip of Sonoma county. From the beginning, the family was committed to making wine without the use of pesticides, fertilizers or additives. Eventually, they also practiced biodynamic methods, becoming certified as both organic and biodynamic in 1991 and 2000, respectively. When the Coturris met with potential distributors, they were often confronted by skepticism. Tony later remembered, "When we went to San Francisco to sell wines to retail shops, one [shop owner] wouldn't carry our bottles because he was afraid of exploding bottles that would spew biological contamination in his wine shop." In 2010, Coturri let his organic and biodynamic certifications lapse. Tony explained, "There are a lot of farmers who are definitely organic but are not certified. Certification is an expensive process – it costs money to be involved, and you don't get any [additional money] for being organic. I used to be certified organic and biodynamic, and it didn't make any difference."[41]

Indeed, one widely cited study that analyzed the retail market outcomes for organic wine found that adding the words "organic" or "biodynamic" to the label of a wine bottle was associated with a 20 percent reduction in price. However, the same study found that organic and biodynamic certification were associated with higher quality (as measured by ratings from the US-based magazine *Wine Spectator*), and if environmental claims were left off the label, certified organic or biodynamic wine enjoyed an average price premium of 13 percent. Perhaps because of this, the study's authors suggested, as many as two-thirds of California vintners of certified organic wine decided not to advertise their wine as such.[42]

There has been much debate about the origin of consumer confusion regarding organic wine. This might be seen as one dimension of the multiple definitions of the meaning of natural which Belasco has observed in late-twentieth-century American food culture.[43] One study found that consumers may have erroneously believed that organic and biodynamic winemaking methods resulted in wine of lower quality due to an imagined trade-off between quality and environmental goals. The same study found that among low-cost wines from low-quality regions, consumers preferred wine with environmentally friendly claims on their labels to conventional wine, but this preference was reversed among wines of higher prices from higher-quality regions.[44]

There was also the persistent issue of the reputational damage done by a handful of early organic wines. In particular, during the 1970s and 1980s, organic red wines were prone to quickly turn to vinegar in the absence of preservatives such as sulfites.[45] This bad reputation lingered, and journalists writing about wine continued to refer to its inauspicious beginning for several decades. Surprisingly, this poor reputation persisted even as organic wines began winning awards, including awards at every prize level at the Decanter World Wine Awards, a leading global wine competition organized by the British wine magazine *Decanter*. Indeed, some of the world's most sought-after and expensive bottles of wine were produced in Burgundy at Domaine de la Romanée-Conti, which adopted organic methods in 1985.[46] Biodynamic wines developed a particular reputation for quality, for reasons often debated because of the unusual and esoteric nature of the growing method. Some believed that the key advantage was simply that biodynamic wine-growing was extremely demanding, and so required great attention to the vines.[47]

Conventional winemakers were often an obstacle for the organic winemakers. This was the early experience of the Freys in California. In

1980 Jonathan Frey, along with his wife Katrina, established Frey Vineyards, becoming the first certified biodynamic and organic winery in the country. Jonathan Frey recalled, "At the time, there was no such thing as organic agriculture in Sonoma county. It's a very dry area, very difficult to grow anything here, but modern agriculture was thriving with the use of all these chemicals." The Freys had become interested in organic agriculture when they both studied permaculture and biodynamic methods under an Englishman named Alan Chadwick at the University of California, Santa Cruz. A highly influential figure in the history of organic farming in California, Chadwick was a former Shakespearean actor and devoted horticulturalist who taught classes in farming in the 1960s and 1970s to college students including Jonathan and Katrina Frey.[48] As the Freys were getting their business started, they also benefited from the advice of Tony Coturri. In the early 1980s, Jonathan Frey approached Tony Coturri to learn more about his methods for making organic pinot grigio.[49]

When the Freys introduced their first wines to the region, there was a backlash from the established industry. According to Jonathan Frey, "These large companies would finance scientific studies to prove that organic was a joke and didn't have any health benefits." Nevertheless, the Frey wines found some customers, particularly in "hippy-type" stores and cooperatives selling health-conscious products. Larger grocery stores were initially uninterested, as the wines from Frey Vineyards were more expensive than wines made conventionally. The Freys had to explain the time-consuming process that went into making additive-free wine, as well as the health benefits associated with organic products.[50] Their persistence was rewarded. Eventually, Frey Vineyards experienced substantial growth, increasing from an annual production figure of 2 000 cases to 80 000 cases by 2011.[51]

Another notable organic wine pioneer in California was fourth-generation winemaker Paul Dolan, who joined Fetzer Winery in 1977 as the company's first non-family-member winemaker. Dolan worked at Fetzer for 27 years, and became president in 1992. His journey into organic wine started in the mid-1980s when he and the then-company president tasted the products of an organic garden which had been developed as a strategy to open a high-end restaurant on the vineyard. They were so impressed by the taste that they began growing organic wine in 1989.[52] Subsequently they began offering a premium to the independent growers who supplied Fetzer if they switched to organic. In 1991 they created a new wholly organic wine called Bonterra which led to a deeper engagement with sustainability issues. An initial packaging design was abandoned in preference for more sustainable options, including labels printed with soy-based inks and corks cleaned with a process not employing harmful chemicals.[53] As the company's wines won many awards, Dolan developed an increasingly wide vision of sustainability, based on the insight that "businesses are part of a much wider system," and recognizing the need to pursue sustainability for the local community and using contracts to spread sustainable agricultural practices.[54] Dolan subsequently became engaged with the ideas of Rudolf Steiner, including biodynamic farming, becoming President of Demeter USA and helping to lead an unsuccessful attempt to allow sulfites in US organic standards (discussed later in this chapter).[55]

In contrast to the Freys and Dolan, the world's largest wine companies largely remained on the sidelines of organic wine. By the late 1990s, the wine markets had consolidated to a significant degree in New World countries, including the United States, Australia and South Africa where the top ten wine brands commanded 25 percent or more of the market. The markets remained relatively fragmented in Old World countries.[56] By the mid-2000s, E. & J. Gallo, Constellation Brands, the Wine Group and Bronco alone accounted for two-thirds of wine production in the United States.[57] Globally, the top ten companies accounted for 13 percent of the world wine market by 2016. The lack of strong support by these mega-wine companies was a further impediment to the growth of the organic wine market.

A number of large companies did promote the category, including E. & J. Gallo Winery, founded in California in 1933 by brothers Ernest and Julio Gallo. Julio Gallo, an organic vegetable gardener, brought his organic methods to the company's vineyards. Beginning in the 1960s, the company experimented with organic methods, including integrated pest management systems. By the early 1990s, E. & J. Gallo owned what was believed to be the world's largest organic vineyard which consisted of 2,700 acres located in the San Joaquin Valley.[58] In 2010, the company began participating in the California Sustainable Winegrowing Alliance's (CSWA) certification program for vineyards and wineries. The CSWA program supported the adoption of sustainable practices with respect to environmental, social and economic concerns. While this program promoted the use of organic methods, it did not have a restriction for added sulfites similar to that of organic certification in the United States.[59] By 2015, E. & J. Gallo had withdrawn from organic certification.[60]

A number of other large companies entered the category. In 1992 Kentucky-based Brown-Forman Corp, a leading spirits company, acquired Fetzer and Bonterra. As the family left the business, Dolan was promoted to company president, and encouraged to continue with organic wine.[61] However wine remained a modest component of Brown-Forman's spirits business, and in 2011 it sold Fetzer (including Bonterra) to the Chilean company Viña Concha y Toro for $238 million.[62]

Concha y Toro was a wine producer and exporter founded in Chile in 1883 by Melchor de Santiago Concha y Toro and his wife Emiliana Subercaseaux. In the 1990s the company began to develop markets outside Chile, and in 1993 shares of the company were floated on the New York Stock Exchange.[63] That same year, a subsidiary of the company named Cono Sur was formed and eventually many of its vineyards became certified organic.[64] By 2011, Concha y Toro was Chile's top wine producer and exporter by both sales volume and value, which were 271 million liters and over $874 million, respectively.[65] By 2017 the company was the sixth-largest vintner in the world.[66] The latest CEO of Concha y Toro is Eduardo Guilisasti Gana, a member of Chile's powerful Guilisasti family. It is noteworthy that this same family owned Emiliana Vineyards, the world's largest organic and biodynamic vineyard as of 2017.[67] Emiliana Vineyards was named after Emiliana Suber-caseaux, but was operated separately from Concha y Toro.[68]

A recurring theme among pioneers of organic wine around the world was that they were largely united in one of two missions. The first was a mission to keep foods and land clear of harmful chemicals that threatened human health and the natural balance and processes of the environment. The second mission was to create wine that expressed its provenance vividly through its *terroir*, which became a highly sought-after sociohistorical and environmental attribute of wine beginning in the 1970s in Europe. Since organic winemaking did not tend to command higher profits, monetary motivations rarely played a role in the industry's development. Rather, they were passionate wine growers and makers, motivated – especially bio-dynamists such as Frick and Dolan – by broad and holistic visions of sustainability.

III PIONEERING RETAIL AND DISTRIBUTION OF ORGANIC WINE

As bottles of organic wine entered the marketplace, distributors and retailers interested in the category encountered many of the same opportunities and challenges that winemakers encountered in the vineyards and winery, as well as several new ones. In significant part, it was due to the efforts of these individuals that organic winemakers were able to find an audience.

Kermit Lynch, who opened his wine store in Berkeley, California in 1972, was to become a forerunner in the organic wine industry, although he did not know it at the time. Lynch did not start his company with the plan of selling organic wine. Instead, he was drawn to it over the course of his business. To learn more about the wine industry and identify the best wines, Lynch undertook road trips in France and Italy. As Lynch met with more and more wine producers, he developed expertise – and a strong opinion – on winemaking methods in the vineyard and winery. In his 1988 book, *Adventures on the Wine Route*, Lynch asserted, "Chemicals increase production, they protect the wine from nature's quirks, but they also muck up the elemental statement the wine is capable of making."[69] Yet, Lynch acknowledged the shortcomings of organic wine as a product. He wrote, "'Organic' is a word that does not work in a wine shop … The word seems to have a negative impact on most wine connoisseurs."[70]

Lynch's views of organic wine changed over time. Since Lynch actively sought out wines that expressed *terroir*, his taste preferences led him to import wine made using organic methods. Indeed, upon discovering the Gang of Four, Lynch was very pleased that the "spirit of Chauvet" lived on in Beaujolais.[71] Lynch, who would eventually earn France's celebrated *Legion d'Honneur*, became a notable importer of wines produced by the Gang of Four, as well as many other organically-produced bottles of wine.[72] By the 2010s, his company's website would clearly indicate the farming methods used by the winemakers whose products he sold, marking a departure from his earlier belief that wine sellers should avoid using the term "organic."

A little over a decade after Lynch launched his business, Ursula and Erich Hartl established Germany's first commercial enterprise to sell organic wine. Erich had grown up in rural Bavaria, and worked in the conventional restaurant and catering business. Becoming more concerned over time about the use of fertilizers in foods, the family decided to start a business in organic wine distribution. The problem was supply; Germany didn't produce a large quantity of organic wine. Erich Hartl later recalled:

> When we started in the early 1980s, there was no "catalog" of organic wines, and finding an organic winemaker in Germany was impossible … It was by accident that I came across this organic winemaker in France. I established a relationship with the producer, I tried his wines, I liked them and started importing them by small quantities in Germany. Then I traveled around to meet with organic winemakers, and started importing more and more wines from different countries."[73]

In this way, the Hartls helped broaden consumer exposure to organic wine, motivated by their desire to sell only "pure" wine. Eventually, Germany would become the world's leading importer of organic wine.[74]

In 1986, just a few years after the Hartls established their importing company, another pioneering organic wine distribution company began in Britain. Three friends – Peter Greet, Neil Palmer and Lance Pigott – were each in their mid-twenties when they decided to start an organic wine distribution company called Vintage Roots in the middle-sized town of Reading outside of London. Greet, Palmer and Pigott had known each other from their time at university and from traveling together in France the previous year, when they harvested grapes together in the Loire Valley. In France, the three travelers learned about the new trend of organic winemaking in Bordeaux and the Loire Valley, which was a novelty to them at the time. Many of the organic winemakers with whom they spoke had switched to these methods after seeing family members endure the negative health consequences of synthetic chemicals in their vineyards.[75]

Inspired by what they learned in France and by their broader interest in healthful foods, Greet, Palmer and Pigott founded their company as a way of working for themselves while promoting a product they firmly believed in. To get their business off the ground, the three founders began with a short list of addresses of organic vineyards in France, and just as Lynch had done, they traveled to France to conduct research for their first wine list, which consisted of just twelve wines. Eventually, they took on wines from Italy and Spain, and later, they also began to source wine from Chile, Australia and South Africa, among other countries.[76]

Initially, Vintage Roots tried to establish relationships with small, independent healthful-lifestyle shops in Britain. Few of these kinds of shops tended to have licenses to sell alcohol, which made matters difficult. For small shops, it was often not worth their while to take on all of the paperwork and fees in order to sell alcohol. When the founders of Vintage Roots were able to find shops that could sell alcohol, often the shops' employees had no prior experience with organic wine and would ask whether there was alcohol in it, or whether it was made from carrots or lentils. The Vintage Roots founders would have to explain the environmental and human health benefits of organic wine, relative to conventional wine, in attempts to win their business.[77]

Vintage Roots found their early customers in small independent stores. Eventually, they also formed business relationships with major supermarkets, including Asda, Sainsbury's, Tesco and Waitrose. However, Palmer later noted, these relationships dwindled over time, as the supermarkets demanded lower prices from Vintage Roots and eventually decided to deal directly with wineries to source their products. Even without strong support from supermarkets, Vintage Roots grew into a sizeable business, eventually employing over 15 staff members and expanding its inventory to include other types of organic spirits and foods.[78] In 2016, the company's annual turnover was approximately $6.9 million.[79]

The employees that the Vintage Roots founders encountered who thought organic wine might contain carrots or lentils touched on a broader error in consumer perception of the product. Beyond not knowing what exactly went into organic wine, some consumers also assumed that organic wine must somehow be less enjoyable than conventional wine. Since wine was historically viewed as an indulgence both psychologically and physically, attaching a health-related term such as "organic" may have tainted consumer perception of the pleasurable sensory and cultural experience wine was often expected to provide. As Adam Morganstern, Editor of the *Organic Wine Journal* later noted, "With organic vegetables it seems great – who doesn't want organic asparagus? But with wine … it causes a momentary question – such as, 'What did they remove to make it organic? Did they take something fun away? Is this like "diet" soda?'"[80]

Organic wine reached Japan decades later than in the West. This was not surprising, given that drinking Western wine was not widespread until the 1990s. The country had its own traditional beverages, including the rice wine known as sake. Japan was also a large consumer of beer, which had been introduced from the West during the second half of the nineteenth century. Imported and domestically-made spirits, especially whiskey, were also very popular. There were particular challenges in the organic sector. In Japan, the traditional translation of "organic" was "yuki," but unfortunately, this word was also associated with radical political groups during the 1960s and 1970s. Organic food consumption was, and remained, quite limited, even as it grew in the West. Japan did not enact a national policy to define organic food until the early 2000s.[81]

Nevertheless, as elsewhere, there were entrepreneurial pioneers who set out to create a market for organic products in Japan. In 1998, Yasushi Tamura started an organic wine distribution business in Tokyo called Mavie, which began as an ecommerce website. Tamura had first encountered organic wine in the late 1980s on a business trip to Germany, when he was a marketing manager for the Japanese soy sauce company Kikkoman. At the time, he did not find the beverage to his liking. However, after moving to France in the early 1990s, he tried an award-winning organic wine from Bourgogne that reminded him of world-renowned Romanée-Conti wine, and the experience stayed with him. After quitting Kikkoman, Tamura worked for a brief time for his father's company, a Japanese culinary school, but soon decided to leave in order to found his own company and conduct business in the international market. To better inform his decision about what kind of company he wanted to build, Tamura looked at the statistics for different food trends in Europe, and it appeared that the only kind of food with favorable projections was the organic category. Based on its growth figures, Tamura expected that the job of selling European organic products to the Japanese would be straightforward.[82]

By the time Tamura entered the industry in 1998, there were plenty of organic wine producers to choose from in Europe. He began by using all of his money to buy 20,000 bottles of organic wine, which left him with nothing to spend for marketing.[83] Further complicating prospects for his business, Tamura discovered that, at that time, people in Japan thought that conventional wine was healthful, due to studies praising the polyphenol content of red wines. This mirrors an important lesson from Chapter 5: in New Zealand, purveyors of organic food found that the "imagined greenness" of conventional food was a difficult perception for consumers to overcome. This was a challenge that Tamura and other organic winemakers and retailers had to contend with to achieve market growth.

Like the large wine companies, supermarkets, too, largely failed to take a leadership role in helping organic wine gain broader appeal among the public and establish legitimacy as a genuine category. Even organic supermarkets were reluctant to stock organic wine. For example, Whole Foods Market, which by 2010 accounted for over half of organic food sales in the United States, did little to promote organic wines, which made up a modest fraction of its wine section.[84] Instead, the company favored conventional and "sustainably"-produced wines, and added in other selections of organic wine only in response to customer demand for it in the 2010s.[85] Supermarkets in Britain, too, acted largely in reaction to the rise in organic wine's popularity, rather than spurring its initial growth.[86] In the face of consumer confusion around the product, as well as negative perceptions of its quality, supermarkets often didn't know how to effectively market the product, prior to its surge in popularity. Andy Howard, who worked as a wine buyer for the large British food retailer Marks & Spencer from 2007 until 2013, observed,

> In the wine category, we used to think, how do you best display wines? Most people display wines by country of origin, or by type of wine, then different price points. We used to have a very good organic Chablis at Marks & Spencer from a producer called Domaine [Jean-Marc] Brocard. It sold reasonably well. Then we decided to put all organic wines in a separate

section and call it the "organic wine section." And at that point, the sales plummeted. It would appear that people didn't really understand or didn't want to get diverted to what was seen as this, perhaps, slightly dangerous area where they weren't sure what organic meant. Then we moved the organic Chablis back into its parent group, and sales recovered.[87]

Thus, organic wine faced significant adversity in the vineyard and winery, all the way to the marketplace where it struggled to sell, at least when consumers were aware of the organic methods used in its production. While organic winemakers gained the sponsorship of small maverick distributors and retailers, it wasn't until much later that larger companies would take a more active role in the marketplace.

IV EMERGENCE OF ORGANIC WINE CERTIFICATIONS

Over time, certification schemes emerged as a way to define organic and biodynamic winemaking methods, as well as to validate claims made by winemakers about their production methods. Though Demeter's biodynamic trademark and farming standard emerged in 1928, it was not until the 1970s that other organic farming standards were introduced.[88] Although certification schemes were intended to provide clarity and reassurance to consumers, they often led to great confusion about the nature of the term "organic." Across the different countries in which certification schemes developed, varying standards emerged to define organic winemaking processes. Complicating matters for organic winemakers, it would take until the 2010s for matters to settle regarding organic wine processing standards and trade equivalents in major wine markets, including the United States and the EU.

Germany was a site of important activity for efforts to standardize organic viticulture. In 1977, organic wine producers from Germany, Switzerland and France convened in order to exchange information on the subject and make organic methods more accessible to others. Following this meeting, regional groups of organic farmers published standards for organic viticulture and winemaking methods in an early attempt to encourage standardization of practices.[89] In 1985 a further attempt to achieve some coherence in Germany came when the *Bundesverband Ökologischer Weinbau* (Federation of Organic Viticulture) was formed by Rudolf Trossen and 34 other small organic producers in Germany. Membership grew rapidly, and the federation launched the ECOVIN trademark five years later.[90] Since then, ECOVIN has become the largest association of organic winemakers in Germany, requiring its members to abide by EU organic regulations as well as its own stricter regulations, and undergo yearly inspections to uphold the ECOVIN seal's integrity.[91]

Within Britain, the Soil Association served as a highly important organic certification and advocacy group.[92] The Soil Association launched its organic certification scheme in 1973 as a way to address the market need for third-party verification of food integrity. As was the case in all EU countries before 2012, winemakers in Britain were not allowed to use the term "organic wine," and instead were limited to writing "made from organic grapes" on their labels, as the EU lacked an official definition for an "organic" winemaking process. The Soil Association, too, was constrained by these EU regulations. Lee Holdstock, Trade Relations Manager at the Soil Association, said this labeling requirement was "inevitably confusing to consumers." He added, "We always felt we were tackling a challenge of helping consumers to understand the benefits and definitions of 'organic.' To add an extra layer of complexity by having products labeled in this slightly more unwieldy way was really unhelpful."[93]

In France, the first national policy concerning organic farming was enacted in 1980, and five years later the organic certification *Agriculture Biologique* (AB) with an accompanying logo was introduced.[94] AB was administered by *Agence BIO*, a French national agency responsible for the development and promotion of organic farming. In 1992, the *Association des Vins Naturels* (AVN) was founded to create a framework for organic wine production that went beyond the simple cultivation of organic grapes to include activities in both the vineyard and winery.[95]

Within the United States, a number of private organizations offered organic certification for decades. For example, California Certified Organic Farmers (CCOF) was established in 1973, making it the first organic certifying entity in the US.[96] It was not until the 1990s that the federal government stepped up to introduce a regulatory framework within the industry. As part of the US Farm Bill, the Organic Foods Production Act of 1990 called for the establishment of the National Organic Program (NOP) and National Organic Standards Board (NOSB). After much debate, the final rules for the NOP were written and implemented in the fall of 2002.[97]

Under the rules laid out by the NOP and the Alcohol and Tobacco Tax and Trade Bureau, wine may be certified organic if it was made from organic grapes and contained no added sulfites, along with other, more subtle requirements. Sulfites were commonly used in wine as a preservative of flavor and quality. If a winemaker wished to add sulfites, then provided that the added sulfites numbered less than 100 parts per million, the wine may then be sold as "made with organic grapes."[98] Wines made from organic grapes that contained added sulfites in the United States were required to feature a label that stated, "Contains sulfites." The US Department of Agriculture (USDA) mandated that wine bottles carry sulfite statements in order to properly warn consumers who may have an allergy to the substance. One study published by the Journal of the American College of Nutrition found that 0.05 percent of the US population had an allergy to sulfites, of which the most common adverse reactions were asthma symptoms.[99]

Following the implementation of the initial rules for organic wine, debate over the use of sulfites became heated. Paul Bonetti, president of an organic import business in Colorado, along with the winery Barra of Mendocino, winemaker Paul Dolan and Redwood Valley Cellars, petitioned the NOSB to allow the use of added sulfites in certified organic wine.[100] The group, which had formed several months before the yearly NOP meeting, argued that prohibiting the addition of sulfites in organic wine made obtaining organic certification more difficult.[101] This added roadblock, they believed, would reduce the number of winemakers who chose to undergo certification, thereby indirectly increasing their use of substances the group perceived as more nefarious than sulfites, such as pesticides and fungicides.[102]

Among the opposing group's especially vocal members were Jonathan and Katrina Frey, co-owners of Frey Vineyards. Speaking before the NOSB weeks before the vote on an amendment proposing the addition of sulfites to organic wine, Jonathan Frey noted that "every winemaking problem can be solved with methods … that don't involve sulfites."[103] For her part, Katrina Frey appeared on the San Francisco-based radio show Organic Conversation to advocate her views, noting that sulfites were a "very useful winemaker tool," but that they should not be allowed under organic standards, since sulfites were synthetic and a known allergen – two properties that some organic food consumers wanted to avoid. She also noted that the NOP's rule clearly stated that if a food can be made without additives, then that "should be the standard operating procedure."[104]

In December 2011, the NOSB voted to reject an amendment to the rules that would have allowed sulfites to be added to wine certified as organic, up to a total of 100 parts per million, including naturally occurring sulfites.[105] Steve Finkel, owner of Organic Vintages, a distribution company based in New York, observed after the ruling that "this victory has insured the continuation of clear, honest, and forthright labeling of organic wine."[106] Paul Dolan, who had petitioned in support of the amendment, later observed, "I believe it was simply the power and influence of those no sulfite folks who had the ear of the Board."[107]

In the EU, the rules for organic certification developed quite differently. In 1991, just a year after the United States introduced its Organic Food Production Act, the European Commission introduced its first regulatory framework for organic food, but there were no standards for organic alcohol. As a result, wines in the EU could only claim to be "made from organic grapes." Private organizations and non-profit agencies such as Demeter and the Soil Association could continue to offer organic certifications to winemakers, although they were constrained by the EU's organic regulations for wine.[108]

In 2005, the EU introduced legislation that required wine containing sulfites over 10 parts per million to include a label bearing a sulfite statement.[109] That same year, the European Commission made a call to understand the science underlying organic winemaking methods, which led to the establishment of the ORWINE Project in 2006. The purpose of the ORWINE Project was to determine the implications of organic winemaking practices on wine quality and the environment, identify market demand for organic wine and its requirements for labeling, develop a code of best practices for viticulturists, and provide recommendations for future EU regulations, among other related activities. The Project involved an array of partners from major wine-producing countries in the EU, including Germany's ECOVIN and IFOAM EU from Britain and Belgium. During the course of the project, its members took into account organic regulations developed by other countries that were considered major export markets for wine from the EU, including the United States and Japan. The ORWINE Project surveyed nearly 500 organic winemakers, representing about a fifth of EU organic wine producers at the time. In the summer of 2009, the Project submitted a set of recommendations for a future regulatory framework on organic winemaking in the EU.[110]

In 2009, the Commission began working to implement regulations for organic winemaking, but as was the case in the United States, debate over the use of sulfites became so heated that, the next year, the Commission suspended the rules. After significant prompting from individuals in the organic sector, the Commission recommenced discussions to develop and finalize regulations for organic wine. The group was able to achieve compromise regarding the use of sulfites by developing different categories of organic wine based on residual sugar content and varying levels of sulfite limitations. According to the new framework, a wine could be certified organic if it was made from certified organic grapes and if the sulfite level remained below 100 parts per million, whether naturally occurring or added. The new regulations were formally introduced in the EU in 2012, allowing organic wine to be labeled as such, along with the EU organic logo.[111]

That same year, the EU and United States developed an organic equivalency agreement that would allow certified organic products to be traded freely among their member states. Wine that was certified organic in the EU but contained sulfites could be sold as "made with organic grapes" in the United States, while wine sold as "made with organic grapes" in the United States could be sold as organic in the EU.[112] This agreement paved the way for easier trading of organic wine between many major wine markets.

Table 6.2 Maximum sulfite use by wine category, 2017

Wine category	Maximum sulfite use by wine category	
	United States	EU
Organic	"Organic" wine may contain up to 10 ppm of sulfites. Wine "made with organic grapes" may contain up to 100 ppm of sulfites.	"Organic" wine with less than 2g/l residual sugar: Red: 100 ppm Whites and rosés: 150 ppm. "Organic" wine with more than 2g/l residual sugar: Red: 130 ppm Whites and rosés: 180 ppm
Biodynamic	Total maximum measured sulfites at bottling cannot exceed 100 ppm.	Wine with less than 5g/l residual sugar: White: 140 ppm Red: 110 ppm Wine with greater than 5g/l residual sugar: White: 180 ppm Red: 140 ppm
Conventional	Total maximum measured sulfites at bottling cannot exceed 350 ppm.	Red wine: Total maximum measured sulfites at bottling cannot exceed 150 ppm. Whites and rosés: Total maximum measured sulfites at bottling cannot exceed 200 ppm.

Sources: Demeter International e.V., "Standards"; Demeter USA, "Demeter"; European Commission, "New"; Nigro, "U.S."

The multiple layers of organic wine regulations that emerged over time amounted to a bureaucratic maze of paperwork and headaches for many organic winemakers. For example, Pierre Frick had to comply with guidelines set by the region in which he worked, the French Ministry of Agriculture, European Commission, and private certifying organizations such as *Nature et Progrès* or Demeter. Adding further complexity, states within the United States defined the term "sulfite-free" differently, which had implications for organic claims made by winemakers. Frick noted:

> [On our wine bottles] when our sticker said 'sulfite-free wine' it was enough for some states to qualify as organic, while other states required us to put 'no added sulfite' on our stickers to be more accurate. For example, our wines are accepted in California as 'organic,' but not in the state of New York. Sometimes all it takes is a change of employee in an administration, and the rule changes again.[113]

This situation meant that Frick had to spend a great deal of time and energy working to comply with these regulations, which otherwise he would have devoted to winemaking.

The complex regulatory landscape for organic wine largely served to slow its growth. As Andy Howard remarked, "I think for organic, the problem's almost been, there've been too many different certifications ... I think organic has suffered a bit from this confusion as to knowing exactly what the official standard is, and what exactly does that mean."[114]

In contrast, biodynamic certification retained a relatively stable, cohesive image over time, as Demeter trademarked the term and kept a tight rein on its use in international markets. Furthermore, Demeter USA adopted standards that allowed its certified wines to contain up to 100 ppm of sulfites, which was much less rigid than the organic certification criterion for sulfites in the United States.[115]

The NOP's decision to disallow the use of sulfites in organic wine made the path to producing organic wine significantly more difficult. Following the NOP's decision, Bonetti asserted, "If we could put everyone into the same category who is using 100 percent organic grapes, there could have been about 800 more winemakers around the world who could get into the US market and use the USDA Organic seal."[116] Although organic wine could, in fact, be made without sulfites (as winemakers like Jonathan and Katrina Frey demonstrated), the complex process involved dissuaded many winemakers from attempting to do so.

Even the EU's much higher limits on the use of sulfites were a challenge for some winemakers to comply with. The British organic winemaker Will Davenport later commented, "In the winery it required a bit of a rethink about how we use sulfites. This took me a year or two to adapt to the 100 mg/L maximum limit and work out how I could guarantee to be below the total sulphite limit every year with every wine."[117] Evidently, organic certification requirements for wine made winemaking processes even more convoluted and reduced the appeal of entering the market.

Within the United States, some winemakers decided against becoming certified organic by the USDA because they viewed sulfites as essential to ensuring the reliability and quality of their wine. According to organic winemaker Tony Coturri, "When you ask a winemaker why they add sulfites to wine, they often say, 'I have a big investment in my company, and I can't afford to lose it.'"[118] Since winemakers were worried that their wines would have a shorter shelf life, demonstrate inconsistencies in flavor over time and oxidize more quickly, they were apprehensive about adopting organic methods.

Adding further to the list of reasons why some winemakers were not compelled to undergo certification was their desire to retain control over their methods in the vineyard. These winemakers feared that undergoing certification would obligate them to adhere strictly to the organic requirements. Jim Clendenen, owner of the California-based organic winery Au Bon Climat, said he was put off organic certification, since it would restrict his ability to respond quickly to local vineyard pests which seriously threatened his crops.[119] Additionally, many winemakers decided not to pursue certification because they felt that conventional winemakers – not those producing organic wines – should be the ones to take on the burden of certification.[120]

While organic certification provided some degree of legitimacy to organic claims on wine labels, they added great confusion to the marketplace and scared many prospective winemakers away from organic methods, due to their restrictive criteria and what was sometimes perceived as an unfair burden.

V THE CONTRAST WITH ORGANIC TEA

The market for organic tea developed differently to the organic wine market. The tea industry as a whole has a different geographical distribution than that of wine, with the major tea growing nations in South Asia, China and East Africa.[121] In the mid-2010s, the biggest markets for tea were China, Russia, Japan, the United States and India, although in per capita terms Turkey, Ireland and Britain were among the highest consumers of tea.[122]

As with wine, tea was originally produced organically until the advent of synthetic fertilizers and pesticides. Beginning in the 1940s, the Indian government pushed for rapid industrialization, and tea gardens were no exception. In an effort to make tea gardens more profitable, plantation owners demolished tea terraces which had helped to protect the soil, removed trees and other vegetation in order to add more tea bushes, and embraced the synthetic chemicals of the West.[123]

By 1986, Indian tea producers in the highly-regarded Darjeeling region began returning to their organic origins, spurred on by shifts in their markets. First, when the Soviet Union – which had been a major destination for India's tea exports – collapsed in the 1990s, India suffered from a severe drop in the price of tea. The Soviet market, to which vast quantities of tea had been exported, had maintained minimal quality requirements, and the quality of tea had declined precipitously.[124] At the same time, due to the absence of strict standards regarding the labeling of tea in India, many tea producers were selling tea blends labeled as "Darjeeling" but which actually included lower-quality tea from other regions.[125] Finally, in the early 1990s, some countries in Europe, particularly Germany, had begun to monitor pesticide levels in tea imports more carefully. Due to diminished consumer confidence in the quality of Darjeeling tea, as well as due to heightened demand in Europe for organic tea and consumer willingness to pay a price premium for the product, tea producers in Darjeeling began to convert to organic methods, with others in Assam and other regions soon following suit.[126] Sanjay Bansal, a prominent figure in the Indian tea industry and passionate enthusiast for the ideas of Rudolf Steiner and biodynamic agriculture, began purchasing tea gardens in distress and converting them to biodynamic methods to bring them back to healthy production.[127] Additionally, tea producers in Darjeeling, in partnership with the government, developed a geographical-origin trademark for the region in order to protect their product from fraud.[128]

Within the large American market, organic tea also attracted the attention of entrepreneurial start-ups such as Honest Tea, a ready-to-drink tea company founded in 1998, which introduced the world's first organic bottled tea in 1999. By 2001, half of Honest Tea's products were organic.[129] The company was successful in marketing organic tea as an approachable product.[130] In 2008, Coca-Cola purchased, for $43 million, a 40 percent stake in the company.[131] By 2010, Honest Tea's sales had tripled to total $72 million, and the next year, Coca-Cola purchased the company outright.[132] In 2015, Honest Tea reached $178 million in sales – about 3.2 percent of the United States ready-to-drink tea market.[133]

The market for organic tea strengthened considerably over time. While India led the production of organic black tea, China emerged as a powerhouse for the production of organic green tea.[134] In the mid-2000s, India exported three-quarters of its organic tea production to France,

Germany, Japan, Britain and the US, while China exported slightly under half of its production to countries in the EU, as well as Japan and the US.[135] By the mid-2010s, nearly all of the world's top tea brands, including Twinings, Tazo and Harney & Sons, sold varieties of organic tea. In 2014, the American herbal tea company Celestial Seasonings partnered with Whole Foods Market to distribute its organic line of teas on a national scale.[136] In 2015, two companies that comprised more than half of the tea market in India announced a joint initiative to invest in research to evaluate the economic and environmental feasibility of phasing out the use of conventional pesticides in tea production in India.[137] That same year, "organic coffee and tea" was ranked as the top category in the international market for organic beverages.[138] Unlike organic wine, large corporations such as Coca-Cola were increasingly prominent in organic tea. In 2017 Unilever, whose Lipton brand was already active in organic tea, acquired Pukka Herbs, a British organic tea start-up inspired by Ayurvedic philosophy, which had reached $39 million in sales by that year.[139]

Organic tea also benefited greatly from lower barriers to entry than organic wine. The product did not require a special license to sell in supermarkets or independent stores, as alcohol did. Furthermore, its organic certification process was straightforward, relative to that of wine. Even though bottled organic tea involved a process of steeping, this did not lead to complicated additional layers of regulations that made the process difficult or financially risky, as was the case with organic wine processing standards.[140]

By 2017, third-party certification of sustainable practices for tea seemed to be crumbling. That year, British supermarket retailer Sainsbury's decided to withdraw from Fairtrade certification of tea and instead follow an in-house standard, which the company termed "fairly traded." The decision prompted speculation that Sainsbury's and other major retailers would use their own ethical standards for a broader array of products in the future, potentially including organic products. If this were to happen, the market for organic tea would become highly fragmented, similar to that of organic wine.[141]

VI THE CONTEMPORARY PERIOD

Consumer interest in organic wine began to accelerate in the mid-2000s, leading the category to achieve modest niche popularity in the 2010s, perhaps as a result of what one winemaker described as a "combustion reaction between ethics and aesthetics."[142] Organic wine emerged as popular in wine bars and fine-dining restaurants in cosmopolitan big cities around the world, including the restaurant Rouge Tomate in New York, Terroir in San Francisco, and Vivant and La Crèmerie in Paris.[143]

The Copenhagen-based restaurant Noma, which was named the World's Best Restaurant in 2010, 2011, 2012 and 2014, developed a wine program with a special focus on organic wine.[144] Shortly after Noma opened in 2003, its owner René Redzepi recruited Pontus Eloffson to develop a wine program. The initial program was relatively conventional, but after the first few years Eloffson slowly began to add in wines with a "more green profile"[145] as they became increasingly available on the market in Copenhagen. When Mads Kleppe took over as Head Sommelier in early 2010, he was initially frustrated by the unusual experience of drinking organic and biodynamic wines, which offered a very different set of flavors and textures than those of conventional wines. However, he quickly learned "to taste all over again," and rebuilt the wine program to have a clearer "profile" by working exclusively with organic and biodynamic winemakers.[146]

Aside from the wines he selected for the wine program, Kleppe also took an unconventional approach to the way in which Noma served wines. In 2017, he worked with a glassmaker to develop customized glasses for the restaurant that featured rounded rather than cut lips – a more natural shape for glass to take. Additionally, when serving guests, Kleppe chose not to use terms such as "organic," "biodynamic" or "natural" to describe the wines he poured, nor provide obscure information about the wine's origin, since the technical details of winemaking were often confusing to guests. Instead, Kleppe chose to explain why he selected the wines he did in simple terms, and if guests did not find the wine to their taste, he offered alternative options. Kleppe stressed that this way of communicating with guests about unusual wines was a better way of introducing wines that otherwise might feel too provocative to them.[147]

Acceptance of organic wine was, however, patchy. In New World regions, production of organic wine failed to become mainstream, perhaps as a result of the lack of domestic demand for the product, absence of organic wine regulations in many of those countries and the often-enormous scale of vineyards.[148] Another possible factor contributing to the slow growth of organic wine in New World regions may have been the lack of local winemaking traditions, which would have helped to support claims of *terroir* expressed by New World wines. Since *terroir* represented both environmental idiosyncrasy and local sociohistorical tradition, and many New World winemakers were unable to make claims about following a longstanding local tradition of winemaking, the organic methods that were so often used by Old World winemakers who sought *terroir* may not have been seen as particularly useful to New World winemakers, from a marketing perspective. As Trubek observed, "The weight of history ends up serving as the gatekeeper for truly tasting *terroir.*"[149]

In the United States, organic wine continued to be distinctly niche. In 2017 only 2 percent of vineyard acreage in California was organic, representing a 10 percent decline in organic vineyard acreage over the previous four years.[150] In contrast, northwest Europe stood out as an epicenter for organic wine, although with considerable variations between countries. The British market remained modest, even if some London-based millennials bought more than they had in the past.[151] In contrast, Germany's market for organic wine was worth $245 million in 2012, while France's market was worth $511 million that year.[152]

A particularly strong market for organic wine emerged in Scandinavia. In Denmark, by 2014, sales of organic wine exceeded $13 million. By contrast, Italy, with a population ten times bigger than that of Denmark, consumed just five and a half times as much organic wine, by value.[153] Meanwhile, in Sweden, organic wine consumption strengthened, due to an effort on the part of Systembolaget, the state-owned alcohol monopoly, to increase sales of organic products to 10 percent of overall sales by 2020. In pursuit of its goal, Systembolaget's employees strategically placed organic wine around its stores.[154] While 6 percent of the wine sold at Systembolaget in 2011 was organic, by 2014 the company described seeing a "sea change" in consumer preferences for organic products.[155] Organic wine accounted for 21 percent of Systembolaget's overall wine sales in 2016.[156] Just as consolidation in a marketplace (such as the overall wine industry, or even New Zealand's food retail sector) can prevent take-up of the organic category, areas in which just one or two companies control the market can also dramatically turn the tide in favor of organic.

VII CONCLUSIONS

In comparison to organic tea (and some other organic beverages, such as milk), organic wine might be seen as a case study of failed new category creation. For decades, the anticipated additional costs of organic farming and certification, in combination with the lower price points at which (labeled) organic wine tended to sell, discouraged most conventional winemakers from entering the organic industry. Early experiments performed by less-savvy winemakers created a negative reputation for organic wine which proved a challenge to overcome. Of the winemakers who did adopt organic methods, many were derided for their efforts, as conventional winemakers felt threatened by their claims to "natural" or "organic" winemaking. Additionally, organic winemakers encountered great complexity in their work, as organic winemaking required close attention to detail and a sophisticated understanding of environmental and chemical processes in the vineyard and winery. Since organic methods were often used by those who wanted their wines to express *terroir*, and since *terroir* represented both environmental and sociohistorical attributes, winemakers in New World regions may have been less inclined to adopt organic methods, as their lack of regional, longstanding winemaking traditions precluded them from claiming that their wines expressed "true" *terroir*. As such, the ideology of *terroir* served to support the historical supremacy of Old World wines – which included organic wines – in the face of increasing competition from New World wines.

The development of organic wine in different countries with various winemaking traditions resulted in little common agreement regarding the definition of "organic" wine, with the exception of the biodynamic wine growers. In contrast with some other organic agricultural products, organic wine standards took a great deal of time to develop. This reflected that organic wine was a more complex product due to the way in which it was processed. After a great deal of heated debate regarding the use of sulfites, differing organic wine standards emerged. This necessitated further policy development, as the United States and EU had to work to develop equivalency agreements for organic wine. For winemakers, distributors and retailers, the complex layers of regulations regarding organic wine required a great deal of time and effort to understand and address. Many winemakers avoided organic certification so as to avoid the bureaucratic paperwork, risk, cost and in some cases the perceived unfairness of the program. The contrast with organic tea was striking.

Organic wine finally attained modest popularity in the 2010s, particularly in northwest Europe, and in metropolitan areas elsewhere where fine-dining restaurants and wine bars sought artisan-made wines with clear *terroir*. As in tea, biodynamic methods resulted in wines of exceptional quality, as well as testifying to a wider and holistic vision of sustainability. After all of the time that had passed, there was evidence that the negative consumer perceptions that had haunted the organic wine industry had begun to dissipate, even if certified organic wine remained a tiny percentage of the world wine market.

NOTES

1. DiMaggio and Powell, "Iron Cage"; Aldrich and Fiol, "Fools"; Santos and Eisenhardt, "Constructing;" Khaire, "Fashioning."
2. Simpson, *Creating*.
3. Anderson, *The World's*, 3–10; Merrett and Whitwell, "Empire," 173–85.
4. Jones, *Profits*, 24.
5. Unsworth, "History."
6. Legeron, *Natural*, 68–9.
7. Feiring, "Naked," 43–4.
8. The "natural" term is a broadly used term that remains unregulated in most major wine markets.
9. Woolf, "How big."
10. Smith, "Revealed."
11. A number of countries, including the United States, make provisions for the use of synthetic fertilizers and pesticides under certain circumstances.
12. Jones, *Profits*, 28–9, 58.
13. Wine Guide, "About."
14. Ökokiste, "Winery." See Chapter 5 for the origins of the Demeter trade mark and the biodynamic movement.
15. Cadiou et al., *L'agriculture*; Jones, *Profits*, 99–100.
16. Interview by Loubna Bouamane with Pierre Frick, winemaker, Pfaffenheim, November 19, 2011 (hereafter, Frick interview).
17. Frick interview.
18. Cohen, "The Artifice."
19. Feiring, "Dear."
20. Atkin, "The new."
21. Chaptalization is a procedure whereby sugar is added to must if there is not a sufficient quantity of natural sugar in the grapes, sometimes due to the fact that they were not ripe enough when picked. Chaptalization increases the alcohol content of wine. See Toussaint-Samat, *A History*, 257.
22. Kermit Lynch Wine Merchant, "Marcel."
23. Atkin, "The new."
24. Demossier, "Beyond."
25. Fisher, "Organic."
26. Organic Winegrowers NZ, "Final"; Wheeler, "Review," 885–913; Döring et al., "Growth."
27. Email interview by Emily Grandjean with Roberto Stucchi Prinetti, winemaker, Badia a Coltibuono, June 18, 2017.
28. Rossetto, "Marketing."
29. Estreicher, "A Brief," 209–39.
30. Albet i Noya, "Going organic."
31. Smith, "Spanish."
32. Duren, "Spain."
33. Sedlescombe, "Sedlescombe."
34. Jackson, "History"; Waldin, "Sedlescombe."
35. Interview by Geoffrey Jones with Andy Howard, Master of Wine, London, June 8, 2017 (hereafter, Howard interview). The Institute of Masters of Wine was founded by London wine merchants in 1953. In 2018 it had around 300 Masters, two-thirds of them British, who have to pass rigorous examinations on their wine knowledge.
36. Sedlescombe, "Biodynamic wines."
37. Trubek, *The Taste*, 98.
38. Jones, *Profits*, 95-6.
39. Belasco, *Appetite*, Part 1.
40. Taber, *Judgement*, 81.

41. Telephone interview by Emily Grandjean with Tony Coturri, winemaker, Coturri Winery, May 25, 2017 (hereafter, Coturri interview).
42. Delmas and Grant, "Eco-labeling," 6–44.
43. Belasco, *Appetite*, Part 2.
44. Delmas and Lessem, "Eco-premium," 318–56.
45. Boone and Kurtz, "Contemporary," 456.
46. Coates, *Côte*, 122.
47. Interview by Geoffrey Jones with Neil Palmer, cofounder, Vintage Roots, Reading, June 8, 2017 (hereafter, Palmer interview).
48. Interview by Loubna Bouamane with Jonathan Frey, cofounder, Frey Vineyards, Redwood Valley, October 11, 2011 (hereafter, Frey interview); Jones, *Profits*, 96.
49. Email interview by Emily Grandjean with Jonathan Frey, cofounder, Frey Vineyards, June 19, 2017.
50. Frey interview.
51. Quackenbush, "Spotlight"; Demeter-USA, "Directors."
52. Dolan, *True*, 113–14.
53. Ibid., 119–20.
54. Ibid., 43–6.
55. Demeter-USA, "Directors"; Nigro, "U.S."
56. Roberto, "The Changing."
57. Franson, "Consolidation."
58. Fisher, "Organic."
59. Email from Allison Jordan, Vice President, Environmental Affairs, Wine Institute and Executive Director, California Sustainable Winegrowing Alliance, September 8, 2017.
60. California Sustainable Winegrowing Alliance, "E. & J. Gallo Winery"; California Certified Organic Farming, "Gallo Vineyards, Inc."
61. Dolan, *True*, 115.
62. This is Chile, "Concha."
63. Viña Concha y Toro, "History."
64. Viña Concha y Toro, "Sustainability."
65. Viña Concha y Toro S.A., "Form."
66. Euromonitor International, "Viña."
67. Reeder, "The World's."
68. Banfi, "Emiliana."
69. Lynch, *Adventures*, 165.
70. Ibid., 164.
71. Napjus, "Beaujolais."
72. Kermit Lynch Wine Merchant, "About."
73. Telephone interview by Loubna Bouamane with Erich Hartl, founder, Biowein[pur] Hartl, January 27, 2011.
74. CBI (2013).
75. Palmer interview.
76. Ibid.
77. Ibid.
78. Ibid.
79. Ibid. All conversions into US dollars use exchange rate in respective year.
80. Email interview by Emily Grandjean with Adam Morganstern, Editor, *Organic Wine Journal*, August 24, 2017.
81. Jones, *Profits*, 189
82. Interview by Geoffrey Jones and Mayuka Yamazaki with Yasushi Tamura, CEO/President, Mavie Corporation, Tokyo, May 24, 2010 (hereafter, Tamura interview).
83. Ibid.
84. Jones, *Profits*, 362; Strayer, "Why."
85. Ettinger, 'Whole."
86. Smithers, "Grape."

87. Howard interview.
88. Demeter-USA, "History."
89. Willer, "Organic."
90. ECOVIN, "Idea."
91. ECOVIN, "Why."
92. For the Soil Association, see Jones, *Profits*, 60.
93. Telephone interview by Geoffrey Jones and Emily Grandjean with Lee Holdstock, Trade Relations Manager, Soil Association, June 14, 2017.
94. Padel and Lampkin, "The Development," 96; Bioagricert, "AB France."
95. L'Association des Vins Naturels, "The commitment."
96. California Certified Organic Farmers, "Our history."
97. Sustainable Agriculture Research and Education, "History."
98. United States Department of Agriculture, "Organic."
99. Lester, "Sulfite," 229–32; Cleveland Clinic, "Sulfite."
100. Nigro, "U.S."
101. Email interview by Emily Grandjean with Paul Dolan, President, Demeter-USA, June 22, 2017 (hereafter, Dolan interview).
102. Nigro, "U.S."
103. United States Department of Agriculture, "Meeting."
104. Frey, "Katrina."
105. National Organic Standards Board, "Petition."
106. Frey Vineyards, "The NOSB."
107. Dolan interview.
108. IFOAM EU Group, "EU Rules."
109. Finch, "Allergens."
110. Micheloni, "ORWINE."
111. IFOAM EU Group, "EU rules."
112. Organic Trade Association, "EU–US."
113. Frick interview.
114. Howard interview.
115. Demeter-USA, "Demeter."
116. Nigro, "U.S."
117. Email interview by Emily Grandjean with Will Davenport, Winemaker, Davenport Vineyards, June 17, 2017.
118. Coturri interview.
119. Alley, "New."
120. Karlsson and Karlsson, "Biodynamic."
121. Deutscher Teeverband, "Tea."
122. Bailey, "The US"; Quartz, "Annual."
123. Blythman, "The hottest."
124. Koehler, *Darjeeling*, 145; interview by Geoffrey Jones with Sanjay Bansal, Chairman of Ambootia Group, Boston, May 30 2017 (hereafter, Bansal interview).
125. Blythman, "The hottest."
126. Kurian and Peter (2007), *Commercial*, 436.
127. Koehler, *Darjeeling*, 145; Bansal interview.
128. Blythman, "The hottest."
129. Honest Tea, "Honest timeline."
130. Gompers, 'Honest Tea."
131. Walker, "Drink."
132. Ziobro, "Coke."
133. Honest Tea, "Honest Timeline"; Goggi, "The state."
134. Bolton, "Insight."
135. Kurian and Peter, *Commercial*, 436; Lin, "Development."
136. Celestial Seasonings, "Celestial."
137. Wong, "Are small"; Tata Global Beverages Newsroom, "Tata."

138. Molineaux, "Report."
139. Unilever, "Unilever."
140. Email from Kyla Smith, Certification Director, Pennsylvania Certified Organic, July 14, 2017; European Commission, "Commission."
141. Vidal, "Move."
142. Haskell, "Why wild."
143. Ibid.
144. VisitDenmark, "Noma."
145. Telephone interview by Emily Grandjean with Mads Kleppe, Head Sommelier, Noma, July 24, 2017.
146. Ibid.
147. Ibid.
148. Karlsson and Karlsson, "Biodynamic."
149. Trubek, *The Taste*, 248.
150. Strayer, "The organic."
151. Smithers, "Grape."
152. Pink, "The Sustainable."
153. CBI (2013) and (2016).
154. Park, "Nudging."
155. Euromonitor International, "Wine"; Systembolaget, "2016 Launch Plan."
156. Euromonitor International, "Wine."

REFERENCES

Albet i Noya (n.d.), "Going organic," accessed August 2, 2017 at www.albetinoya.cat/eng/inicis.php.

Aldrich, H.E. and C.M. Fiol (1994), "Fools Rush In? The Institutional Context of Industry Creation," *Academy of Management Review*, **19**, 645–70.

Alley, Lynn (2002), "New USDA rules on organic labeling mean changes for wineries," *Wine Spectator*, April 19, accessed August 2, 2017 at www.wine spectator.com/webfeature/show/id/New-USDA-Rules-on-Organic-Labeling-Mean-Changes-for-Wineries_21261.

Anderson, Kym (2004), *The World's Wine Markets: Globalization at Work*, Cheltenham, UK and Northampton, USA: Edward Elgar.

Atkin, Tim (2007), "The new Beaujolais," *Saveur*, February 7, accessed August 1, 2017 at www.saveur.com/article/Wine-and-Drink/The-New-Beaujolais.

Bailey, Sharon (2015), "The US is the fourth largest tea market in the world," *Market Realist*, June 4, accessed August 14, 2017 at www.marketrealist.com/2015/06/us-fourth-largest-tea-market-world/.

Banfi (n.d.), "Emiliana," accessed August 2, 2017 at www.banfiwines.com/winery/emiliana/.

Belasco, Warren J. (2007), *Appetite for Change: How the Counterculture Took on the Food Industry*, Ithaca, NY: Cornell University Press.

Beverage Trade Network (n.d.), 'Let's talk about organic wines and its demand," accessed August 2, 2017 at www.beveragetradenetwork.com/en/Organic-Wines-229.htm.

Bioagricert (n.d.), "AB France," accessed August 2, 2017 at www.bioagricert.org/en/certification/organic-production/ab-france.html.

Blythman, Joanna (2007), "The hottest cuppa in the world," *The Guardian*, April 28, accessed July 24, 2017 at www.theguardian.com/lifeandstyle/2007/apr/29/foodanddrink4.

Bolton, Dan, (2015), "Insight: Organic tea imports," *World Tea News*, July 20, accessed August 2, 2017 at www.worldteanews.com/insights/industry-insight/insight-organic-tea-imports.

Boone, Louis E. and David L. Kurtz (2011), *Contemporary Business*, Malden, UK: John Wiley & Sons.

Brandl, Thomas (n.d.), "Organic wine boom continues," *Prowein Magazine*, accessed August 2, 2017 at www.prowein.com/cgi-bin/md_prowein/lib/pub/tt.cgi/Organic_wine_boom_continues.html?oid=29664&lang=2&ticket=g_u_e_s_t.

Brodt, Sonja, Karen Klonsky and L. Ann Thrupp (2009), "Market Potential for Organic Crops in California: Almonds, Hay, and Winegrapes," Giannini Foundation Information Series Report 09-1, accessed August 14, 2017 at s.giannini.ucop.edu/uploads/giannini_public/ff/12/ff12d172-0808-4a70-866a-21012c227695/091_organic.pdf.

Cadiou, Pierre and André Lefebvre, Yves Le Pape, François Mathieu-Gaudrot, Stéphane Oriol (1975), *L'agriculture biologique en France, écologie ou mythologie*, Fontaine, France: Presses universitaires de Grenoble.

California Certified Organic Farmers (n.d.), "Gallo Vineyards, Inc.," accessed August 2, 2017 at www.ccof.org/members/gallo-vineyards-inc-4.

California Certified Organic Farmers (n.d.), "Our history," accessed August 2, 2017 at www.ccof.org/ccof/history.

California Sustainable Winegrowing Alliance (n.d.), "E. & J. Gallo Winery," accessed June 23, 2017 at www.sustainablewinegrowing.org/certified participant/8/EJ_Gallo_Winery.html.

CBI Ministry of Foreign Affairs (2013), "CBI product factsheet: Organic wine in Europe," accessed August 3, 2017 at www.cbi.eu/sites/default/files/market_information/researches/product-factsheet-organic-wine-europe-wine-2013.pdf.

CBI Ministry of Foreign Affairs (2016), "CBI trends: Wine in Denmark," accessed September 13, 2017 at www.cbi.eu/sites/default/files/market_information/researches/trends-denmark-wine-2016.pdf.

Celestial Seasonings (2014), "Celestial Seasonings introduces new line of organic, Fair Trade certified estate tea," Press release, accessed August 2, 2017 at www.celestialseasonings.com/press-releases/715.

Cleveland Clinic (n.d.), "Sulfite sensitivity," accessed August 14, 2017 at www.my.clevelandclinic.org/health/articles/sulfite-sensitivity.

Coates, Clive (1997), *Côte d'Or: A Celebration of the Great Wines of Burgundy*, Berkeley, CA: University of California Press.

Cohen, Paul (2013), "The Artifice of Natural Wine: Jules Chauvet and the Reinvention of Vinification in Postwar France," in Rachel E. Black and Robert C. Ulin (eds.), *Wine and Culture: Vineyard to Glass*, New York: Bloomsbury Academic, 261–78.

Delmas, Magali A. and Laura E. Grant (2014), "Eco-labeling Strategies and Price-premium," *Business & Society*, **53**, (1), 6–44.

Delmas, Magali A. and Neil Lessem (2017), "Eco-premium or Eco-penalty? Eco-labels and Quality in the Organic Wine Market," *Business & Society*, **56**, (2), 318–56.

Demeter International e.V. (2008), "Standards for Demeter/biodynamic wine," accessed August 2, 2017 at www.organicstandard.com.ua/files/standards/en/demeter/st_wine_e08.pdf.

Demeter-USA (2017), "Demeter Association Inc. biodynamic processing standard," accessed August 2, 2017 at www.demeter-usa.org/downloads/Demeter-Processing-Standards.pdf.

Demeter-USA (n.d.), "Directors," accessed July 14, 2017 at www.demeter-usa.org/about-demeter/directors.asp.

Demeter-USA (n.d.), "History," accessed August 2, 2017 at www.demeter-usa.org/about-demeter/demeter-history.asp.

Demossier, Marion (2011), "Beyond Terroir: Territorial Construction, Hegemonic Discourses, and French Wine Culture," *Journal of the Royal Anthropological Institute*, **17**, 685–705.

Deutscher Teeverband (n.d.), "Tea production worldwide from 2006 to 2016, by country (in metric tons)," Statista – The Statistics Portal, accessed August 14, 2017 at https://www-statista-com.ezp-prod1.hul.harvard.edu/statistics/264188/production-of-tea-by-main-producing-countries-since-2006/.

DiMaggio, P.J. and W.W. Powell (1983), "The Iron Cage Revisited: Institutional Isomorphism and Collective Rationality in Organizational Fields," *American Sociological Review*, **48**, 147–80.

Dolan, Paul (2003), *True to Our Roots. Fermenting a Business Revolution*, Princeton, NJ: Bloomberg Press.

Döring, Johannah, Matthias Frisch, Susanne Tittmann, Manfred Stoll and Randolf Kauer (2015), "Growth, Yield and Fruit Quality of Grapevines under organic and Biodynamic Management," *PLoS ONE*, **10** (10).

Duren, James (2015), "Spain dominates bio wine industry," accessed August 31, 2017 at www.snooth.com/articles/spain-dominates-bio-wine-industry/?viewall=1.

ECOVIN (n.d.), "Idea," accessed August 11, 2017 at www.ecovin.de/wissen.

ECOVIN (n.d.), "Why ECOVIN?" accessed August 2, 2017 at www.ecovin.de/wissen/mitglied-werden.

Estreicher, Stefan K. (2013), "A Brief History of Wine in Spain," *European Review*, **21**, (2), 209–39.

Ettinger, Jill (2012), "Whole Foods Market to carry first sulfite-free wines from Italy and Spain," *Organic Authority*, January 13, accessed July 31, 2017 at www.organicauthority.com/blog/organic/whole-foods-market-to-carry-first-sulfite-free-wines-from-italy-and-spain/.

Euromonitor International (2017), "Viña Concha y Toro SA in wine (world)," accessed September 24, 2017 at www.portal.euromonitor.com.

Euromonitor International (2017), "Wine in Sweden," accessed August 2, 2017 at www.euromonitor.com/wine-in-sweden/report.

European Commission (2008), "Commission regulation (EC) no 889/2008," accessed August 20, 2017 at http://eur-lex.europa.eu/legal-content/EN/TXT/PDF/?uri=CELEX:32008R0889&from=EN.

European Commission (2012), "New EU rules for 'organic wine' agreed," Press release, February 8, accessed August 2, 2017 at www.europa.eu/rapid/press-release_IP-12-113_en.htm.

Feiring, Alice (2010), "Dear Marcel (to whom all roads lead)," accessed July 20, 2017 at www.alicefeiring.com/blog/2010/10/dear-marcel.html.

Feiring, Alice (2011), *Naked Wine: Letting Grapes Do What Comes Naturally*, Boston, MA: De Capo Press.

Finch, Graham (2016), "Allergens labeling for wine," *Food Standards Agency*, April, accessed June 4, 2016 at www.food.gov.uk/sites/default/files/multi media/pdfs/enforcement/wineallergenlabeloct13.pdf.

Fisher, Lawrence M. (1991), "Organic wines enter the mainstream," *The New York Times*, November 19, accessed July 14, 2017 at www.nytimes.com/1991/11/19/business/organic-wines-enter-the-mainstream.html?pagewanted=all.

Franson, Paul (2006), "Consolidation in changing the business of wine," *Napa Valley Register*, November 2, accessed August 4, 2017 at www.napavalley register.com/business/consolidation-is-changing-the-business-of-wine/article_ 8cbf2ddf-56c8-52ef-97bf-a77ff69b0eb4.html.

Frey Vineyards (2011), "The NOSB voted: No added sulfites in organic wines," accessed July 21, 2017 at www.freywine.com/?method=blog.blogDrill down&blogEntryID=72CDBE33-0EA3-8A6B-BB53-F7E537C4F8B5&original MarketingURL=blog/The-NOSB-voted–no-added-sulfites-in-Organic-Wines.

Frey, Katrina (2011), "Katrina Frey talks about sulfites and the battle to keep them out of organic wine on the Organic Conversation Radio Show," accessed August 2, 2017 at www.freywine.com/blog/Katrina-Frey-talks-about-sulfites-and-the-battle-to-keep-them-out-of-organic-wine-on-the-Organic-Conversation-Radio-Show.

Goggi, Peter F. (2017), "The state of the US tea industry," Tea Association of the U.S.A. Inc., accessed July 31, 2017 at www.teausa.com/14654/state-of-the-industry.

Gompers, Paul G. (2001), "Honest Tea," *Harvard Business School Case 201-076* (revised October 2001).

Haskell, Rob (2016), "Why wild, chemical-free, 'natural' wines are taking the industry by storm," *Vogue*, April 21, accessed August 2, 2017 at www.vogue. com/article/natural-wine-industry-chemical-free.

Honest Tea (n.d.), "Honest timeline," accessed August 4, 2017 at www.honesttea. com/about-us/timeline/.

IFOAM EU Group (2013), "EU rules for organic wine production: Background, evaluation, and further sector development," accessed August 14, 2017 at www.itr.si/uploads/LW/AJ/LWAJRgGe_kylvigPDidvmg/ifoameu_reg_wine_ dossier_201307.pdf.

Jackson, Evelyn (n.d.), 'History of English wine," accessed June 10, 2017 at www.greatenglishwines.co.uk/history-of-english-wine.

Jones, Geoffrey (2017), *Profits and Sustainability: A History of Green Entre-preneurship*, Oxford: Oxford University Press.

Karlsson, Britt and Per Karlsson (2016), *Biodynamic, Organic, and Natural Winemaking*, Stockholm: Floris Books.

Kermit Lynch Wine Merchant (n.d.), "About Kermit," accessed July 12, 2017 at www.kermitlynch.com/about-kermit/.

Kermit Lynch Wine Merchant (n.d.), "Marcel Lapierre," accessed August 12, 2017 at www.kermitlynch.com/our-wines/marcel-lapierre/.

Khaire, Mukti (2014), "Fashioning an Industry: Socio-cognitive Processes in the Construction of Worth of a New Industry," *Organization Studies*, **35**, (1), 41–74.

Koehler, Jeff (2015), *Darjeeling: The Colorful History and Precarious Fate of the World's Greatest Tea*, New York: Bloomsbury.

Kurian, A. and K.V. Peter (2007), *Commercial Crops Technology*, Delhi: New India Publishing Agency.

L'Association des Vins Naturels (n.d.), "The commitment of the winemaker for an AVN wine," accessed August 14, 2017 at www.lesvinsnaturels.org/category/L-association/Engagement.

Legeron, Isabelle (2014), *Natural Wine: An Introduction to Organic and Biodynamic Wines Made Naturally*, London: CICO Books.

Lester, Mitchell R. (1995), "Sulfite Sensitivity: Significance in Human Health," *Journal of the American College of Nutrition*, **14**, (3), 229–32.

Lin, Zhi (2010), "Development, production, and trade of organic tea (China part)," Food and Agriculture Organization of the United Nations, accessed September 16, 2017 at www.fao.org/fileadmin/templates/est/COMM_MARKETS_MONITORING/Tea/Documents/China_CFC_project_for_FAO_19th_session_May13_2010_.pdf.

Lynch, Kermit (1988), *Adventures on the Wine Route: A Wine Buyer's Tour of France*, New York: North Point Press.

Merrett, David and Greg Whitwell (1994), "The Empire Strikes Back: Marketing Australian Beer and Wine in the United Kingdom," in Geoffrey Jones and Nicholas J. Morgan (eds.), *Adding Value: Brands and Marketing in Food and Drink*, London: Routledge, 162–88.

Micheloni, Cristina (2009), "ORWINE: Publishable final activity report," accessed August 2, 2017 at cordis.europa.eu/docs/publications/1238/1238 69711-6_en.pdf.

Millésime Bio (2017), "Overview: An increase in visitors and in international presence," accessed August 31, 2017 at www.millesime-bio.com/files/download/644.

Millésime Bio (2017), "Press kit," accessed August 31, 2017 at www.millesime-bio.com/en/press/press-kits.

Molineaux, Sam (2017), "Report predicts growth in market for organic tea," *World Tea News*, January 24, accessed August 4, 2017 at www.worldtea news.com/news/report-predicts-growth-in-market-for-organic-tea.

Napjus, Alison (2010), "Beaujolais loses top winemaker Marcel Lapierre at 60," *Wine Spectator*, October 13, accessed July 21, 2017 at www.winespectator. com/webfeature/show/id/43806.

National Organic Standards Board (2011), "Petition to amend annotation for sulfur dioxide on 205.605," accessed August 2, 2017 at www.ams.usda.gov/sites/default/files/media/Sulfur%20dioxide%20recommendation%202011.pdf.

Nigro, Dana (2012), "U.S. and Europe have different definitions of organic wine," *Wine Spectator*, February 24, accessed August 2, 2017 at www.wine spectator.com/webfeature/show/id/46432.

Ökokiste (n.d.), "Winery Sander, Demeter, Rhineland-Palatinate," accessed July 18, 2017 at www.oekokiste.de/lieferanten/lieferant/125.html.

Organic Trade Association (n.d.), "EU–US equivalency agreement," accessed July 31, 2017 at www.ota.com/resources/global-market-opportunities/trade-access-barriers/trade-agreements/eu-us-equivalency.

Organic Winegrowers NZ (2015), "Final results of the organic focus vineyard project," accessed July 12, 2017 at www.organicfocusvineyard.com/2015/06/22/final-results/.

Padel, Susanne and Nicolas Lampkin (2007), "The Development of Governmental Support for Organic Farming in Europe," in William Lockeretz (ed.), *Organic Farming: An International History*, Oxfordshire, UK: CABI.

Park, Juan (2015), "Nudging consumers to do good, Swedish style," Wine Intelligence, April 8, accessed August 15, 2017 at www.wineintelligence.com/nudging-consumers-to-do-good-swedish-style/.

Pekic, Branislav (2016), "Italian organic wine exports grow by 38%," *European Supermarket Magazine*, August 17, accessed August 14, 2017 at www.esmmagazine.com/italian-organic-wine-exports-grow-38/31058.

Pink, Małgorzata (2015), "The Sustainable Wine Market in Europe – Introduction to a Market Trend and its Issues," *Oeconomia*, **14**, (2), 131–42.

Quackenbush, Jeff (2011), "Spotlight on leaders at independent wine companies," *North Bay Business Journal*, June 27, accessed August 20, 2017 Małgorzata www.northbaybusinessjournal.com/csp/mediapool/sites/NBBJ/IndustryNews/story.csp?cid=4179872&sid=778&fid=181.

Quartz (n.d.), "Annual per capita tea consumption worldwide as of 2016, by leading countries (in pounds)," Statista – The Statistics Portal, accessed August 14, 2017 at https://www-statista-com.ezp-prod1.hul.harvard.edu/statistics/507950/global-per-capita-tea-consumption-by-country/.

Reeder, Jessica (2012), "The world's largest organic & biodynamic vineyard: Chile's Emiliana Vineyards," *Organic Authority*, June 12, accessed August 14, 2017 at www.organicauthority.com/juicy-spirits/eco-winery-emiliana-vineyards-chile.html.

Roberto, Michael A. (2011), "The Changing Structure of the Global Wine Industry," *International Business & Economics Research Journal* (IBER), **2**, (9).

Rossetto, Luca (2002), "Marketing Strategies for Organic Wine Growers in the Veneto Region," 8th Joint Conference on Food, Agriculture and the Environment, accessed July 18, 2017 at ageconsearch.umn.edu/bitstream/14363/1/wp02-04.pdf.

Santos, F.M. and Eisenhardt, K.M (2009), "Constructing Markets and Shaping Boundaries: Entrepreneurial Agency in Nascent Fields," *Academy of Management Journal*, **49**, 643–671.

Sedlescombe, "Biodynamic wines of England," accessed January 20, 2018 at http://englishorganicwine.co.uk/pages/history of sedlescombe.

Sedlescombe (n.d.), "Sedlescombe: Vineyard tours & wine tasting," accessed August 2, 2017 at www.englishorganicwine.co.uk/.

Simpson, James (2011) *Creating Wine: The Emergence of a World Industry, 1840–1914*, Princeton, NJ: Princeton University Press.

Smith, Adrienne (n.d.), "Spanish wines go organic," *Food & Wines from Spain*, accessed August 2, 2017 at www.foodswinesfromspain.com/spanishfoodwine/global/products-recipes/products/more-about-products/spanish-wines-go-organic.html#.

Smith, Oliver (2017), "Revealed: The countries that quaff the most wine per capita," *The Telegraph*, February 17, accessed August 2, 2017 at http://www.telegraph.co.uk/travel/maps-and-graphics/wine-consumption-per-capita-by-country.

Smithers, Rebecca (2017), "Grape Britain: UK merry on organic wine as sales soar," *The Guardian*, April 3, accessed July 28, 2017 at www.theguardian.com/environment/2017/apr/03/grape-britain-uk-merry-on-organic-wine-as-sales-hit-nearly-6m.

Strayer, Pam (2015), "Why is Whole Foods so lame about organically grown wine?" accessed July 31, 2017 at winecountrygeographic.blogspot.com/2015/07/why-is-whole-foods-so-lame-about.html.

Strayer, Pam (2017), "The organic opportunity: Will the U.S. wine industry miss out?" *Wines & Vines*, January, accessed August 17, 2017 at www.winesandvines.com/columns/section/26/article/178258/The-Organic-Opportunity-Will-the-US-Wine-Industry-Miss-Out.

Sustainable Agriculture Research and Education (n.d.), "History of organic farming in the US," accessed August 2, 2017 at www.sare.org/Learning-Center/Bulletins/Transitioning-to-Organic-Production/Text-Version/History-of-Organic-Farming-in-the-United-States.

Systembolaget (2015), "2016 launch plan," accessed August 3, 2017 at www.systembolaget.se/imagelibrary/publishedmedia/zi1hli7jhiaxxylfzb7d/Launch_plan_2016.pdf.

Systembolaget (2016), "2017 launch plan," accessed August 19, 2017 at www.systembolaget.se/imagelibrary/publishedmedia/77fj20gd52sp7wdvqinb/Launch_Plan_2017.pdf.

Taber, George M. (2005), *Judgement of Paris. California vs France and the Historic 1976 Paris Tasting that Revolutionized Wine*, New York: Scribner.

Tata Global Beverages Newsroom (2014), "Tata Global Beverages and Hindustan Unilever progress sustainable initiatives for tea industry," Press release, accessed August 4, 2017 at www.tataglobalbeverages.com/media/news/detailed-news/2015/02/24/tata-global-beverages-and-hindustan-unilever-progress-sustainable-initiatives-for-tea-industry.

This is Chile (2011), "Concha y Toro buys largest organic and sustainable vineyards in the US," March 3, accessed August 2, 2017 at www.thisischile.cl/concha-y-toro-buys-largest-organic-and-sustainable-vineyards-in-the-us/?lang=en.

Toussaint-Samat, Maguelonne (1992), *A History of Food*, Chichester, UK: Wiley-Blackwell.

Trubek, Amy B. (2008), *The Taste of Place: A Cultural Journey into Terroir*, Berkeley and Los Angeles, CA: University of California Press.

Unilever (2017), "Unilever acquires Pukka Herbs," accessed September 13, 2017 at www.unilever.com/news/Press-releases/2017/unilever-acquires-pukka-herbs.html.

United States Department of Agriculture (2011), "Meeting of The National Organic Standards Board (NOSB)," accessed July 30, 2017 at www.ams. usda.gov/sites/default/files/media/transcript1ga.pdf.

United States Department of Agriculture (n.d.), "Organic wine: Oversight, labeling + trade," accessed August 2, 2017 at www.ams.usda.gov/sites/default/ files/media/Organic%20Wine%20-%20Oversight-Labeling-Trade.pdf.

Unsworth, John (2010), "History of pesticide use," *International Union of Pure and Applied Chemistry*, accessed August 1, 2017 at www.agrochemicals.iupac. org/index.php?option=com_sobi2&sobi2Task=sobi2Details&catid=3&sobi2Id =31.

Vidal, John (2017), "Move by UK supermarkets threatens to bring Fairtrade crashing down," *The Guardian*, accessed September 13, 2017 at www. theguardian.com/global-development/2017/jun/24/fairtrade-crashing-down-sainsburys-tesco-tea-growers-nairobi.

Viña Concha y Toro (n.d.), "History," accessed August 2, 2017 at www. conchaytoro.com/concha-y-toro-holding/quienes-somos-cat/history/.

Viña Concha y Toro (n.d.), "Sustainability," accessed August 4, 2017 at www. conchaytoro.com/concha-y-toro-holding/sustainability/.

Viña Concha y Toro S.A. (2012), "Form 20-F: Annual report," United States Securities and Exchange Commission, accessed August 14, 2017 at www. conchaytoro.com/wp-content/uploads/2014/07/2011.pdf.

VisitDenmark (n.d.), "Noma – Four-time world's best restaurant!" accessed August 2, 2017 at www.visitdenmark.com/copenhagen/places-eat/noma-four-time-worlds-best-restaurant.

Waldin, Monty (n.d.), "Sedlescombe," accessed August 2, 2017 at www.drink britain.com/visits/sedlescombe.

Walker, Andrea K. (2008), "Drink maker finds Coke its cup of tea," *The Baltimore Sun*, April 16, accessed August 2, 2017 at web.archive.org/web/ 20110522195656/http://www.baltimoresun.com/features/green/sns-honest-tea-coke-green%2C0%2C4779978.story.

Wheeler, Sarah (2011), "Review of Organic Farming Policy in Australia: Time to Wipe the Slate Clean?" *Journal of Sustainable Agriculture*, **35**, (8), 885–913.

Willer, Helga (2008), "Organic viticulture in Europe: Development and current statistics," 16th IFOAM Organic World Congress, accessed August 11, 2017 at www.orgprints.org/10909/2/willer-2008-viticulture%5D.doc.

Willer, Helga and Julia Lernoud (eds.) (2017), *The World of Organic Agriculture: Statistics & Emerging Trends 2017*, Frick and Bonn: FiBL & IFOAM – Organics International. Accessed August 2, 2017 at shop.fibl.org/CHen/ mwdownloads/download/link/id/785/?ref=1.

Willer, Helga and Minou Yussefi (2006), *The World of Organic Agriculture. Statistics and Emerging Trends 2006*, Frick and Bonn: Research Institute of Organic Agriculture FiBL & IFOAM – Organics International.

Wine Guide (n.d.), "About Weingut Sander," accessed July 11, 2017 at wineguide.wein-plus.eu/weingut-sander/about.

Winemonitor (2013), "Press release," accessed August 4, 2017 at www.wine monitor.it/images/PDF/Comunicati%20stampa/CS%20Wine%20Monitor%20 Nomisma%20organic%20EN.pdf.

Wong, Kristine (2015), "Are small farms in India the key to taking tea organic?" *The Guardian*, February 5, accessed July 31, 2017 at www.theguardian.com/sustainable-business/2015/feb/05/tea-farm-india-sustainable-organic.

Woolf, Simon (2016), "How big is the market for natural wines?" *Meininger's Wine Business Journal*, September 15, accessed August 2, 2017 at www.meininger.de/en/wine-business-international/how-big-market-natural-wines.

Ziobro, Paul (2011), "Coke buys rest of Honest Tea," *The Wall Street Journal*, March 1, accessed July 31, 2017 at www.wsj.com/articles/SB1000142405274 8704506004576174282892481392.

PRIMARY MATERIALS

Interviews by Geoffrey Jones with Sanjay Bansal, Boston, May 30, 2017; Andy Howard, London, June 8 2017; Neil Palmer, Reading, June 8, 2017.

Interview by Geoffrey Jones and Mayuka Yamazaki with Yasushi Tamura, Tokyo, May 24, 2010.

Telephone interview by Geoffrey Jones and Emily Grandjean with Lee Holdstock, June 14, 2017.

Interviews by Loubna Bouamane with Jonathan Frey, Redwood Valley, October 11, 2011; Pierre Frick, Pfaffenheim, November 19, 2011.

Telephone interview by Loubna Bouamane with Erich Hartl, January 27, 2011.

Telephone interviews by Emily Grandjean with Tony Coturri, May 25, 2017; Mads Kleppe, July 24, 2017; Adam Morganstern, August, 24, 2017.

Email interviews by Emily Grandjean with Will Davenport, June 17, 2017; Roberto Stucchi Prinetti, June 18, 2017; Jonathan Frey, June 19, 2017; Paul Dolan, June 22, 2017.

7. Creating ecotourism in Costa Rica*

With Andrew Spadafora

I INTRODUCTION

This chapter explores how the Central American nation of Costa Rica became a global center for ecotourism during the late decades of the twentieth century. This was an era when the country flourished as an overall tourist destination. Total tourist arrivals to the country increased from 155 000 in 1970 to 435 000 in 1990, and reached 1.1 million in 2000, with revenues generated by tourism growing from US$21 million to $1.15 billion over that period.[1] The distinctive feature of this tourism boom, however, was that much of it appeared driven by ecological interests.

As in the case of organic wine, discussed in Chapter 6, ecotourism's identity is ill-defined. There are porous boundaries between conventional tourism and ecotourism, which emerged as a defined concept quite recently. It was only in the 1990s that the nonprofit International Ecotourism Society (TIES) articulated what became the mostly widely accepted definition of ecotourism: "Responsible travel to natural areas that conserves the environment and improves the well-being of local people."[2] There were much longer antecedents to the phenomenon, stretching back to nature- and wildlife-based tourism in the nineteenth century.[3]

Leaving aside for the moment definitional vagaries, it is evident that Costa Rica experienced a rapid growth of ecotourism during the last decades of the twentieth century. Visits to protected forest areas increased from 287 000 in 1987 to 866 000 in 1999.[4] By the late 1990s, a survey suggested that the average foreign tourist spent approximately two-thirds of his or her time in Costa Rica in protected areas or traveling to them.[5] International surveys came to place Costa Rica regularly at or near the top of ecotourism destinations.[6] A standard text on ecotourism published in 2008 noted that "the country was perceived internationally as the world's prime ecotourist destination," ahead of such forerunners as Kenya, Nepal and the Galapagos Islands.[7] The website IndependentTraveller.com notes: "Costa Rica is practically synonymous with the term 'ecotourism,' and for good reason."[8]

The existing literature on the emergence of Costa Rican ecotourism has focused on the role of the state, especially the creation of the national park system.[9] While acknowledging the role of public policy, the growth of the ecotourism industry is better seen as a case of co-creation, involving small entrepreneurial start-ups operating private reserves, tours and accommodations, as well as environmental and scientific NGOs. This chapter draws on new primary sources, especially two sets of oral histories conducted in different time periods.

Section II examines Costa Rica's natural endowment and institutional foundations for tourism; Section III turns to the role of scientists, NGOs and the national parks. Section IV examines the role of entrepreneurs and firms in the creation of the industry, and Section V discusses the advent of ecolodges and private reserves. Section VI turns to the overall impact of ecotourism on the country. A final section concludes.

II NATURAL ENDOWMENT AND INSTITUTIONAL FOUNDATIONS

Costa Rica's natural endowment was a mixed blessing for the emergence of an ecotourism industry. The country allegedly contains 4–5 percent of the world's biodiversity in 0.035 percent of its territory; about the size of West Virginia in land area, it has more bird species than all of the United States.[10] It boasts 20 separate "life zones"; some 850 species of birds; 1,260 species of trees; 237 species of mammals; and 361 species of reptiles.[11] However, Costa Rica's bounty also invited intensive logging, ranching, monoculture plantations of agricultural commodities and over-development of some of its sunny beaches, all of which wreaked havoc on its forests and shorelines after the 1950s. Between 1940 and 1980, Costa Rica lost 2.5 million hectares of forest, with annual average deforestation rates reaching a height in the 1970s of approximately 60,000 hectares per year.[12] The country's primary forest cover fell from 90 percent in 1950 to just over 25 percent by 1990.[13]

Costa Rica developed a growing domestic beach tourism market between 1950 and 1980, and began to improve its transportation infrastructure to service it. The completion of rail lines and expansion of the Pan-American Highway after 1946 eased access from the central population centers to the Pacific beaches of Guanacaste, which later became the most heavily overdeveloped tourism center.[14] The country constructed more roads, raising its total to 30 000 kilometers by 1983.[15] In 1957 the government opened a modern international airport near San José.[16] Work began on a second airport to serve the Guanacaste tourist region in the mid-1970s, but it was not opened to international air traffic until 1996.[17] The national airline, LACSA, was established in 1945 by the US airline Pan American, the Costa Rican government and private investors, and operated routes to Miami and Latin American capitals. During the 1980s, LACSA became the largest Central American carrier.[18]

The government created the National Tourism Council in 1931, and replaced it in 1955 with the Costa Rican Tourism Institute (ICT), both of which mainly promoted domestic travel.[19] The ICT was explicitly permitted to declare and protect national parks, but it never moved beyond preliminary studies.[20] What international tourism there was – approximately 6,000–7,000 tourists annually in 1953–54[21] – generally concentrated at beaches, museums, churches and visits to "typical towns."[22]

In later years, the national legislature passed a package of tax incentives, delivered through the ICT, for large-scale tourism investment in 1985, including moratoria on property taxes and import duties for construction materials and vehicles. These incentives did not apply to smaller-scale enterprises, which would soon include most ecotourism developments,[23] and even where they did, the government sometimes revoked the privileges prematurely.[24] Tourism policies were often not consistent; for example, new visa legislation in 1986 created high administrative barriers to tourist entry.[25] The ICT tried to involve the private sector in its decisions by creating a joint Tourism Marketing Committee in 1986, but then alienated the entrepreneurs by spending the entire budget it had promised to the committee, which resigned en masse. One such entrepreneur stated that he "refuse[d] to be part of an organization [the ICT] dedicated to the destruction of foreign tourism in Costa Rica."[26] Once ecotourism had taken off, its advocates regularly denounced the ICT's lack of interest in the category, and its willingness to seize on "green" rhetoric while speeding up the approval of large and environmentally destructive developments like the beach resorts at Playa Tambor and Papagayo.[27]

The growth of all varieties of tourism was, however, promoted by a level of political stability that set the country apart from its neighbors. Costa Rica has a long tradition of national elections and has suffered few disruptions in the democratic selection of presidents since 1920.[28] The major exception was a civil war in 1948, in which the "founding father" of modern Costa Rica, José Figueres Ferrer, used temporary rule to abolish the military, nationalize the banks, weaken Communist militancy and insist on free elections after 18 months of stabilization. In the following decades, Costa Rica alternated peacefully between presidential administrations of Figueres's National Liberation Party (PLN) and several opposition parties. Both the PLN and the opposition pursued economic policies based on state-led social development, partial industrialization and continued agricultural exports.[29]

Following Costa Rica's severe debt crisis in the late 1970s and early 1980s, both factions embraced privatization and other liberalizing reforms. During this difficult period of adjustment, demilitarized Costa Rica avoided the civil wars and dictatorships that had engulfed its neighbors, Nicaragua and Panama.[30] Though poverty and surrounding Central American instability disrupted Costa Rica's still-nascent tourism industry in the early to mid-1980s, it subsequently recovered, particularly after President Arias was awarded a Nobel Peace Prize in 1987. The prize provided a strong global signal of the country's commitment to peace, stability, and cosmopolitan and democratic traditions, and generated widespread interest in Costa Rica.[31]

By 1987 the country had also become well known among biologists and conservationists. Statutory and regulatory attempts at environmental protection dated back to the nineteenth century, but for decades execution was poor.[32] Beginning around 1960, however, a series of public and private initiatives, both domestic and international, began to build up the scientific ideas, organizations and the national parks that would serve as a major impetus to ecotourism.

III SCIENTISTS, NGOS AND THE NATIONAL PARKS

The institutional basis for the scientific understanding of both the country's biodiversity and the need to protect it were laid quite early. The National School of Agriculture, integrated into the new University of Costa Rica in 1940, served as a locus for incipient conservation thought.[33] So, too, did the locally-based Inter-American Institute of Agricultural Sciences, established in 1942 and later known as Tropical Agricultural Research and Higher Education (CATIE), which would prove to be both a major source of scientific understanding of Costa Rican biodiversity and of conservation activism after 1960.[34] Biologists from Costa Rica and the United States soon established a series of other institutions that would educate a new generation of conservationists, and protect forests and wildlife in more than name only.

In 1959, drawing on US philanthropy, the American herpetologist Archie Carr established the Caribbean Conservation Corporation, Costa

Rica's first NGO, to provide funds for the protection of the sea turtle nesting beach at Tortuguero.[35] Two other institutions founded by US scientists are of particular significance for the later development of ecotourism, as they subsequently came to operate private reserves. In 1962, Leslie Holdridge, Robert Hunter and Joseph Tosi established the Tropical Science Center (TSC). It was designed to conduct research in biology, agronomy and forestry; to consult with other organizations like CATIE; and to promote conservation through lobbying and direct land management.[36] The following year, a consortium of six US universities and the University of Costa Rica, guided by Rafael Rodríguez Caballero and Jay Savage, founded the Organization for Tropical Studies (OTS) to create a research station for their tropical biologists.[37] These institutions and others would soon provide both education in biology and conservation, and also support for the creation of parks and private reserves.

Beyond Costa Rica, scientists in this era were developing new ideas of conservation biology and biodiversity. The latter concept was intimately connected with scientists' and environmentalists' efforts to preserve tropical rainforests from at least 1972 onward.[38] Biodiversity received a formal definition in 1980, and considerable attention and funding from US universities, government agencies and the media after a series of publications and conferences such as the National Forum on Biodiversity.[39] It connected especially well in the 1980s with the "Save the Rainforest" campaigns, backed by various environmental NGOs, including the World Wildlife Fund, Rainforest Alliance and Rainforest Action Network. Building on the international orientation of environmentalism in the 1970s, and through media reports and boycotts of companies whose supply chains were enmeshed with rainforest destruction, these organizations promoted public awareness in the United States and Europe of developing nations' deforestation.[40] These NGO campaigns and media reporting unquestionably increased nonscientists' demand for travel to experience the rainforest in the 1980s, as public perception underwent a transition from considering the region as hot and hostile jungles to rainforests that contained beauty and amazing biodiversity. Ornithology enthusiasts, too, soon followed the scientists and conservationists in expanding their international horizons in an attempt to add to their lists of bird sightings. Various companies began to cater to them after 1960,[41] and local tour operators and private reserve owners in Costa Rica found that birdwatching became one of their first strong market segments.[42]

Scientists and NGO activists were not the only émigrés concerned with preserving nature in Costa Rica. In the early 1960s, Olof Wessberg and Karen Mogensen, a couple who had immigrated to Costa Rica from Sweden in 1954 in search of a natural, tropical paradise, secured funding from international conservation NGOs to protect the Cabo Blanco region of the Nicoya Peninsula. In 1965 this became the first formally protected biological reserve in the country.[43]

Even earlier, in 1951, a group of American Quakers had moved to Costa Rica and begun dairy farming in the remote and sparsely populated mountain community of Monteverde.[44] At the outset, they agreed to set aside a 500-hectare preserve of cloud forest to protect their watershed, and out of inspiration for the area's natural beauty named it the *bosque eterno* (eternal forest). In 1972 a visiting graduate student named George Powell persuaded the TSC to solicit grants to purchase the land and neighboring forests, where incursions by squatters and loggers threatened the habitat of the resplendent quetzal, one of Costa Rica's most notable birds. Holdridge, Hunter and Tosi also sought to cover the costs of protecting the area by generating revenue through visitation – they built a field station for researchers and a visitors' center, and constructed a trail system and camping area. Scientific researchers sometimes volunteered their services in exchange for lodging, and the reserve became so popular with them and their students that it was the subject of a BBC documentary in 1978, which launched Monteverde's career as an ecotourism destination more broadly. Two thousand visitors in 1978 became nearly 7,000 in 1983, and reached a temporary plateau at 50 000 throughout the early 1990s. As a private reserve, Monteverde was able to charge visitors more than the national parks, and could generate enough revenue to pay for its upkeep even before the ecotourism boom.[45]

Holdridge had also bought some land on the Sarapiquí River, north of the capital. In 1968 he agreed to sell the reserve, known as La Selva, to OTS for use as a tropical biology field station, and it was eventually connected by a corridor to the Braulio Carrillo national park.[46] At least 1,600 researchers stayed at La Selva between 1963 and 1988, but they also averaged more than three return trips per visitor, and a sample claimed a high level of influence on colleagues by word-of-mouth recommendations.[47] Although La Selva provided only basic accommodations and permitted only narrowly limited tourist occupancy at a relatively high price,[48] it helped to generate much of the awareness of the potential for nature travel to Costa Rica, which was later directed to Monteverde, the national parks and to commercial ecotourism enterprises.[49] Altogether, "science tourism" generated an estimated US$1 million in revenues in 1976, and a decade later La Selva and OTS alone brought in $1.5 million, or approximately 1.3% of overall tourism spending in the country.[50]

Scientists not only cataloged Costa Rica's biodiversity, promoted conservation, and protected and operated important private reserves but also, in pioneering classes and publications, the American biologist

Kenton Miller of CATIE and his Venezuelan-Costa Rican student Gerardo Budowski articulated the notions of "ecodevelopment" and park-based conservation driven by revenues from responsible nature tourism. Miller and Budowski sought to combat a common attitude within the scientific and conservation communities that biologically valuable forest and marine areas should be cordoned off from human visitation. Instead, they argued in favor of a "symbiotic" relationship between nonextractive land use and nature protection, in which the former would generate revenue and lead to community acceptance of conservation in place of agricultural development. Through their influence on a young graduate student, Mario Boza, these ideas led directly to the national park system and the rise of ecotourism.[51] Boza, inspired by Miller's teaching and a visit to US national parks in 1967, developed a concrete plan for creating a park at Poás Volcano. He then took to Costa Rica's daily newspapers to weigh in on the forestry law under debate in 1969 and to advocate seriously for a Costa Rican park system that would generate revenues from international tourism, much as was done in East Africa.[52]

The Costa Rican legislature passed the Forestry Law in 1969, which envisioned a multiuse approach to the nation's forests embracing conservation, tourism, controlled extraction and research. It explicitly allowed for the creation of the National Parks Department within the agriculture ministry, and the 27-year-old Boza became the head of the new department.[53] Supported by Alvaro Ugalde, then still a student and later Boza's successor, and by influential political figures including Karen Figueres (wife of President Figueres) and later President Daniel Oduber, Boza began a process of declaring protected areas throughout the country and gathering the money to buy the land within them. At the end of the 1980s, under a new leader, Alvaro Umaña, and recognizing the need to include local people in the financial benefits of the parks, the park service shifted from merely nature protection to the idea of sustainable development.[54] Sustainability became a central concern of the Costa Rican government in 1994, when President Figueres explicitly integrated it into the country's development strategy and reformed the forestry law. In the same year, the park service raised entrance fees from $1.50 to $6 for noncitizens to increase funds,[55] and by 1998 the state financed 50 percent of the park system's operating costs while the entrance fees financed 30 percent.[56]

Boza was always more enthusiastic than Ugalde and others about allowing tourism within the parks and using the revenues generated for their conservation.[57] Some believed that the parks should be devoted to nature preservation alone, and looked askance at the perceived over-development around some US national parks. But there were also persistent funding problems, which intensified after 1980 and made the total exclusion of visitors unworkable. The bulk of the government's funds and international aid and donations were devoted to purchasing land within the declared park boundaries, leaving negligible budgets for park infrastructure and security. No lodges or guided tours, and few visitors' centers or trails, were made available anywhere by the park service.[58]

Without national parks, ecotourism in Costa Rica would have been a smaller and more precarious business. The parks were always a significant draw for private tour companies, making it worth investing to operate tours. As one entrepreneur put it in the early 1990s, a major reason why nature tourism was better business in Costa Rica than elsewhere in Central America "was that there were parks here, that there was good reason to believe that the resources would stay protected, so as to justify the investment of time and energy to get the parks known."[59] Nevertheless, without private accommodations and tour companies, few international or even Costa Rican tourists would have visited the parks and paid admission fees. As they had benefited from the work of the scientists, conservationists and park officials who had come before them, an array of environmentally-minded entrepreneurs helped secure those protected areas as well as private lands. The next section turns to these entrepreneurs.

IV ENTREPRENEURIAL PIONEERS

As travel to the parks and to nonprofit private nature reserves such as Monteverde and La Selva began to grow in the mid-1970s, a small number of for-profit nature tourism enterprises appeared as well, often on an informal basis within sharply limited geographic areas. Then, beginning in 1978, several tour operators and private reserve proprietors with strong environmental principles and international connections led the way in creating the commercial market, joined by a wave of other companies after 1985, when the country's recovering economy and reputation for ecotourism began to attract a growing numbers of visitors. These early businesses were started both by Costa Ricans and by expatriates from the United States who had been drawn to Costa Rica in the 1970s.

Regardless of their nationality, the interests and attitudes of many of these entrepreneurs had been shaped by new cultural developments of the late 1960s and early 1970s, including the counterculture, the increasing availability of international travel and adventure in the jet age and the growth of popular environmentalism. The international counterculture, which reached beyond the small bohemian communities of earlier generations to embrace millions of educated, middle-class youths in the 1960s, emphasized the search for personal authenticity, opposition to materialism and the mores of elders and Cold War leaders, and the "unrealized spiritual and ideological demands" of prosperous youth and adults with access to leisure.[60] Many of these desires found expression in international travel and allowed for increased feelings of mobility, independence and cross-cultural understanding, supported institutionally by the growth of youth hostel networks and relaxation of some visa and travel restrictions.[61] They were also reflected in the 1960s environmental movement and the growth of expatriate communities of young Americans and other nationalities who sought to build alternative lifestyles abroad, where they believed conditions were less constricting.[62] The former was propelled not only by popularization of ecological ideas such as Rachel Carson's book *Silent Spring* (1962), but also by the involvement of student protesters and middle-class women who shared countercultural goals of authentic living, communing with nature and opposition to some forms of capitalism.[63] As this section will suggest, ecotourism entrepreneurs – and particularly tour operators – often drew inspiration from these ideas in operating businesses that allowed them to share and promote their values.

Table 7.1 lists the major tourism enterprises in the country that were established for, or converted to, a primary focus on ecotourism between 1975 and the year 1993, which can be regarded as approximately the end of the truly pioneering era and the start of the mainstreaming of ecotourism in the country. There is no claim that the table is fully comprehensive as this section focuses on some of the earliest and most innovative tour operations. It examines how the entrepreneurs who founded them came to their environmental convictions and addressed a set of threats and challenges to expand their businesses, and in the process facilitate the creation of the ecotourism industry.

Early domestic tourism in Costa Rica had long focused on the country's beaches, and so it is perhaps unsurprising that the first internationally oriented nature tour operators had their start along the Caribbean and Pacific coasts. In 1972 the Florida-born tourism entrepreneur Archie Fields established Swiss Travel, which would become one of Costa Rica's largest mainstream and nature tour operators in the 1980s. Fields also bought a wooden cabin that year on the mouth of the Colorado River, which he converted into a tarpon fishing lodge. Not yet a true ecotourism enterprise, the Río Colorado Lodge emphasized its

Table 7.1　Ecotourism enterprises in Costa Rica, 1975–93

Name of enterprise	Founder(s)	Founder's original nationality	First year in ecotourism
Papagayo Excursions	Mary Ruth, Louis Wilson	United States	1975
Caminos de la Selva	Carlos Coles	Costa Rican	1976
Costa Rica Expeditions	Michael Kaye	United States	1978
Tikal Tours	Bary Roberts	Costa Rican	1978
Rara Avis	Amos Bien	United States	1983
Horizontes	Tamara Budowski, Margarita Forero	Costa Rican	1984
Ríos Tropicales	Rafael Gallo, Fernando Esquivel	Salvadoran	1985
Marenco Biological Station	Guillermo and Sergio Miranda	Costa Rican	1985
Selva Verde	Giovanna Holbrook	United States	1985
GeoTur	Sergio Volio	Costa Rican	1985
Savegre Mountain Lodge	Efraín Chacón	Costa Rican	1986
Hacienda Baru	Jack and Diane Ewing	United States	1987
Arenal Observatory Lodge	John Aspinall	Costa Rican	1987
Tiskita	Peter Aspinall	Costa Rican	1987
Hotel Si Como No	Jim Damalas	United States	1993
Lapa Rios Ecolodge	John and Karen Lewis	United States	1993

Source:　Author research.

air-conditioned comforts, but Fields was also involved in marine conservation efforts, offered early nature trips known as "Jungle Tours" and advertised widely to build a celebrity-studded clientele that brought Costa Rica to the attention of international sport-fishing tourists.[64]

On the Pacific coast, too, boating and fishing drew young, counter-cultural US nationals seeking an alternative lifestyle in Costa Rica. Californians David and Cecelia Reid began offering group sightseeing cruises of the coastline and small islands in 1975, despite travel agents' skepticism.[65] In the same year, two young Americans, Louis Wilson and Mary Ruth, first took patrons of the Hotel Tamarindo on boat trips up the Playa Grande estuary and on "turtle tours" to view the large nesting populations of leatherback sea turtles then present near Tamarindo. An informal operation known at first as Papagayo Vagabonds, financed by an heiress friend and designed to support their lifestyle of surfing, fishing and living in harmony with nature, the business was eventually incorporated as Papagayo Excursions. Although this might be regarded as one of the very first truly ecotourist ventures, it faced formidable challenges. As Wilson later pointed out, the local residents and San José travel agents initially mocked the company's prospects. "We were considered to be the fringe," he observed, as the existing tourism industry expected international tourists to be interested in urban sights, but "they didn't realize that what people really wanted to see was nature." The ICT was no better, insisting that nature tours were unlikely to generate any interest.[66]

Nonetheless, Papagayo Excursions began to draw international tourists, especially from the United States, but also Canadians and Europeans, and even managed to expand visits from abroad during the early 1980s amid a recession by marketing their environmentally friendly catch-and-release deep-sea fishing expeditions.[67] The turtle-watching tours remained Papagayo's focus until the second half of the 1980s, when larger companies captured market share, and numerous unlicensed boat tours operated by former turtle-egg poachers lowered both safety and ecological standards.[68] Beginning in 1986, Wilson and the Costa Rican Marianela Pastor worked together to establish a wildlife conservation area at Tamarindo, and they constructed the Hotel Las Tortugas, building in protections for minimal impact on the beaching turtles. It opened to guests in 1991.[69] Ruth continued to run Papagayo, which possessed a seven-boat fleet and employed 18 by 1992, but she had become disillusioned with the possibilities of ecotourism, reflecting on the growing ignorance of the tourists and the damage done by unlicensed ("pirate") operators and overcrowding.[70]

A year after the first turtle-watching trips at Tamarindo, a young Costa Rican nature enthusiast and entrepreneur, Carlos Coles, established the first company in Costa Rica devoted to rainforest tours. Coles had studied biology and hiked the country's coasts and mountains in the early 1970s. He first began putting this familiarity with the land to use in guiding family friends who had come to visit from the United States, and inspired by a friend who had worked in wildlife conservation in Kenya, he decided to create and market tours that emphasized Costa Rica's flora and fauna. His company, Caminos de la Selva, or Jungle Trails, operated only in the dry months from December to April, and took three or four groups on multiweek camping excursions. With Coles as guide and with two other employees, Jungle Trails drew mainly wealthy British tourists who had developed an interest in nature tourism. Coles continued his studies in the other months of the year, and the company did not operate year-round until 1986. Jungle Trails remained small, and although it survived into the 1990s, it employed no more than seven. In fact, between 1978 and 1980, Coles himself worked most of the year as a guide for another travel company, Costa Rica Expeditions, which was engaged in promoting a new form of nature tourisms.[71]

Michael Kaye founded Costa Rica Expeditions in 1978 as a whitewater rafting company, and quickly developed his business into the largest ecologically oriented nature tourism enterprise in Costa Rica. Kaye had been raised in Manhattan, New York, but was devoted to the outdoors, and began whitewater rafting in California in the early 1960s.[72] At first working as a road manager for 1960s music bands,[73] Kaye and a partner then established a successful low-cost, high-volume rafting company in California called Mother Lode. After three years, Kaye sold his shares and subsequently traveled to Central America to explore new rafting opportunities in the mid-1970s.[74] There he met a Salvadoran woman who became his wife, and the couple found themselves drawn to Costa Rica by its political stability, openness and potential as a rafting destination.

When Kaye established Costa Rica Expeditions shortly thereafter, he partnered with a Costa Rican citizen in order to satisfy the governmental licensing requirement, eventually buying out this nominal partner when he himself became a Costa Rican citizen. He also hired a Salvadoran, Rafael Gallo, as an engineer and river guide. Kaye, Gallo, Coles and others scouted rivers around Costa Rica and led rafting parties. But Kaye recognized that the high-volume model he had used in California would not be workable in a country where rafting was as yet largely unknown. Using his expatriate status to his advantage, Kaye focused instead on drawing smaller numbers of North American tourists to an unfamiliar but highly promising destination and providing them premium service. He later noted that he "didn't have enough cultural knowledge, even with all the time in Latin America, to sell to this market" in the early years.[75] Many local residents were also underserved owing to the firm's emphasis on small numbers and premium pricing. This left room for Gallo to leave Kaye's operation amicably in 1985 to start his own ecologically sensitive rafting enterprise, Ríos Tropicales, with partner Fernando Esquivel, to focus more on the domestic market.[76]

By 1985 Costa Rica Expeditions was much more than a rafting company. Kaye had quickly found that the US and Canadian tourists he brought in wanted to see more of Costa Rica after several days' rafting. He had observed the potential for "natural history tours," or scientifically guided forest hikes, when taking groups to cloud forests in Guatemala in the mid-1970s, and saw them as an opportunity for new business. The risks such tours had faced in Guatemala – he had once scheduled a tour to an area that turned out to have been unexpectedly clear-cut – were obviated by Costa Rica's system of parks and private reserves. In 1979 he hired Jim Lewis, a US biologist who had been consulting with the TSC, to become a guide and director of natural history tours. By 1980 Kaye's company offered tours to the Santa Rosa, Corcovado, Chirripó, Tortuguero and Isla de Coco parks,[77] and by 1988 its staff of 50 included naturalists, ornithologists, entomologists, horticulturalists and other trained guides.[78]

Costa Rica Expeditions thus brought increased revenue to the parks and provided the guiding and accommodations services that the park service could not afford to budget. As demand grew rapidly, Kaye found it difficult to provide satisfactory accommodations for his tour groups owing to the lack of control over the service standards of local lodges. Consequently, when the opportunity arose to buy a hotel in Tortuguero where Costa Rica Expeditions had been sending clients, Kaye arranged a loan from a US-backed private bank and bought the hotel in 1986.[79] Eventually the company vertically integrated by purchasing several other properties, including building a hotel in Monteverde in 1991 to guarantee lodging at the popular destination during the ecotourism boom.[80] Kaye intended to invest in long-term operations in Costa Rica, rather than to repatriate his profits to the United States, and the purchase of hotels was one step in that direction.[81]

By 1991 some 75 percent of Kaye's 20 000 annual clients came to Costa Rica for natural history ecotours, spending an average of US$148 per day in the country.[82] In 1994 his company had 180 employees, the great majority of them Costa Ricans.[83] It continued to grow throughout the 1990s, taking advantage of the new opportunities for direct marketing by becoming a partner in one of Costa Rica's first Internet service providers in 1994.[84] Although it was widely regarded as a green company and Kaye became involved with TIES, local chapters of environmental NGOs occasionally criticized Costa Rica Expeditions for its relatively high volume. On one occasion, the Rainforest Alliance ecotourism project even refused to rate the company in its first green travel certification program (discussed below) over a difference of opinion about the "social" component of responsible ecotourism.[85]

Nonetheless, Kaye's early environmentalism, which was at first aesthetically and then ecologically motivated, had strongly influenced his view of how nature tourism should be conducted. He had spent significant time at Yosemite National Park, and shared the growing countercultural consciousness that environmental problems required active protest and opposition. He became involved with Martin Litton, a fellow rafter, Sierra Club board member and important figure in environmentalist circles. Kaye particularly came to share Litton's longstanding opposition to river dams for their destruction of riparian ecology and natural beauty, despite the highly positive common opinion of hydroelectric projects at that time. He opposed several dams on California rivers, but the protests merely delayed construction, which was the major factor prompting Kaye to sell his shares in Mother Lode and leave the state. Not for the last time, Kaye's environmental views and his business interest in protecting the rivers for rafting were aligned.[86] In a 1980 interview, after moving to Costa Rica, Kaye said his vision of the industry was that "tourism should contribute to, rather than exploit [the land]."[87] He later argued explicitly that operating in an environmentally and culturally sensitive way made both business sense and ethical sense. Costa Rica Expeditions hired local people as guides and installed solar-powered heaters and sound waste treatment systems, such as biodigesters, at its properties.[88] Over industry opposition, the company argued that park fees should be raised in the 1990s to increase funds for conservation, and it donated more than US$100 000 to the parks and NGOs for environmental protection, which Kaye regarded as "money well spent, keeping our product attractive and worthwhile."[89]

Not long after Costa Rica Expeditions diversified from rafting into ecotourism, it was joined by other travel companies run by Costa Ricans with international connections. As Kaye led his first rafting groups in 1978, the 28-year-old Costa Rican Bary Roberts was pondering how to expand inbound tourism without generating destructive overdevelopment. Roberts was the son and grandson of Protestant missionaries with roots in Canada, and he had discovered a passion for travel in North America, Africa and Europe during the 1960s. As a teenager, he had shared the counterculture's wanderlust to the degree that he had hitchhiked from Costa Rica to Los Angeles, and sought, as he remarked, to be "open to the world." While completing his degree in economics at the University of Costa Rica at the beginning of the 1970s, he took a position with Pan Am but also cultivated a farm. He enjoyed working in the travel industry, the international orientation of which aligned with his personal goals and values, and when given the opportunity in 1975 to sell his farm in exchange for a small existing travel agency known as Tikal Tours, he took it.[90]

At the time, Tikal's principal business involved ticketing Costa Rican outbound tourists and packaged bus tours to sights elsewhere in Central America, but Roberts sought to bring more international visitors to Costa Rica. He had a cautionary experience in 1976, however, when a trip to the Spanish town of Sitges revealed the damage caused by intensive beach tourism in the decade since his first visit there. Motivated by his family's Christian vision of stewardship and by his friendship with Mario Boza and Alvaro Ugalde, Roberts was determined to avoid creating a new Sitges in Costa Rica. Through his stepbrother, who worked in the government, he arranged a meeting in 1978 with Maurice Strong, the Canadian businessman and organizer of the first UN conference on the environment in Stockholm in 1972, who was visiting Costa Rica.[91] Strong had bought some beachfront property on the Caribbean coast, which he would later develop into a resort, creating a minor controversy during the 1992 UN Earth Summit in Rio de Janeiro.[92] At the time of his meeting with Roberts in 1978, Strong sought to preserve the property from destruction and had incorporated a company to hold the land, which he named *Ecodesarrollos S.A.* (Eco-Development). Roberts impressed Strong with his vision of increasing inbound tourism without causing cultural or environmental damage; to encourage the younger man, Strong offered him an investment equal to a quarter of the value of the company. The Canadian would serve as a silent partner until Roberts reacquired the shares from Ecodesarrollos in 1992.[93]

Buoyed by this investment and by what he learned from Strong about environmentally friendly development, Roberts weathered the threats to tourism from the recession and Central American instability of the early 1980s. At Strong's suggestion, he began to explore the idea of "eco-logical tourism" for inbound tourists.[94] "There was a lot that could be done that was not being done, particularly in the way of educating the clients themselves, and creating a positive impact on the [natural] areas instead of destroying them like most tourist centers," Roberts reflected in 1992.[95] He attempted to develop nature tourism packages for inter-national clients, and taking a cue from the name of Strong's enterprise, Tikal was the first travel company to use the word "ecotourism" in Costa Rica. Indeed, Roberts registered the term as a trademark in 1985, as the general concept was becoming popular. The trademark led to controversy with other tour operators and TIES, who regarded it as an attempt to co-opt a common enterprise, while Roberts argued that it was a way to protect the concept from being watered down by widespread use.[96]

Roberts also faced skepticism from some competitors and environmental organizations over his other innovation during the mid-1980s: the introduction of ecotourism itineraries to large chartered tours that had previously been focused on beaches and urban sights. For several years, the Smithsonian Institution, National Geographic, the World Wildlife Fund, the Audubon Society and numerous US universities had brought small groups of people to Costa Rica; generated business for Tikal, Costa Rica Expeditions and other firms; and subsequently advertised Costa Rica's natural wonders in their magazines and television programs.[97] "But," noted Roberts, "the great majority of the people are not getting to see" what the environmental organizations' members saw. He sought to create a "mass production [form of] tourism that could present the natural resources, but at the same time be a way of funding and protecting [them], and be a way of raising consciousness of the ecological problems."[98]

In 1986 Roberts convinced the Canadian wholesaler Fiesta Wayfarers Holidays Ltd., which at the time brought 13 000 clients to Costa Rica annually on chartered flights, to include ecotours operated by Tikal in its itineraries. The following year, Tikal managed about a third of Fiesta's business in Costa Rica, providing its own guides and buses but subcontracting hotels. Roberts named the tours "eco-safaris," and offered four throughout the country, including one devoted to rafting and horseback riding. The clientele was quite different from those traditionally attracted to ecotourism: Roberts occasionally had to explain that there would be no elephant sightings on a Costa Rican ecosafari. They expected greater comfort, and Roberts eventually built his own ecolodge at Lago Coter in order to exert greater control over the quality of the experience while maintaining ecological standards. At first, Tikal's competitors saw Roberts's approach as conceding too much to a purely "commercial" form of ecotourism, and he was not able to generate as much new business from environmental groups as he had hoped.[99] As ecotourism grew in the 1990s, this view of Tikal began to change even as the company drew ever-larger numbers of tourists from Canada, the United States and Germany, and competitors would later view Roberts's enterprise as a genuine green company rather than a "greenwasher."[100]

A different path to leadership in the ecotourism industry was traced by Tamara Budowski and Margarita Forero. The two women, both aged 24, established Horizontes Nature Tours in 1984. Budowski was the daughter of the forest biologist Gerardo Budowski and a Panamanian mother, and Forero's grandparents were Colombian and German immigrants to Costa Rica.[101] When young, Budowski had lived in Berkeley, California, as well as in France and Switzerland; changing schools and languages with such frequency led her to feel "more a citizen of the world than a citizen of any country" and to appreciate the emphasis on cross-cultural harmony and understanding that marked the 1960s counterculture. She later described herself as "very much influenced" by the counterculture, the peace movement and the environmental movement of that era.[102] Her father's work also exposed her from an early age to biological and ecological studies, and particularly to the developing idea of biodiversity, as well as to the connected normative drive to protect threatened natural environments, all of which she later pursued at college. Her childhood was, moreover, marked by prolonged and repeated international nature travel.[103] She later recalled that while abroad "we would go to national parks in different areas of the world, like northern Africa or Kenya, Tanzania, Sri Lanka, [and] Latin America. So I grew up, in a way, doing ecotourism."[104] Both Budowski and Forero broke with family expectations in order to work in the travel business. They met and became friends at the technical college in Cartago, which offered a new degree program in tourism; they camped in the Costa Rican national parks and then pursued further business training abroad. Budowski studied marketing in Miami, Florida, where she was alerted to the problems of mass tourism development, and Forero specialized in tourism administration at Salzburg, Austria.[105]

Upon their return to Costa Rica, Budowski worked at the student travel organization OTEC for a year, while she and Forero traveled to various Costa Rican parks, enjoying the adventure of backpacking and throughout 1983 planning the opening of their own conservation-oriented travel company.[106] Lacking capital, they secured an outbound-only license and initially focused on ticket sales as they continued to research and explore destinations for future inbound clients.[107] Throughout 1984 and 1985, they built their capital and reputation, and developed an alliance with Sergio Miranda, a family friend of Forero, who was beginning to develop the Marenco private reserve near Corcovado National Park (discussed below). This arrangement, and Miranda's financial resources, allowed Budowski and Forero to devote themselves to "leading naturalists to the country's most attractive wildernesses," while the Miranda family gained a channel through which to market Marenco.[108] As Budowski later reflected, "They didn't have the travel knowhow, but they had financial resources and they had a hotel. We had the knowhow – we didn't have money, and we didn't have other assets, and it seemed like the perfect alliance ... And we created Horizontes together."[109] In 1986 Horizontes began offering nature tours of the national parks and Monteverde to the wholesale travel trade, primarily in the United States.[110]

In its first decade, Horizontes was heavily reliant on group business from the United States and Canada, creating tours for conservation and educational organizations. Budowski estimated that such groups made up about 75 percent of their business in 1992, at which time Horizontes had expanded to employ 28 full-time staff, a majority of them women. The attraction for the conservation organizations was not only the company's well-scouted destinations and intimate knowledge of Costa Rican business customs, which allowed for minimal disruptions, but also its commitment to environmentalism. Horizontes donated to numerous local causes, including the national zoo, as well as scientific and conservation organizations, including the TSC, OTS, Caribbean Conservation Corporation (CCC) and Centro de Estudios Ambientales. It offered a free training course to 40 guides from all companies to improve the level of biological and ecological knowledge passed on to tourists.[111] In 1992 it combined with Costa Rica Expeditions to establish a US $25 000 fund to meet some of the needs of park service personnel as a way of helping ensure the parks' continuing viability. Like Kaye, Budowski publicly argued in the early 1990s that environmental sensitivity and the protection of nature from overdevelopment was simply good business.[112]

In the 1980s and 1990s, Budowski saw private business and the nonprofit scientific organizations such as the TSC and OTS building the new ecotourism industry largely in the face of indifference from the government, especially the ICT.[113] She argued that for the first decade of ecotourism, "it was private enterprise (hotels, lodges, travel agencies) that got behind it, both nationally and internationally, using advertising and such public relations tools as promotional trips to attract attention to Costa Rica's natural riches," and she particularly credited the airline LACSA.[114] Although she later interpreted this positive attitude toward the private sector as a function of 1980s "yuppie" culture, she and Forero also tried to cultivate a company culture that prioritized values such as sustainability, philanthropy and trust, and thus had much in common with the values they detected in their clients.[115] Budowski observed at the 1988 conference of the International Union for the Conservation of Nature that the idea of ecotourism arose from the "search for profound and enriching experiences that characterized the decade of the sixties," which came especially to embrace "outdoor activities" in the 1970s and health, natural foods and exercise in the 1980s.[116]

In short, tour operators such as Papagayo Excursions, Caminos de la Selva, Costa Rica Expeditions, Tikal, Horizontes and Sergio Volio's GeoTur were major actors in the creation of Costa Rican ecotourism. Whether their founders were Costa Rican or American, they sought to incorporate the values they had drawn from the countercultural, spiritual or environmentalist ideas and experiences of their youth into the guiding purposes of their firms. They also possessed international connections that allowed them to market effectively to potential North American and European consumers interested in the fate of the rainforests and wildlife. Their businesses in turn brought the national parks much-needed funding through an ever-increasing stream of such international visitors.

V ECOLODGES AND PRIVATE RESERVES

None of the tour companies could provide sufficient lodging for guests in all of their areas of operation. They relied, as a result, on the growth of private reserves and ecolodges to house their clients and supplement trips to national parks. Private reserves in turn and on their own drew many ecotourists to the country; and as they directly conserved natural areas outside of the national parks, they often served as "buffer zones" to protect the territorial integrity of the latter. These reserves and ecolodges were often connected with scientific research, but frequently evolved to offer their own tours of their private land and local areas, especially when in the vicinity of national parks. Many such reserves opened to the public at the same moment, between 1986 and 1987.[117]

The first of these concerted efforts to establish a for-profit reserve in order to protect a local area was that of the US biologist Amos Bien.[118] Bien had studied biology at the University of Chicago, where he had initiated a program of community recycling in the early 1970s. Inspired by a course in tropical botany that had introduced him to the deforestation crisis, he later enrolled in a graduate program that brought him to Costa Rica through OTS. While studying at La Selva, Bien began looking for a way to align the incentive to preserve the rainforest with continued economic development.[119] In April 1983 he decided to open the Rara Avis Lodge as an experiment to prove that intact rainforest could be more profitable than clear-cut land. He formed a Costa Rican corporation, bought a 485-hectare property in 1986 with both bank loans and equity capital, and developed rudimentary accommodations in a former prison building on the grounds. Bien sourced food and other products locally, and employed mostly community residents – 14 full-time and 4 part-time in 1992 – and gave them an equity stake in the business after two years' employment.[120] Rara Avis was estimated to have brought around $80,000 a year to the neighboring town of Horquetas in 1991.[121]

Bien welcomed this involvement by the local community because he felt that "if the chainsaw wielders were not part of the project, then it would never work." He brought in students and birdwatchers as guests beginning in 1986; built a lodge that could house 32 in 1989; and added running water, but never electricity, outside the lodge's common space. Rara Avis attracted guests from the United States, Canada, Germany, Switzerland, the Netherlands and Scandinavia throughout the late 1980s and 1990s; provided discounts to draw Costa Ricans; and was an early convert to Internet marketing in 1995. It offered guided hikes, bird-watching, a small orchid garden and butterfly farm, and through the assistance of biologist Don Perry of OTS, a climbing cable-car system with platform viewing opportunities at the top of the canopy.[122] Perry received the income for his device, but it served as a marketing tool to put Rara Avis on the map from the late 1980s until 1994, when Perry relocated the system to a more accessible site than Bien's remote lodge, and started a larger, $2 million eco-friendly educational enterprise under the name "Rainforest Aerial Tram."[123] Without Perry's contraption, guest numbers at Rara Avis peaked in 1996 and subsequently fell modestly. Nevertheless, the continued survival of the enterprise as a business alongside its success in conserving the property bore out Bien's eco-tourism hypothesis.

As Bien was raising capital to buy the original Rara Avis property in 1985, the Costa Rican Miranda family was exploring the possibility of bringing tourists to their remote landholdings on the Osa Peninsula. Guillermo Miranda had bought 400 hectares of primary forest from the government in 1974, intending to start a cattle ranch. He cleared three or four hectares before coming to the conclusion that the property and its wildlife were too beautiful and unique to destroy.[124] Corcovado National Park was established bordering their property in the following year, and when the Mirandas traveled from San José to visit it in the late 1970s and early 1980s, they often encountered biologists seeking transportation and lodging in the area of the park. Recognizing an unserved market, they overcame their doubts about the viability of a business in such a remote location and decided to establish Marenco Biological Station. The name was chosen so as to attract biologists seeking to work in Corcovado or the nearby Isla de Caño National Park, and groups of students doing fieldwork for tropical biology courses.[125]

Nevertheless, through the connection with Horizontes that Guillermo Miranda's son Sergio developed in the mid-1980s, the Mirandas began to attract nonacademic American clients interested in ecology. Starting with small groups of 55- to 65-year-old professionals in lodgings with eight bedrooms and shared bathrooms,[126] Marenco saw a major increase in tourist visitation beginning in 1988, and by 1992 they could offer 25 separate rooms, a main lodge building with a restaurant and shop.[127] In these years, they received bookings through Horizontes but also marketed both the region and their lodge at trade shows, and advertised in US magazines until the sudden popularity of Costa Rica made advertising an unnecessary expense.[128] The alliance between Horizontes and Marenco was an easy one, as both were committed to the environmental cause. The Mirandas saw providing buffer-zone protection for Corcovado as one of the major purposes of their enterprise, offered three regular nature excursions on their reserve and the nearby parks, and sought to include as many local residents as possible among their 60 to 70 high-season employees. The family determined that it would be better to offer more luxurious accommodations than to expand the footprint of their property, which remained at 25 rooms in 2001, despite demand from visiting cruise ships.[129]

Inland to the north, in the quetzal-filled cloud forest of San Gerardo de Dota, the Chacón family also perceived an opportunity brought about by visiting biologists. Efraín Chacón and a group of hunting companions had first explored the Río Savegre Valley in 1954, when it was untouched primary forest. They constructed a dirt trail to the Pan-American High-way in 1961, and Chacón brought his family to build a house and to farm and fish for trout.[130] The Chacóns became accustomed to feeding visiting fishermen, and in 1971 they built a small cabin for guests, shortly followed by two more. Although they could not advertise, word spread and tourism gradually supplanted agricultural pursuits as their primary business. In 1978 two researchers from Harvard University were impressed by the profusion of quetzals in the area, published photographs in the United States, and the Chacóns began to host increasing numbers of American birdwatchers. They formally incorporated their business, and registered with the ICT under the name *Albergue de Montaña Savegre* (Savegre Mountain Inn) in 1980.[131]

Two years later, Efraín Chacón came to an agreement with a US university to build a field station on the property for visiting biologists and students.[132] When the travel companies began searching for destin-ations at this time, they contacted the Chacóns, who provided accommo-dations for Costa Rica Expeditions, Horizontes and Caminos de la Selva, among others.[133] The strong interest of the visitors and conversations with biologists caused the Chacóns to see their lands through an environmentalist lens for the first time. Efraín, who originally had to live in a cave when settling the area, adapted very quickly to the conserva-tionist convictions expressed by foreign guests, who had never known a comparable level of need. He recognized that ecologically sound tourism could be beneficial on several fronts. "If we know how to conserve the forests, and work with the least impact possible," he later remarked, Savegre would maintain both its natural resources and its visitors.[134]

Another of the first ecolodges was also the work of individuals who had no initial commitment to conservation. The American Jack Ewing arrived in Costa Rica in 1970 to work in the cattle business, was soon joined by his wife Diane, and by 1976 came to manage a ranch for a US-based investor group. Called Hacienda Baru, it was a 330-hectare property with three kilometers of beachfront on the Pacific Ocean.[135] Ewing became a partner with a one-seventh interest in the land in the late 1970s,[136] and engaged first in ranching and then farming until 1982. While living on the property, he grew increasingly interested in the surrounding primary forest, and noticed how modern agriculture led the plant life and wildlife to become "out of balance."[137] He was moved by the killing of a beautiful ocelot and ended hunting on the property, which gave him a reputation as an environmentalist. "And at some point – I don't remember exactly when – I guess I just stepped into the role," he later reflected. He and Diane joined the Costa Rican conservation organization known as ASCONA, and contacted OTS to seek reforestation advice.[138]

Beginning in 1982, the Ewings secured the region's first zoning plan to protect the property, beachfront and ecologically sensitive areas such as mangroves. Their neighbors' interest in beachfront tourism led them at first to look askance at tourism in general.[139] After some acquaintances insisted on paying for a guided hike in 1987, the couple began to discuss the idea of running rainforest tours for profit. Both local property owners and the Ewings' own partners thought the idea ridiculous,[140] but made no objection. Hacienda Baru first catered to foreign tourists in 1988, bringing in US$4,500 in its third year and becoming profitable in 1991.[141]

Hacienda Baru's commercial success helped change the local property owners' attitudes toward conservation, and several sought to start their own ecotourism businesses.[142] Expatriate US businessman Steve Stroud bought out the other investors of Hacienda Baru and provided further capital for ecotourism development. The Ewings added four new cabins in 1994 for visitors wishing to stay overnight. Jack Ewing continued to offer guided rainforest tours, horseback riding and a "Night in the Jungle" tour with camping on a raised platform.[143] He added a canopy tour that involved climbing into the treetops in 1993 and a zip-line tour in 2000. Stroud and the Ewings secured National Wildlife Refuge status for the property in 1995, further improving its reputation as an ecotourism destination, and drew a steady stream of US and especially European visitors after the advent of Internet marketing.[144] "It's not going to make us rich," Jack Ewing remarked in 1992, but by providing access to a sizeable private rainforest to biologists, students and limited numbers of tourists, "we can guarantee the people something they can't get in the national parks. We can guarantee them that they're not going to see anybody else when they're in there."[145]

Rara Avis, Marenco, Savegre, Hacienda Baru and equivalent reserves and lodges provided the accommodations necessary for ecotourists who visited nearby parks, increasing the flow of travelers to Costa Rica while remaining devoted to environmental sustainability. The entrepreneurs who converted these businesses to ecotourism were, on balance, motivated less by countercultural and environmentalist values or enthusiasm for travel (as compared to their tour operator colleagues) and more by the importation of American biological and ecological scholarship and the need to serve visiting scientists, birdwatchers and subsequently broader categories of ecotourists. They did, however, adopt the conservation orientation of most visiting naturalists, and became proud of the fact that their businesses directly protected valuable or representative lands and supported some scientific research.

VI ECONOMIC AND SOCIAL OUTCOMES

Ecotourism delivered significant economic and environmental benefits to Costa Rica. Tourism became Costa Rica's principal export and source of foreign exchange in 1993, surpassing bananas, and remained so apart from a few years in which it was outpaced by microchip production from an Intel plant.[146] The category was estimated to represent a cumulative investment of nearly US$1 billion from 1986 to 1998, and it employed 10 percent of Costa Ricans in 2000,[147] even though large majorities of the nation's tourism businesses remained small in scale and located in rural areas.[148] Even as tourism grew, public and private parks and reserves together protected over a quarter of Costa Rica's land area.[149] A virtuous circle of investment and new policies played a role in the recovery of Costa Rica's forests, which had been restored to cover more than 40 percent of the country's land area by 2002.[150] The cohort of small but successful entrepreneurs in ecotourism exercised a strong demonstration effect, proving to skeptics in government and the agricultural sector that nature preservation could be commercially viable.

Outcomes were not, however, wholly positive. Conventional tourism flourished alongside ecotourism. There was continued growth of large international hotel chains in the country.[151] Unsustainable resort projects continued to threaten the beaches of Guanacaste and elsewhere. The sudden interest in the environment that swept the country led to an overuse of the terminology of ecology, providing incentives to engage in "greenwashing," or making false, opportunistic claims of environmental benefits. In terms of Richard Butler's Tourism Area Life Cycle model, Costa Rica as a destination had passed from the "exploration" and "involvement" stages, in which the "science tourists" and committed entrepreneurs had shaped the industry, into the "development" stage of large-scale corporate and governmental involvement. It thereby risked the possibility that the new entrants to the market, driven solely by profit or by the desire to increase national tourism revenues, would overdevelop the industry, jeopardizing the country's natural resources and the position of the pioneering firms.[152] Even for entrepreneurs whose environmental convictions were integrated into their companies' principles, the influx of new and less well-informed tourists created challenges in providing good service and concerns about the potential damage caused by an increase in scale.

Competing for inexperienced international customers with enterprises that offered green rhetoric but little substance was fraught with risks for the ecotourism pioneers. Many individuals both inside and outside of the industry consequently became interested in rating and certification schemes in the 1990s. Richard Holland and Chris Wille, of the Rainforest Alliance, developed voluntary guidelines for ecotourism enterprises in Costa Rica, and distributed them in 1990 at the country's annual tourism trade show, Expotour, whose theme that year was ecotourism. The guidelines consisted of a code of responsible tourist conduct with a commitment to environmental education, and company compliance was to be monitored by student volunteers in exchange for publication in a "recommended" list.[153] Beatrice Blake and Anne Becher, the authors of *The New Key to Costa Rica*, the most influential early English-language guidebook to the country from the 1970s to the 1990s, also decided to rate accommodations on their success in achieving sustainability. After conducting surveys for the 1992 and 1994 editions, they listed hotels and lodges that received passing scores on environmental management and social engagement as sustainable accommodations, and subsequently adopted a three-tiered rating system for those listed in the *New Key*.[154] Several other systems appeared under the aegis of organizations located outside of Costa Rica, including the International Youth Hostel Federation (1991–94) and the International Ecotourism Society (1993–95).[155]

The most important effort at developing standards and certification for sustainable tourism in the country came in the mid-1990s through a cooperative effort between the ICT, the industry and NGOs. By 1992 the ICT was considering establishing its own certification system, first known as *Sello Verde* (Green Seal). The Certification for Sustainable Tourism (CST) was developed from 1994 to 1997 by ICT officials Marco

Picado and Rodolfo Lizano, Bary Roberts, who had become vice president of the ICT under the new government in 1994, Lawrence Pratt, from the Central American Institute for Business Administration and Alfio Piva, of the National Biodiversity Institute. The first version of CST was made available for hotels in 1997 and for tour operators in 2001, and it offered on-site inspections by accredited auditors to verify performance in such areas as water and energy consumption, emissions, waste management, effect on flora and fauna and impact on the local community. By 2001, more than 100 hotels had applied for CST certification.[156]

Despite its popularity, CST was also criticized. Roberts, Pratt, Piva and others were disappointed when a change of government led the ICT to take full ownership of the CST, closing out a continued partnership with the business and environmental NGO communities.[157] Beatrice Blake, and some small and mid-size tourism entrepreneurs, complained that the CST's requirements were unnecessarily expensive and time-consuming, and assisted larger companies at the expense of the more innovative smaller ones.[158] These criticisms were indicative of some of the challenges of codifying what sustainable tourism actually meant, and more broadly of the incentive for certification schemes that sought to be widely adopted and to set metrics at levels that many participants had a realistic chance of meeting. The same issues bedeviled certification of many green industries, from organic wine to building and construction.[159]

The new wave of tourists who were the intended beneficiaries of the CST and other certification systems included demographics that had not ventured to Costa Rica in prior years. They brought the opportunity to extend the educational mission of ecotourism, but there were also trade-offs. In the 1990s, so-called "soft" nature tourists included those interested in nature but also seeking comfortable accommodations, and those who traveled to Costa Rica because it had become fashionable but had little interest in nature beyond beaches. The former, especially, created opportunities for boutique hotels and luxury ecolodges, which were quite different in character from early rustic lodges but equally committed to environmental principles.

Among the most innovative and architecturally dramatic were the Lapa Rios Ecolodge, established by Karen and John Lewis,[160] and Hotel Si Como No, owned by Jim Damalas, both of which opened in 1993 after cooperation between American expatriates and Costa Rican architects, followed a year later by Hotel Punta Islita. The entrepreneurs behind these hotels had much in common with the earlier ecolodge pioneers. For instance, Damalas was a Californian and member of the Sierra Club who had been visiting Costa Rica periodically since 1974. He worked in

Hollywood but also maintained a farm near Manuel Antonio National Park, and had a strong interest in landscape architecture. Making use of the tax incentives provided by the 1985 tourism law, he decided to build a hotel that would fit into the landscape while providing an impressive vista for his guests to replicate the experience he had had when visiting the property for the first time in the 1970s. In 1992 Damalas and architects Ronald Zurcher and Jaime Rouillon began constructing villas along the property's hillside overlooking the Pacific coast, removing no trees and retaining corridors for the movement of monkeys and other animals while substituting natural airflow for energy-consuming air conditioning. The hotel also provided easy access to Manuel Antonio National Park, generating revenue for the park service, and Damalas insisted on keeping the villas free of television sets, air conditioners, and noxious chemicals and detergents.[161]

The green boutique hotels established by Damalas and the Lewises were designed to appeal to "soft" ecotourists – principally couples at Lapa Rios and families at Si Como No – but still aimed to promote education and rainforest tours nearby. With the advent of the worldwide web during the 1990s, new booking travel options opened up, but the challenge for such businesses was to remain committed to sustainability even as online comparison shopping sites focused primarily on price and tourists displayed decreasing interest in environmental quality.[162] Even the most ecologically sensitive international tourists still arrived by air, with all of the associated problems of burning fossil fuels.

Tour operators shared growing skepticism about what could be achieved. Mary Ruth of Papagayo Excursions reflected as early as 1992: "What we started off to do, which was [based on] a love of Tamarindo and the nature, and the beauty – it has definitely been exploited and I have had to reevaluate how I feel about it because you can't stop it."[163] By the early 2000s, Tamara Budowski took the lack of interest of the new ecotourists, the building of golf courses, the polluting practices of cruise ships and the commercialized killing of sharks and other animals as signs that "despite all the efforts," ecotourism "wasn't working." She continued to run her business until 2008, but found herself troubled by it and retired to seek new horizons in esoteric religion and the global ecovillage movement.[164] Michael Kaye, too, saw no sign of client interest in the sustainability practices of tour operators or hotels unless the client was already seriously engaged in environmental causes. Tourists were "happy to get outraged if they think you are doing something wrong," but their actual purchasing patterns and company reviews reflected no desire to put sustainability at a level with price or comfort. Even the international bodies that singled out particular firms for environmental awards –

including Costa Rica Expeditions – operated on the basis of personal connections rather than merit, he concluded.[165] While the multiple gains from ecotourism were evident, by the early twenty-first century the trade-offs and limitations had also become clear.

VII CONCLUSIONS

By 2002, when the UN declared the "International Year of Ecotourism," Costa Rican ecotourism was an impressive success held up as a world-wide model. The country had been rebranded as a natural paradise. The category raised employment and generated considerable income flows.

This chapter has argued that the ecotourism cluster in Costa Rica was a co-creation of the public, private and tertiary sectors. Forest and wildlife biologists and other students of ecosystems and biodiversity were vital at the start of the process, as were national and international conservation NGOs. Without the scientists' and conservationists' work, little would have been known about Costa Rica's rainforests and their denizens, few if any national parks would have been created, and little international interest would have arisen for trekking through steamy tropical jungles before they disappeared in the name of progress.

The private sector was also pivotal. Without entrepreneurship, much of it expatriate, the underfunded park service and NGOs alone would not have been able to bring sufficient numbers of tourists to Costa Rica to contribute to the maintenance of the parks. Multiple small-scale entre-preneurs helped ensure that formally protected areas remained sustain-able parks and reserves, by providing revenues, education in conservation to tourists, community development and jobs, international demand for tourist travel and self-regulation to ensure that tourism was a net benefit to the nation's forests and wildlife. Although the category was highly fragmented, and spread over different locations, clustering within the country created positive externalities for new entrepreneurs to enter the industry, who could also learn from knowledge spillovers. The perceived commercial viability of many ventures reinforced the case to policy makers and others that forests and wildlife could be worth more when preserved than when used for ranching or farming.

Many of the original ecotourism entrepreneurs were not born in Costa Rica. They were often expatriate Americans who came to the country in search either of biological riches to study or a peaceful society to live in. They brought ecological ideas, whether at the level of academic biology or environmentalist convictions, and together with Costa Rican biologists and environmentalists helped to spread these ideas widely. Costa Rica's stability and openness to foreigners allowed these entrepreneurs as well as Costa Rican nationals to start the businesses that created the industry.

At the same time, the creation of the national image of a natural paradise enabled many businesses that were not environmentally sustainable to free-ride on the growing demand for ecotourism. In this regard, although the country's emergent national image was a huge positive for green businesses compared to the case of New Zealand, discussed in Chapter 5, it also carried potential downsides. Mass tourism has continued to grow, particularly on the beaches of Guanacaste. Greenwashing constitutes a serious threat to principled ecotourism businesses. Even the latter faced the dilemma that arose when they expanded the scale of their operations in the 1990s beyond the small number of already committed ecotourists. By 2000 some of the original ecotourism entrepreneurs were concluding that they could not alter the nature of tourism entirely. They were left with preserving their own forests and wildlife, maintaining a high level of sustainability in their own operations, and hoping to convey their message one tourist at a time.

NOTES

* The chapter appeared in an earlier version as Jones, Geoffrey and Andrew Spadafora, "Entrepreneurs and the Co-creation of Ecotourism in Costa Rica," *Harvard Business School Working Paper* 16-136 (August 30, 2013). A shorter version of that paper was published as Jones, Geoffrey and Andrew Spadafora (2016), "Creating Eco-tourism in Costa Rica, 1970–2000," *Enterprise & Society*, **18**, (1), 146–83. Many thanks are due to Laura Alfaro, René Castro, Andrew Popp and Megan Epler Wood for insightful comments on earlier drafts.

1. For 1970, see Weaver, *Ecotourism*, 84; for 2000, see Capitán, *Costa Rica*, 255.
2. Honey, *Ecotourism*, 6–10, 15–16.
3. Jones, *Profits*, 151–61.
4. Gámez and Obando, "La Biodiversidad," 179.
5. Deshazo, "Linking," 253. The survey was conducted in 1997.
6. Inman, "Tourism," 110.
7. Honey, *Ecotourism*, 160.
8. Independent Traveler, "Top".
9. Fournier, *Desarrollo*; Wallace, *Quetzal*; Evans, *Green*.
10. Honey, *Ecotourism*, 160; Steinberg, *Environmental*, 150.
11. Weaver, *Ecotourism*, 81.
12. Gámez and Obando, "La Biodiversidad," 151. The rate dropped to an average of 43 000 hectares annually in the 1980s, to 13 000 hectares in 1993, and to 3 000 hectares in 2000.
13. Evans, *Green*, 40.
14. Marín Hernández and Viales Hurtado, "Turismo y ambiente," 185; Honey, *Ecotourism*, 162.
15. Creedman, *Historical Dictionary*, 139.
16. Rankin, *History*, 117, 153.
17. Barahona, "Aeropuerto de Liberia aún no despega."
18. Davies, *Airlines*, 94, 98–102;
19. Observatorio del Turismo del Pacifico Norte, "El origen."

20. Evans, *Green*, 56–7.
21. Observatorio del Turismo del Pacifico Norte, "El origen," 51.
22. See, for instance, Jean Hopfensperger, "Wilderness Adventures Spice Up Local Travel," *Tico Times*, October 10, 1980, cited in Honey, *Ecotourism*, 15.
23. Honey, *Ecotourism*, 162–3.
24. Interview with Louis Wilson by Royal G. Jackson, May 4, 1992 (hereafter, Wilson interview); interview with Mary Ruth by Royal G. Jackson, August 21, 1992 (hereafter, Ruth interview).
25. Ruhlow, "Tourism groups," 1, 8.
26. Ruhlow, "Tourism to get," 1, 3; Ruhlow, "Tourism committee," 1, 4.
27. Honey, *Ecotourism*, 164–7. For impressions of the ICT, see below.
28. Wilson, *Costa Rica*, 11–14, 18–23.
29. Wilson, *Costa Rica*, Chapter 4; Rankin, *History*, Chapters 8 and 9.
30. For a relatively favorable account of these reforms, see Hidalgo Capitán, *Costa Rica*, Chapters 2 and 3; for a negative view, see Weinberg, *War*, Chapter 12.
31. Weaver, *Ecotourism*, 84; Rovinski, "Private," 56.
32. Fournier, *Desarrollo*, 22–51; Evans, *Green*, 54–7.
33. Fournier, *Desarrollo*, 40–43, Steinberg, *Environmental*, 52–4.
34. Evans, *Green*, 23–5; Steinberg, *Environmental*, 54.
35. Davis, *Man*, esp. 111–17; Wallace, *Quetzal*, 41–2.
36. Evans, *Green*, 26; Fournier, *Desarrollo*, 58–9.
37. Fournier, *Desarrollo*, 58.
38. Farnham, *Saving*, 214.
39. Ibid., Chapter 1.
40. Rawcliffe, *Environmental*, 28; Dauvergne, *Historical Dictionary*, liii, 148.
41. Moss, *Bird*.
42. Interview with Efraín Chacón by Andrew Spadafora, June 7, 2014 (hereafter, Chacón interview); interview with Carlos Coles by Royal G. Jackson, August 26, 1992 (hereafter, Coles interview); and interview with Peter Aspinall by Royal G. Jackson, October 13, 1992, RGJ Papers.
43. Wallace, *Quetzal*, 6–10.
44. For Monteverde, long the most popular Costa Rican ecotourism destination, see especially Aylward et al., "Sustainable," 323–8; Honey, *Ecotourism*, 184–9; van Gulik, *Green or Gold*, 89–93.
45. Boo, *Ecotourism*, 38.
46. Wallace, *Quetzal*, 108–11; Honey, *Ecotourism*, 193.
47. Laarman and Perdue, "Science," 206, 211–12.
48. Blake, Becher and Earle, "Evaluating Ecotourism," 126, observed that a day at La Selva, including access to the trails, three meals and rustic accommodations, cost $60 in 1986.
49. Honey, *Ecotourism*, 194.
50. Budowski, "Tourism," 30; Laarman and Perdue, "Survey," 17.
51. Evans, *Green*, 24; Miller, *Planning*; Budowski, "Tourism."
52. Evans, *Green*, 73–5; Wallace, *Quetzal*, 14–15.
53. Evans, *Green*, 64–73.
54. See, above all, Evans, *Green*, Chapters 4–8; Wallace, *Quetzal*, 11–106 and Chapter 17; Fournier, *Desarrollo*, 62–75.
55. Evans, *Green*, 229.
56. René Castro, personal communication.
57. Evans, *Green*, 171; Wallace, *Quetzal*, 118, 190–91, 193.
58. Honey, *Ecotourism*, 170–72.
59. Michael Kaye, quoted in Wallace, *Quetzal*, 121.
60. Suri, "Rise," 51.
61. Jobs, "Youth Movements."
62. Churchill, "American Expatriates."
63. Rome, "Earth."

64. Staley, "Archie Fields."
65. Adams, "Discovering."
66. Wilson interview.
67. Ibid.
68. Ruth interview.
69. Wilson interview.
70. Ruth interview.
71. Coles interview.
72. Interview with Michael Kaye by Andrew Spadafora, San José, June 5, 2014, Creating Emerging Markets (CEM) project (hereafter, Kaye interview).
73. Interview with Jim Lewis by Royal G. Jackson, November 2, 1992 (hereafter, Lewis interview).
74. Ibid; Kaye interview.
75. Ibid.
76. Interview with Fernando Esquivel by Royal G. Jackson, July 30, 1992 (RGJ Papers).
77. Lewis interview; Castro and Serrano, *Ambiente*, 346.
78. *Wall Street Journal*, "Vast tourism."
79. Kaye interview; Ruhlow (1986a), "Tour operators," 17.
80. Kaye interview.
81. Lewis interview.
82. Rovinski, "Private," 46–7.
83. Costa Rica Expeditions Archives, Sales Manual, "Profits."
84. Kaye interview.
85. Interview with Richard Holland by Royal G. Jackson, August 28, 1992 (hereafter, Holland interview).
86. Kaye interview.
87. Cited in Honey, *Ecotourism*, 15; Kaye, "Responsible travel."
88. Kaye interview.
89. Costa Rica Expeditions Archives, Sales Manual, "Profits"; Kaye quoted in Bangs, "Meet."
90. Interview with Bary Roberts by Andrew Spadafora, San José, June 9, 2014, CEM (hereafter, Roberts interview, CEM). On the Roberts-Strachan family, see Roberts, *One Step*.
91. Roberts interview, CEM. On Strong and the Stockholm meeting, see Jones, *Profits*, 89; Strong, *Where*, Chapter 6.
92. Sheaff, "Summit Organizer," 1.
93. Interview with Bary Roberts by Royal G. Jackson, September 9, 1992, RGJ Papers (hereafter Roberts interview, RGJ).
94. Ibid.
95. Ibid.
96. Roberts interview, CEM.
97. Ibid.; Young, "Eco-enterprises," 362.
98. Roberts interview, RGJ.
99. Ibid.
100. Ibid.; interview with Tamara Budowski by Andrew Spadafora, Escazu, June 6, 2014 (hereafter, Budowski interview, CEM).
101. Budowski interview, CEM; Rodriguez Chaverri, *Mujeres pioneras*, 140.
102. Budowski interview, CEM.
103. Ibid.; interview with Tamara Budowski by Royal G. Jackson, September 21, 1992, RCJ Papers (hereafter, Budowski interview, RGJ).
104. Budowski interview, CEM.
105. Ibid.; Rodriguez Chaverri, *Mujeres pioneras*, 141–6.
106. Budowski interview, CEM.
107. Budowski interview, RGJ; Rodriguez Chaverri, *Mujeres pioneras*, 151–2.
108. Ibid., 147–8. Quotation cited in Evans, *Green*, 222.

109. Budowski interview, CEM.
110. Rodriguez Chaverri, *Mujeres pioneras*, 154.
111. Budowski interview, CEM; Galizzi, *Environment*, 113–16.
112. Budowski interview, RGJ.
113. Budowski, "Ecotourism," 52.
114. Ibid.
115. Budowski interview, CEM.
116. Budowski, "Ecotourism," 50.
117. Langholz, "Cowboys."
118. This account of Rara Avis relies on the following source unless otherwise noted: interview with Amos Bien by Royal G. Jackson, October 2, 1992, RGJ Papers (hereafter, Bien interview).
119. Honey, *Ecotourism*, 196; Bien interview.
120. Ibid.
121. Evans, *Green*, 222.
122. Bien interview.
123. On Perry, see Honey, *Ecotourism*, 198, 200.
124. Interview with Pedro Miranda by Royal G. Jackson, October 14, 1992, RGJ Papers (hereafter Miranda interview); for the correct date of 1974, see Miranda, "Estación," 58.
125. Miranda, "Estación," 58.
126. Ibid., 59.
127. Miranda interview.
128. Ibid.; Miranda, "Estación," 58.
129. Miranda interview; Miranda, "Estación," 59.
130. Chacón interview.
131. Rodríguez Chaverri, *Efraín Chacón*, 25–9.
132. Chacón interview.
133. Rodríguez Chaverri, *Efraín Chacón*, 29.
134. Chacón interview.
135. Interview with Jack Ewing by Andrew Spadafora, Hacienda Baru, June 3, 2014, CEM (hereafter, Ewing interview, CEM).
136. Interview with Jack Ewing by Royal G. Jackson, November 4, 1992, RGJ Papers (hereafter, Jack Ewing interview, RGJ).
137. Ibid.
138. Ewing interview, CEM.
139. Jack Ewing interview, RGJ.
140. Interview with Diane Ewing with Royal G. Jackson, November 5, 1992, RGJ Papers (hereafter, Diane Ewing interview, RGJ).
141. Ewing interview, CEM.
142. Interview with Diane Ewing, R Diane Ewing interview, RGJ GJ.
143. Jack Ewing interview, RGJ.
144. Ewing interview, CEM.
145. Jack Ewing interview, RGJ.
146. Honey, *Ecotourism*, 162.
147. Inman, "Tourism," 18.
148. Gámez and Obando, "La Biodiversidad," 177.
149. Evans, *Green*, 7.
150. Porras et al., *Learning*, 8–9.
151. Gámez and Obando, "La Biodiversidad," 177; Honey, *Ecotourism*, 164–7.
152. Butler, "Tourist."
153. Holland interview.
154. Blake, Becher and Earle, "Evaluating ecotourism," 141–3.
155. Bien, "Environmental certification," 138–9.
156. Ibid., 147–9; Roberts interview, CEM.
157. Ibid.

158. Bien, "Environmental certification," 150; interview with Jim Damalas by James Spadafora, Quepos, June 4, 2014, CEM (hereafter, Damalas interview, CEM).
159. Jones, *Profits*.
160. On this hotel and competitors like Hotel Punta Islita, see Honey, *Ecotourism*, 167–9, 175–7.
161. Damalas interview.
162. Ibid.
163. Ruth interview.
164. Budowski interview, CEM.
165. Kaye interview.

REFERENCES

Adams, Barbara (n.d.), "Discovering Costa Rica," accessed May 30, 2017 at http://calypsocruises.com/history.php.

Aylward, Bruce, Katie Allen, Jaime Echeverría and Joseph Tosi (1996), "Sustainable Ecotourism in Costa Rica," *Biodiversity & Conservation*, **5**, (3), 315–43.

Bangs, Richard (1999), "Meet the godfather of ecotourism," accessed May 1, 2014 at http://www.costaricaexpeditions.com/Articles/article.php?id=43.

Barahona, Hazel (1996), "Aeropuerto de Liberia aún no despega," *La Nación*, May 27.

Bien, Amos (2002), "Environmental Certification for Tourism in Central America: CST and other Programs," in Martha Honey (ed.), *Ecotourism & Certification: Setting Standards in Practice*, Washington, DC: Island Press, 133–59.

Blake, Beatrice, Anne Becher and Jane Segleau Earle (1996), "Evaluating Ecotourism Lodgings in *The New Key to Costa Rica*," *Yale School of Forestry & Environmental Studies Bulletin*, **99**, 141–52.

Boo, Elizabeth (1990), *Ecotourism: The Potentials and Pitfalls*, vol. 2, Washington, DC: World Wildlife Fund.

Budowski, Gerardo (1976), "Tourism and Environmental Conservation: Conflict, Coexistence, or symbiosis?" *Environmental Conservation*, **3**, (1), 27–31.

Budowski, Tamara (1992), "Ecotourism Costa Rican style," in Valerie Barzetti and Yanina Rovinski (eds.), *Toward a Green Central America: Integrating Conservation and Development*, West Hartford, CT: Kumarian Press, 48–62.

Butler, R.W. (1980), "The Concept of a Tourist Area Cycle of Evolution: Implications for Management of Resources," *Canadian Geographer*, **24**, (1), 5–12.

Churchill, David (2010), "American Expatriates and the Building of Alternative Social Space in Toronto, 1965–1977," *Urban History Review*, **39**, (1), 31–44.

Coldwell, Norma (1970), "The History of Braniff in Peru," Masters thesis, North Texas State University, Denton, TX.

Creedman, Theodore S. (1991), *Historical Dictionary of Costa Rica*, 2nd edn, Metuchen, NJ: Scarecrow Press.

Dauvergne, Peter (2009), *Historical Dictionary of Environmentalism*, Lanham, MD: Scarecrow Press.

Davies, R.E.G. (1984), *Airlines of Latin America since 1919*, London: Putnam.

Davis, Frederick R. (2007), *The Man Who Saved Sea Turtles: Archie Carr and the Origins of Conservation Biology*, Oxford: Oxford University Press.

Deshazo, J.R. (2001), "Linking the Growth of Tourism with the Conservation of Protected Areas," in Theodore Panayotou (ed.), *Environment for Growth in Central America*, Cambridge, MA: Harvard University Press, 231–56.

Evans, Sterling (1999), *The Green Republic: A Conservation History of Costa Rica*, Austin, TX: University of Texas Press.

Farnham, Timothy (2007), *Saving Nature's Legacy: Origins of the Idea of Biological Diversity*, New Haven, CT: Yale University Press.

Fournier, Luis (1991), *Desarrollo y perspectiva del movimiento conservacionista costarricense*, San José: Editorial de la Universidad de Costa Rica.

Galizzi, Paolo (2008), *The Role of the Environment in Poverty Alleviation*, New York: Fordham University Press.

Gámez, Rodrigo and Vilma Obando, 2004, "La Biodiversidad," in Eugenio Rodríguez Vega (ed.), *Costa Rica en el siglo XX*, vol. 2, San José: EUNED, 139–91.

Hidalgo Capitán, Antonio Luis (2003), *Costa Rica en evolución: Política económica, desarrollo y cambio estructural del sistema socioeconómico costarricense, 1980–2002*, San José: University of Costa Rica.

Honey, Martha (2008), *Ecotourism and Sustainable Development: Who Owns Paradise?* 2nd edn, Washington, DC: Island Press.

Independent Traveler, "Top Five Destinations for Ecotourism," accessed June 11, 2016 at http://www.independenttraveler.com/travel-tips/none/top-five-destinations-for-ecotourism.

Inman, Crist (2002, March), "Tourism in Costa Rica: The Challenge of Competitiveness," Researcher-Consultant of the Latin American Center for Competitiveness and Sustainable Development (CLACDS) Working Paper.

Jobs, Richard Ivan (2009), "Youth Movements: Travel, Protest, and Europe in 1968," *American Historical Review*, **114**, (2), 376–404.

Jones, Geoffrey (2017), *Profits and Sustainability: A History of Green Entrepreneurship*, Oxford: Oxford University Press.

Kaye, Michael (2002), "Responsible Travel to Natural Areas," *Condé Nast Traveler*, November.

Laarman, Jan and Richard Perdue (1989), "Science Tourism in Costa Rica," *Annals of Tourism Research*, **16**, 205–15.

Laarman, Jan and Richard Perdue (1987), "A Survey of Return Visits to Costa Rica by OTS Participants and Associates," Working Paper, Research Triangle Park, NC: Southeastern Center for Forestry Economics Research.

Langholz, Jeff (1999), "Conservation Cowboys: Privately-owned Parks and the Protection of Biodiversity in Costa Rica," PhD dissertation, Cornell University, Ithaca, NY.

Marín Hernández, Juan José and Ronny Viales Hurtado (2012), "Turismo y ambiente en la 'Perla' del Pacifico, 1946-1980," *Diálogos: Revista Electrónica de Historia* (October), 151–205.

Miranda, Sergio (2001). "Estación Biológica Marenco y Marenco Beach & Rainforest Lodge," in *Realidades y Visiones en la Gestión ambiental y ecoturística: Memoria del primer simposio internacional*, Red Interamericana de Formación-Gestión Ambiental y Ecoturismo, San José: University of Costa Rica, 57–60.

Miller, Kenton (1978), *Planning National Parks for Ecodevelopment*, Madrid: Fundación para la Ecologia y para la Protección del Medio Ambiente.

Moss, Stephen (2004), *A Bird in the Bush: A Social History of Bird-watching*, London: Aurum Press.

Observatorio del Turismo del Pacifico Norte (2008), "El origen de la actividad turística en Costa Rica: de la junta nacional de turismo al ICT," *Revista Umbral*, **22**, 42–52.

Porras, Ina, David Barton, Adriana Chacón-Cascante and Miriam Miranda (2013), *Learning from 20 Years of Payments for Ecosystem Services in Costa Rica*, London: International Institute for Environment and Development.

Quesada Castro, Renato and Estrella Guier Serrano (2014), *Ambiente y turismo sostenible*, San José: EUNED.

Rankin, Monica (2012), *The History of Costa Rica*, Santa Barbara, CA: Greenwood.

Rawcliffe, Peter (1998), *Environmental Pressure Groups in Transition*, Manchester, UK: Manchester University Press.

Roberts, W. Dayton (1996), *One Step Ahead: The Innovative Strachans and the Birth of Latin American Mission*, Miami: Latin American Mission.

Rodríguez Chaverri, Camilo (2008), *Efraín Chacón: El padre de San Gerardo*, San José: Maya & PZ Editorial.

Rodríguez Chaverri, Camilo (2006), *Mujeres pioneras del turismo en Costa Rica*, San José: Maya & PZ Editorial.

Rome, Adam (2003), "'Give Earth a chance': The Environmental Movement and the Sixties," *Journal of American History*, **90**, (2), 525–54.

Rovinski, Yanina (1991), "Private Reserves, Parks, and Ecotourism in Costa Rica," in Tensie Whelan (ed.), *Nature Tourism: Managing for the Environment*, Washington, DC: Island Press, 39–57.

Ruhlow, Jerry (1986a), "Tour operators: Don't overlook our fishing!" *Tico Times*, October 3.

Ruhlow, Jerry (1986b), "Tourism committee resigns," *Tico Times*, August 29.

Ruhlow, Jerry (1986c), "Tourism groups to battle law," *Tico Times*, August 15.

Ruhlow, Jerry (1986d), "Tourism to get private push," *Tico Times*, August 1.

Sheaff, Michelle (1992), "Summit organizer charged with violating national laws," *Tico Times*, June 5.

Steinberg, Paul F. (2001), *Environmental Leadership in Developing Countries: Transnational Relations and Biodiversity Policy in Costa Rica and Bolivia*, Cambridge, MA: MIT Press.

Strong, Maurice (2000), *Where on Earth are We Going?* New York: Texere.

Suri, Jeremi (2009), "The Rise and Fall of an International Counterculture, 1960–1975," *American Historical Review*, **144**, (1), 45–68.

Staley, Todd (2011), "Remembering Archie Fields," *Tico Times*, July 18.

Van Gulik, Ilse (1999), *Green or Gold? Sustainable Tourism in Costa Rica and the Actors Involved*, Nijmegen, the Netherlands: Catholic University of Nijmegen Press.

Wall Street Journal (1988), "Vast tourism resources untapped in Costa Rica," October 20.

Wallace, David Rains (1992), *The Quetzal and the Macaw: The Story of Costa Rica's National Parks*, San Francisco: Sierra Club.

Weaver, David (1998), *Ecotourism in the Less Developed World*, New York: CABI.

Weinberg, Bill (1991), *War on the Land: Ecology and Politics in Central America*, London: Zed Books.

Wilson, Bruce M. (1998), *Costa Rica: Politics, Economics, and Democracy*, Boulder: Lynne Rienner.

Young, A.M. (1986), "Eco-enterprises: Eco-tourism and Farming of Exotics in the Tropics," *Ambio*, **15**, (6), 361–3.

PRIMARY MATERIALS

Creating Emerging Markets project, Baker Library Historical Collections, Harvard Business School, http://www.hbs.edu/businesshistory/emerging-markets. Interviews by Andrew Spadafora with Jim Damalas, Quepos, June 4, 2014; Jack Ewing, Hacienda Baru, June 3, 2014; Michael Kaye, San José, June 5, 2014; and Bary Roberts, San José, June 9, 2014.

Interviews by Andrew Spadafora with Tamara Budowski, Escazu, June 6, 2014; and Efraín Chacón, San Gerado de Dota, June 7, 2014.

Royal G. Jackson Papers, Series II.1, Oregon State University Special Collections, interviews by Royal G. Jackson with Peter Aspinall, Amos Bien, Tamara Budowski, Carlos Coles, Fernando Esquivel, Diane Ewing, Jack Ewing, Richard Holland, Jim Lewis, Pedro Miranda, Bary Roberts, Mary Ruth, Louis Wilson.

Costa Rica Expeditions Archives, Costa Rica Expeditions Sales Manual (1995), "Profits, prestige, and repeat business: A message from Michael Kaye, president of Costa Rica Expeditions."

8. Alternative paths of green entrepreneurship: Yvon Chouinard, Doug Tompkins and Kristine McDivitt Tompkins*

With Ben Gettinger

I INTRODUCTION

This chapter examines the impact of entrepreneurs who offered alternative paths to reach their shared goal of a more sustainable world. Yvon Chouinard and Doug Tompkins were founders of the prominent outdoor apparel brands Patagonia and The North Face, respectively. Chouinard pursued incremental sustainability strategies over decades at his firm. Tompkins, who went on to manage the fashion company Esprit, opted to exit business entirely in 1989, concluding that capitalism could never be sufficiently sustainable to reverse environmental degradation. He and his wife, Kristine McDivitt Tompkins, a former chief executive at Patagonia, purchased 1.5 million hectares of land in Chile and Argentina, which they converted to protected areas and national parks.

The previous chapters examined the impact of green entrepreneurs in a variety of industries and countries, and these green entrepreneurs have been contrasted with their conventional counterparts. In contrast, this chapter raises the question whether entrepreneurial talents are used more productively in activities beyond for-profit activities. A second question, first broached in Chapter 7 (on ecotourism), is whether a company can credibly fight for sustainability initiatives while simultaneously benefiting from a consumer culture that creates waste and degradation. Section II examines the early entrepreneurial careers of Chouinard and Tompkins. Section III turns to Tompkins and his wife Kristine's investment in conservation in Argentina and Chile. Section IV assesses the evolving commitment to sustainability at Patagonia. Section V compares the environmental impact of the two strategies, and Section VI concludes.

II TWO ENTREPRENEURIAL PATHS

Doug Tompkins was born in 1943 in Conneaut, Ohio, into a wealthy family. A nonconformist from an early age, Tompkins was expelled from prep school and spent several years rock-climbing across Europe and the American West.[1] Wanting to sell premium gear to his compatriot mountaineers and outdoor enthusiasts, Tompkins founded The North Face in 1964, at the age of 21, with an initial investment of US$5,000.[2] He started it as a mail order company for backpacking and climbing equipment; by 1966 he opened a flagship brick-and-mortar retail store in San Francisco, California. He sold the company for $50 000 in 1967, and immediately traveled to the Patagonia region of Argentina for several weeks of climbing and hiking; his traveling companions were fellow climbing enthusiasts and entrepreneurs, including Yvon Chouinard.[3]

While Tompkins was exploring Patagonia, his wife, Susie, and a friend started a clothing label, Plain Jane Dress Company. By the time Tompkins returned from South America, Plain Jane had taken off. He joined the company as a partner, leading marketing and sales.[4] The company, renamed Esprit de Corp, grew tremendously throughout the 1970s. In 1972 manufacturing was offshored to Hong Kong to reduce labor costs, and by 1985 sales had reached $700 million. Esprit was the pioneer of the now-common "shop within a shop" concept by partnering with department stores.[5]

The late 1980s marked turmoil for both Doug and Susie personally and for the company. Sales began to falter as Esprit lost market share to competitors, it incurred its first financial losses and the marriage frayed. In 1989, shortly after filing for divorce, Doug sold his stake in Esprit to Susie for $170 million.[6]

Yvon Chouinard was born in Lisbon, Maine, in 1938. A self-described high school "misfit," Chouinard took more of an interest in falconry than academics, and joined the Southern California Falconry Club. In order to access falcon aeries located on cliff faces, Chouinard learned how to mountain climb, which immediately became his passion.[7] After two years of community college and working part-time for his brother as a private detective, Chouinard taught himself how to blacksmith, and in 1957 he began forging pitons (spikes used in climbing).[8] He initially sold the pitons out of his car in order to fund climbing expeditions. Over time, he expanded manufacturing to include carabineers, a metal loop and other small-form, metal-based climbing tools. By 1970 Chouinard Equipment was the largest supplier of climbing equipment in the United States and had developed a reputation for durability and quality.[9]

The company's subsequent move into apparel had practical beginnings related to climbing needs. According to Chouinard:

> I bought myself a regulation team rugby shirt to wear, thinking it would make a great shirt for rock climbing. Overbuilt to withstand the rigors of rugby, it had a collar that would keep the hardware slings from cutting into my neck ... Back in the States I wore it around climbing, and all my friends asked where they could get one.[10]

The addition of clothing to Chouinard Equipment was to support the existing equipment business that, despite topline success, was still barely profitable, earning only 1 percent net income margin, at best.[11] The company's apparel business was even branded separately from Chouinard Equipment, which was unwittingly fortuitous. The clothing line, started in 1973, was named Patagonia, after the South American region Chouinard and Tompkins had explored a few years earlier, and it used a silhouette of Mount Fitz Roy as its logo.[12]

Patagonia, created as a secondary entity to the primary equipment business, grew to be the dominant of the two companies. Chouinard Equipment experienced legal trouble and ultimately filed for bankruptcy under the American Chapter 11 bankruptcy law; the company was bought out by its employees, renamed Black Diamond and resumed operations.[13] Patagonia traveled a different path. Under the leadership of Kristine McDivitt, who became Patagonia's first titled CEO in 1979, the company boomed. McDivitt had met Chouinard when she was 15 years old, and he had given her a summer job working at Chouinard Equipment.

Under McDivitt's tenure, sales grew from $20 million to $100 million in the 1980s, and the company expanded into Europe and Japan.[14] Major innovations in outdoor apparel were brought to market by Patagonia, including fleece clothing, bright colors (outdoor products had traditionally been tan or green), polyester long underwear, and the concept of wearing base-, mid-, and outer-layers.[15] In 1993 she resigned her position, and went to stay with Tompkins, who had relocated to Chile. They married in the following year, and she became Kristine McDivitt Tompkins. Patagonia continued to grow under new leadership. By 2000 the company had $200 million in net sales;[16] by 2013, despite the global financial crisis, revenues had grown to $600 million,[17] and reached $800 million by 2016. By then it also had 29 standalone stores in the US, 23 in Japan and others elsewhere. Throughout the decades of growth, Chouinard remained deeply involved in Patagonia's strategic and operational decision-making; he and his wife were the sole shareholders of the company.

III DEEP ECOLOGY AND THE TOMPKINS' STRATEGY

Doug Tompkins demonstrated a desire to promote environmentalism throughout his decades of managing Esprit. Early on, Esprit's corporate outings consisted of rafting trips led by both Susie and Doug, along with organized lectures given by environmental activists.[18]

During the late 1970s and early 1980s, Arne Naess, the Norwegian philosopher and mountaineer, and the founder of the "Deep Ecology" movement, deeply affected Tompkins's views on the state of conservation and sustainability. Based on a personal philosophy called ecosophy, Naess emphasized the importance of protecting the environment as a part of ourselves, not as opposition to humanity. He first used the term "deep ecology" in 1972. A decade later, he and his supporters encoded the philosophy into a set of principles. These principles asserted that human beings had no right to reduce the diversity of life forms except to satisfy vital needs, and called for radical steps to reduce human interference in the nonhuman world and for a sharp reduction in the human population. Modern industrial culture was seen as exploiting the Earth to satisfy exaggerated and artificial desires for consumption. Biological diversity was being destroyed, Naess argued, by the demands of business to make profits.[19]

By the late 1980s, influenced by these ideas, Tompkins had become critical of his company's role in what he judged as an environmentally destructive consumer culture. He initially sought change within Esprit through marketing. In a controversial campaign, Tompkins implored Esprit customers not to buy Esprit clothing. This "buy only what you need" strategy was supplemented by warning labels on clothing tags, and designs were created with more muted, traditional colors to disincentivize excessive purchasing.[20] Rather than attempt to bring further sustainability initiatives to Esprit, Tompkins decided instead to exit the corporate world entirely, selling all of his shares in Esprit in 1989. "I just realized," Tompkins remarked, "what I was doing was making a lot of stuff that nobody needed and pushing a consumerist society. So I went to do something else."[21]

In 1990 Tompkins founded the Foundation for Deep Ecology, based in San Francisco, intended as an activist foundation aimed at combating ecological destruction.[22] Over the following two decades, this foundation published more than 20 books, reports and advocacy campaigns to raise awareness of environmental issues in the United States. It also made strategic grants to nonprofit organizations protecting the environments of

Chile and Argentina. By 2012 more than $52 million had been donated to over 1,500 organizations.[23]

Tompkins moved to Chile in 1991. He purchased the 42,000-acre Reñihue farm with the intention to create his own nature reserve protected from deforestation and encroachment from developers. He called it Pumalín Park, after the puma, a familiar predator in the region.[24]

Tompkins chose Chile for a variety of reasons. First, the rules for foreign investors were favorable and easy to understand. Second, it was possible to develop a strategy that minimized the payment of US taxes. Tompkins bought the lands through a Chilean commercial entity and then transferred the ownership to US-based foundations. Third, the area had very low population density – just 1.2 people per square kilometer – with land titles that were often in disarray. Finally, the region contained several tracts of ancient larch forests that could be purchased at a much lower price per hectare compared to land in Europe or North America.[25]

Tompkins established the Conservation Land Trust, a charitable foundation registered in San Francisco, endowing the fund with his personal capital and the charter of acquiring more land to build Pumalín Park. Tompkins and the man who would become his longtime attorney, Pedro Pablo Gutierrez, began to map out their buying strategy in 1991. For the most part, the land purchases Tompkins made were not unduly complicated: a small number of people held most of the land that interested him, and many of those landowners were not especially interested in the properties. Most were absentee owners.[26] Tompkins was a fair but steadfast negotiator, sticking to his offered price for months until sellers capitulated.[27] From 1991 to 1998, the trust purchased close to 700 000 acres, 98 percent from absentee landowners.[28] There were rumors, never confirmed, that Tompkins financed the large sums of money required by earning high returns from investing his capital with conventional San Francisco-based finance houses.[29]

As time passed, Conservation Land Trust became controversial and surrounded by rumors. By the end of 1993, Tompkins had become a major media topic in Chile, just as some of his largest purchases were poised for completion. The Chilean press questioned the "real" nature of his land-acquisition efforts; anti-Semitic rumors circulated that Pumalín Park was ultimately meant as a haven for Jews, an accusation that even led Tompkins to be questioned by representatives from the Chilean government.[30] Some hypothesized that Chileans' growing rejection of Tompkins was perhaps a lasting consequence of the military dictatorship of General Pinochet (1973–90), which had left a widespread suspicion in some parts of Chilean society of the new and foreign. In one observer's words: "No one could come to Chile and buy such a great piece of land so close to the frontier with Argentina for love of nature alone."[31]

Legislators and the press also complained that Tompkins was pushing poor Chileans, many of whom were barely making a living, off their land. At times, landowners who accepted money in exchange for their plots quickly bankrupted themselves, and then cast Tompkins as the villain.[32] Though Tompkins was quick to defend the legality of his actions and to assert that his intentions were good, public opinion against him mounted. As recounted by Chilean journalist Andrés Azócar Zamudio:

> The businessman's efforts to move closer to the community were like tiny boats rowing against the current, and in different directions. The huge number of letters that Tompkins ... sent to the newspaper "El Llanqihue" was irrelevant. In them, he tried to explain and repeat that most of the settlers moved to other lands acquired by the businessman in the area – even though they were not entitled to – that he had no intentions of cutting Chile in two, that his park would not restrict access to the public, [and] that he was not in favor of depopulating Palena.[33]

Tompkins's relationship with the Chilean government evolved over time. Under the government of Eduardo Frei Ruiz-Tagle (1994–2000), relations were difficult. Frei's government tracked his activities for five years in efforts to find grounds to remove him from Chile, but found that nothing Tompkins did was even on the margins of illegality.[34] Ultimately, Tompkins and the government reached an agreement to designate Pumalín Park as a nature sanctuary to be run by an independent foundation. After holding the land privately for 15 years, on August 19, 2005, Pumalín Park was formally designated a nature sanctuary by the president of Chile, and control of its acreage was handed over to Fundación Pumalín, a Chilean foundation.[35]

The improved government relations may have resulted from Tompkins's employment of Enrique Correa, a former member of Chilean government, as a lobbyist.[36] The role of Kristine McDivitt Tompkins was also important. She was more savvy in terms of interpersonal relations and public relations; for example, she brought containers of Patagonia clothes for foundation employees, followed their lives and engaged in many other activities that reduced hostility toward Foundation for Deep Ecology.[37] According to one colleague, "she made [Tomkins] evolve, she humanized him, [and] she turned him into a landholding environmentalist who could also worry about other people."[38]

Kristine and Doug Tompkins executed a large-scale strategy to acquire massive amounts of land for conservation, preservation and eventual repatriation in several wildlife zones beyond the Pumalín sanctuary. As of 2016, the Conservation Land Trust – in conjunction with Conservación Patagónica[39] (founded by Kristine in 2000) – had formed ten national parks in Argentina and Chile, encompassing over two million acres (Table 8.1). As described in the magazine *The Atlantic*:

> They [Doug and Kristine] have purchased enough land in Chile and Argentina to equal an area the size of nearly two Rhode Islands, and they plan to donate these [lands] to the respective governments in the form of national parks. They have protected more land than any other private individuals in history.[40]

Table 8.1 Selected national parks in Argentina and Chile, created or expanded by the Conservation Land Trust and Conservación Patagónica

Park	Size (thousand hectares)	Country
Corcovado National Park	293.8	Chile
Pumalín Park	289.4	Chile
Patagonia National Park	259.4	Chile
Iberá Park	161.9	Argentina
Yendegaia National Park	149.7	Chile
El Impenetrable National Park	128.0	Argentina
Monte León National Park	66.8	Argentina
Cabo León	26.3	Chile
El Rincón	15.2	Argentina
El Piñalito Provincial Park	3.8	Argentina
El Cañi Sanctuary	0.5	Chile

Sources: Conservation Land Trust, http://www.theconservationlandtrust.org/eng/our_mission.htm; Conservación Patagónica, http://www.conservacionpatagonica.org/home.htm.

The whole venture was an unprecedented act of entrepreneurial philanthropy, whose strategy evolved over time. "The process at the beginning was quite intuitive and organic," Kristine Tompkins later observed, "propelled by the desire Doug and I felt to be together and to take this important habitat and protect it in perpetuity."[41]

IV GREEN CAPITALISM AT PATAGONIA

Patagonia's commitment to the environment dated back to the early days of Chouinard Equipment. In 1970 Chouinard realized that steel pitons – the staple product of Chouinard Equipment – were scarring Yosemite and other mountains as more and more climbers hammered the pitons into the rock face. Rather than slowly phase out pitons to ease the hit on topline sales, Chouinard Equipment immediately stopped selling the product. Concurrently, the company introduced aluminum chocks, which served the same function as pitons but without damaging the natural rock surface. In its first catalog, Chouinard Equipment published an article espousing the philosophy of "clean climbing": climbing without leaving a trace on the environment.[42]

As Patagonia scaled, it began donating to small nonprofits devoted to habitat restoration. The company formalized this program in 1986 when it created a policy of annually donating 10 percent of profits to environmentally focused organizations; that metric was later raised to 1 percent of sales.[43] By 2016 the company's donation program had granted $70 million to grassroots activists.[44] Patagonia also began making incremental changes to its internal operation to be more environmentally friendly. Catalogs were printed on recycled paper, and R&D dollars were spent on developing recycled polyester.[45]

From 1991 to 1994, Patagonia mapped the full environmental impact of its supply chain, focusing in particular on the damage caused by using its four main inputs: cotton, wool, polyester and nylon. In the words of Rick Ridgeway, vice president of Public Engagement at Patagonia, and lifelong friend of both Tompkins and Chouinard, "We mapped our supply chain much more thoroughly than our competitors. [We made] direct relationships with the secondary and tertiary companies in that chain, including mills and dye houses and extending to a farm and fiber production level."[46]

Based on this analysis, in 1996 Patagonia began making jackets out of recycled polyester and moved to organically grown cotton, despite the sourcing change "tripling the company's supply costs."[47] In 1998, ignoring customer demands for the technology, anti-odor chemicals were eliminated given the concerns related to the chemicals' impact on the environment.[48]

Patagonia's philosophy of "cause no unnecessary harm" led, over time, to more campaigns that conflicted with the mindset of traditional retail businesses. In 2004 Ridgeway brought the idea of implementing the "buy only what you need" marketing strategy to Patagonia. "It took years to get the ads approved and everybody on board," recalled Ridgeway, but now "asking customers not to buy a new product until they need it fits our business model."[49] Famously, in 2011 on Black Friday, the largest shopping day of the year, Patagonia took out a full-page advertisement in the *New York Times* that boldly stated, "Don't Buy This Jacket."[50]

In support of this campaign, Patagonia launched the Worn Wear Program in 2013. The company began offering repair services to extend the life of its products, while also volunteering to recycle used Patagonia clothing on its customers' behalf. By 2016 the program had grown in size to 40,000 repairs per year, which was handled by a full-time staff of 45 repair technicians, including a team that tours the country in an RV repairing and recycling clothing on location.[51] "It's a loyalty program that doesn't inspire more purchases," Ridgeway observed, "It turns loyalty on its head."[52]

Patagonia's green strategies have more recently evolved beyond apparel. Patagonia Provisions, launched as a new company in 2012, aimed to change the food industry. The start-up invests in bringing to market sustainably-sourced food products, including salmon, bison jerky and organic soups, and advocating for agricultural techniques that have the ability to reduce water consumption, regenerate depleted soil and stop – if not reverse – the industry's deleterious impact on climate change. While still a nascent effort, the environmental impact on revolutionizing farming and food production has the potential to be significantly greater than that of the eco-friendly initiatives promoted by Patagonia's apparel business, especially with regard to reducing carbon emissions and increasing carbon sequestration. In 2016 Chouinard assessed it as "the most important project the company has ever tackled."[53]

V   COMPARING THE ENVIRONMENTAL IMPACT

A comparison of the environmental impact of the Tompkins' deep ecologism and Chouinard's green capitalism is inherently subjective, given the lack of a standardized measurement rubric. There remains no methodology to compare the value of preserving an acre of wetland with extending the life of a fleece jacket by three years. (On the latter point, Patagonia estimated in 2015 that extending the use of clothing nine months resulted in a 20 to 30 percent reduction in related waste.[54]) However, it is possible to develop crude quantitative estimates around the two different strategies.

Doug and Kristine Tompkins, through their organizations and personal endowments, helped protect roughly 1.5 million hectares in South

America. This vast acreage – replete with forests, grasslands and wetlands – slowed the adverse effects of climate change through biomass storage and sequestering of carbon. According to one expert scientist, the soil and vegetation of these protected areas may store anywhere from 30 to 60 tons of carbon per hectare, depending on the topography of the land. In addition, previously degraded and carbon-depleted lands restored by this conservation may restart sequestering carbon from the atmosphere at anywhere from 1.5 to 3 tons per hectare per year.[55] Table 8.2 shows that, based on rough assumptions regarding topography, the total sink capacity of these sanctuaries – that is, the amount of carbon that can be stored – approximated to 80 million tons of carbon at equilibrium. In addition, by protecting these habitats indefinitely, the future emissions of the stored carbon that would have occurred via continued environmental destruction were prevented.

Table 8.2 Estimated impact of protected areas on atmospheric carbon dioxide

Assumptions	
Tons of carbon sequestered per year (forests)	2.5
Tons of carbon sequestered per year (grasslands)	1.5
Tons of carbon sequestered per year (wetlands)	3.0
Tons of carbon stored per hectare in equilibrium (forests)	55.0
Tons of carbon stored per hectare in equilibrium (grasslands)	35.0
Tons of carbon stored per hectare in equilibrium (wetlands)	60.0
Hectares protected	1 500 000.0
Assumed percentage of forest land	50%
Assumed percentage of grasslands	25%
Assumed percentage of wetlands	25%
Total carbon sink capacity (tons)	76 875 000.0

Sources: Author estimates based on interview with Professor Rattan Lal, October 6, 2016.

It is a more challenging task to compare the environmental impact of land preservation with the protection of the habitats of many of the endangered species. Restoring lands that had previously been used for raising livestock, logging or other business purposes rebuilt the natural environment for dislocated species. Iberá Park hosted more than 360 species of birds and serves as a massive source of fresh water for Northeast Argentina.[56] Corcovado National Park – along with providing sanctuary to seals, sea lions and penguins – has been described as a "crucial nursery area for blue whales."[57] Conservación Patagónica, part of the umbrella of the family's collective environmental organizations, became actively involved in recovery programs for nine at-risk species within the Patagonia region. Rewilding strategies included reintroducing tapirs, giant anteaters and green-shouldered macaws.[58] There is no current metric or methodology that enables a quantitative estimate of the environmental benefits of saving and protecting animal species, despite the known key roles of many species in sustaining entire environmental ecosystems. It is equally hard to capture the social and environmental externalities generated by Doug Tompkins. For example, he believed protecting the land would have an enormously positive long-term economic impact on regional tourism, and went so far as to build and establish tourism-specific infrastructure in Iberá.

Despite the sharp rise in awareness of global warming over the last decade, at least beyond some political circles in the United States, there are no tools to capture the value of uncompromised natural habitats. The net present value of new ventures that require incremental deforestation are probably negative when accounting for the long-term environmental costs and not just the immediate economic gains. Doug Tompkins spoke to this under-appreciation of biodiversity loss in one of his early treatises on the rationale for buying rainforests:

> Compromises on ancient forests are never compromises; they are losses ... Ecological concerns are long term; transnational concerns are narrow and short term, exploitive and rarely aimed at preserving integrity and diversity of natural systems. The social justice arguments of jobs versus wilderness always surface – again, short-term thinking versus long-term.[59]

His approach added value by forcing long-term perspectives onto a society that, certainly since the rise in the 1980s of shareholder capitalism models in the United States and elsewhere, has mostly over-emphasized single-stakeholder and short-term results.[60]

In many respects, it is easier to quantify the environmental impact of Patagonia, the clothing line. Several of the company's internal business initiatives can be measured and are made public by the company. Although the nature and limitation of environmental reporting is a topic of active scholarly debate,[61] it would be churlish not to recognize Patagonia's self-assessment of the impact of its environmental programs since their inception. The initiatives listed in Table 8.3 are only a sample of the many changes Patagonia has implemented since the mid-1980s.

Table 8.3   Select examples of Patagonia's environmental initiatives and impact

Initiative	Impact
Renewable energy use	1.2 mil kWh of energy replaced with green sources by 2015
Employee Drive-Less program	500K lbs CO_2 emissions/26K gallons of gas saved in the first year
1% for the Planet	$70 million donations made to environmental groups since 1985
Product recycling	164 062 lbs of products recycled since 2013
$20 million and change fund	10 start-ups focused on environmental initiatives funded since 2013
Sourcing	75 percent of materials are organic/recycled; 30 percent of suppliers deemed environmentally advanced by third party
Patagonia denim	Dying process uses 84 percent less water, 30 percent less energy, and 25 percent fewer CO_2 emissions

Source: Patagonia, "Annual Report."

Beyond the company-specific actions, Patagonia has also pursued active advocacy supporting environmental causes. The impact of this advocacy is hard to measure beyond anecdotal examples. Patagonia has partnered with several firms to launch new organizations dedicated to fighting climate change. For example, in 2002 the company co-launched the nonprofit 1% for the Planet, which is dedicated to expanding Patagonia's pledge of donating 1 percent of gross revenue every year to environmental groups. Twelve hundred companies are now members and have donated in excess of $100 million to over 3,300 different nonprofits.[62]

The company has also served as an outside consultant and role model to firms trying to change their own operations to be more sustainable. For example, Wal-Mart enlisted Patagonia's help in piloting changes to reduce water consumption and packaging waste, and Levi Strauss used Chouinard's supply-chain benchmarking to help save 45 million gallons of water annually through more environmentally friendly production.[63] Patagonia has pioneered and shared standards and methods for incorporating environmental costs into traditional accounting statements. According to Ridgeway, "We have tools that measure footprints and that allow designers to understand the environmental impact of their design choices."[64] Chouinard's and Ridgeway's advocacy even reached the leading practitioner journal *Harvard Business Review*; the two co-authored an article promoting retail-wide rating of products according to measured environmental and social impacts.[65]

Absent an advance in current methodologies and environmental metrics, there is still no rigorous way to quantify and compare the overall environmental impact of protecting Patagonian habitats versus promoting sustainable manufacturing practices. However, it is possible to identify a number of trade-offs in both strategies.

Two significant issues arose from the land-buying strategy. First, Doug and Kristine Tompkins individually determined the optimal use of the land based on their own views, not on those of the surrounding communities. Although this might be considered the norm in governance of private property, both the scale of the purchases and their status as foreigners gave pause for concern. Certainly they legally purchased all the acreage, buying from landowners who were willing to sell at a fair price. Yet even Antonio Horvath, a Chilean senator known for his support of environmental causes, took issue with their lack of consultation with Chilean stakeholders. Horvath viewed the scale of their landholdings and unchecked power to do as they wished with that land as "a blow to sovereignty, to territorial continuity."[66]

The paternalist aspect of this strategy was illustrated by the remodeling of the local villages located on or next to their preservations. Quoting again an article from *The Atlantic*:

> Tompkins has also beautified the homes of the neighbors, as well as the town's gas station, school, supermarket, and bus shelters. "The people were a little hesitant. A gringo shows up and tells us our town is ugly?" ... Tompkins has taken many of the decisions about the design of these renovations into his own hands – the patterns of the houses' trim, the colors of their fences.[67]

While some villages reacted with bemused acceptance to this design overhaul, others reacted with resentment. As one local citizen described, "It bothers me that they call it the Patagonia Park because there's no

Patagonian identity in it. You see the buildings and it looks like you're in London! It's the same in Amarillo – what they did to the houses there. It's not Patagonian. It looks like you're in Germany."[68]

In many ways, this may appear to fit the description of entrepreneurial philanthropy discussed in Chapter 1.[69] Tompkins felt compelled to buy as much land as possible because he believed neither businesses nor governments could be trusted to respect the Patagonian wilderness. There is something alarming about the idea of individual wealthy people from another society being able to reshape landscapes without the support or consultation of any stakeholder beyond the willing sellers of property. The controversy over the philanthropy of Roxanne Quimby, cofounder of the Burt's Bees personal care company, provides another example. In 2016 Quimby, in attempting to donate $100 million for land and facilities to create a new national park in Maine, was met with fierce hostility.[70] Yet motivation and execution matter in an overall assessment. While there is a good case to be made that such classic philanthropists as Andrew Carnegie were seeking social rates of return and seeking to deflect criticisms of the legitimacy of wealth, this hardly seems to fit the Tompkins example. A key tenet of their philosophy was the fact that the ownership of the land was meant to be temporary. As Doug Tompkins outlined in an early editorial, "Our feeling is that land purchases must be seen as interim emergency or preemptive measures only. Within a reasonable time (probably 10 to 20 years) transfer of those purchases should be made to return those lands back to the public commons."[71] As noted in the list of national parks in Table 8.1, this strategy was implemented. Quimby's land was also given the nation. In 2016 then-US President Obama used an executive order to create the 87 500 acre Katahdin Woods and Waters National Monument.

The strategy used by Chouinard's Patagonia was also not without trade-offs and limitations. Although it was an innovator in corporate sustainability, the company continued to thrive on a consumer culture that remained inherently wasteful in environmental terms. That the company has tripled sales since the early 2000s runs counter to Chouinard's stated goal of moderated and sustainable growth, and suggests that the Worn Wear Program and anticonsumerism advertisements were not delivering paradigm shifts. In fact, the "Don't Buy This Jacket" campaign worked to boost Patagonia sales. While the company would claim that growth came from taking market share, it is impossible to quantify how many consumers truly needed a new jacket versus those who bought a new jacket after being inspired by the advertisements. As said by journalist J.B. Mackinnon, "It's quite possible that Patagonia's philosophy has attracted many shoppers to the brand without deeply affecting their buying habits, as suggested by the way that 'Don't Buy This Jacket' translated, for many, into 'Buy This Jacket'."[72]

The company, despite its environmental and social efforts, at times ran into situations in which delivering on its mission to "build the best product" conflicted with the socially and eco-conscious priorities for which Patagonia simultaneously stood. In 2011, an internal audit discovered "multiple instances of human trafficking, forced labor, and exploitation in Patagonia's supply chain."[73] In 2016, Greenpeace, testing a wide variety of outdoor apparel of different brands, found several Patagonia samples that contained hazardous polyflourinated chemicals which were used as water repellents in clothing.[74] Patagonia had struggled with the trade-off between using toxic chemicals and durability for some time.[75] It had opted to prioritize durability. As Ridgeway stated, "Durability becomes the main environmental component of a product ... If we replace our current water resistant chemistry with what Greenpeace advocates, then durability goes way down so the product has to be replaced more frequently causing more harm than what we currently offer."[76]

Certainly, there were some buyers who valued the longevity of Patagonia gear and replaced that equipment only when necessary. However, there were other consumers who were willing to replace a previous year's jacket for the latest version. For those customers, Patagonia's choice to use more toxic components might not, in practice, have an impact on the frequency of product replacement. However, if consumers were willing to discard Patagonia's products well before the products themselves wear out – that is, if consumer preference and not true durability ultimately dictated a product's replacement cycle – then the rationale for using less eco-friendly components was undermined. At the very least, Patagonia's presence in the apparel market afforded consumers the ability to vote for more eco-friendly alternatives by buying the firm's products. Chouinard himself explicitly believed that changing consumer mindsets was key for sustainability. Consumers "have the power," he noted in an interview in 2016, "and corporations will only change when we force them to."[77]

Patagonia's strategy has an evident scalability, far more so than the specific strategy the Conservation Land Trust had of buying huge amounts of land for conservation. The supply-chain initiatives that lower waste, save water and reduce emissions can be, and have been, adopted by other companies. Environmental accounting standards that Patagonia created have been adopted by some other companies, not only as a way to measure true cost but also as a mechanism for making operations more efficient. Finally, the internal capital earned by Patagonia can have a sustained multiplier effect through its ongoing support of new grassroots start-ups, either via grants from Patagonia's 1 percent donation pledge or as seed investments from Patagonia's recently launched "$20 Million & Change" venture capital fund.

Patagonia's systematic and detailed approach to mapping out and tracing the footprint of its products has usefully exposed the often unsustainable and unethical components of the textile manufacturing industry as a whole. The company has worked to improve its supply chain, often going beyond required guidelines to serve as a model for how an apparel operation can and should be managed. As *The Atlantic* explains, "The status quo throughout the industry ... largely requires that companies only look at and remedy labor trafficking issues at their first-tier suppliers. In attempting to monitor and improve the treatment of its second-tier-factory workers, Patagonia is going far beyond that standard."[78]

Importantly, Patagonia set a valuable precedent by being transparent with its own failings. Rather than hide the fact that some of the company's second- and third-tier Taiwanese suppliers were using exploited labor, Patagonia went public. In the words of Ridgeway:

> I was in the meeting when we found out from auditors that we had slave labor in our supply chain. What are we going to do? First thing that came out was we have to go public. We have to tell people about the problem. We have to get the supply chain involved. We have to get government involved. You can't fix a system problem without all players in the system coming together. That is our default reaction.[79]

By shining a public light on grey areas of the apparel industry's supply chain that no firm had yet investigated, and working with companies and governments to address those issues, the company has promoted system-wide change by implementing solutions to problems that other companies, and consumers, had either not identified or chosen to ignore.

Nevertheless, doubts remain on the extent to which Patagonia served as a role model. It was still widely believed that the pursuit of environmental and social sustainability came with a trade-off on bottom-line profitability. Patagonia's evident achievements in successful brand-building served as a compelling counter-example. Of course, because Patagonia's sole shareholder was the Chouinard family, the company had more flexibility than a publicly traded Fortune 500 company, which was mandated to report quarterly returns. A key issue, then, was how far public companies have really learned from Patagonia.

While there was evidence of the willingness of large companies to partner and work with Patagonia – reflected in the considerable interest in understanding the secrets of combining sustainability with profitability – the extent to which the company has functioned as a role model is less clear. In a 2016 interview, Chouinard recalled that in his response when Tompkins urged him to follow his own example, he would say that his aim was "to change the way people do business. I can do far more by showing an example." However, he also commented on his work with large companies:

> They took the low-hanging fruit, recycling plastic, converting their fleet over to natural gas. Things like that. They did everything that ends up making 'em more money. But when it comes down to doing the hard things, anything with a long-term payoff, they backed out … All of these companies, whether it's Dannon or Unilever, they're all greenwashing. They start out making a big deal out of something and they back down. It's like Nike started out doing a little bit of organic cotton, like 1 percent. Now I don't know if they do any at all. The fashion industry, same thing.[80]

While Chouinard's accusations of greenwashing by specific firms must be regarded entirely as his personal value judgement, his broad argument was broadly aligned with studies suggesting that high-profile sustainability campaigns by some large companies were often strategies to boost bottom-line profitability by reducing supply-chain costs. Such strategies, one such study suggested, "is fundamentally aiming for sustainability of big business, not sustainability of people and the planet."[81] A potential solution was to incorporate in a form which required managers to serve a wide range of stakeholders. This was the driver of the B Corporation movement, which certified companies that met rigorous standards of social and environmental performance, and was launched in 2006 by nonprofit B Lab. Patagonia became the first certified B Corp in California in 2012, and acted as an important momentum for the B Corporation movement.[82]

VI CONCLUSIONS

On December 8, 2015, Doug Tompkins was killed in a kayaking accident on Lake General Carrera, which straddles the border between Argentina and Chile. In the weeks that followed, an outpouring of remembrances flowed from newspapers and environmentalists alike. Included in those eulogizing Tompkins was Chouinard, who had been a member of the paddling expedition that tragically claimed Tompkins's life.[83]

Kristine Tompkins continued the mission after her husband's premature death. In March 2017, at a ceremony in Pumalín Park, attended by President Michelle Bachelet, Conservation Land Trust donated just over one million acres to the country's government. This was probably the largest private land donation to a national state in history. The government of Chile agreed to contribute and reclassify roughly ten million acres of federal government lands for conservation; this agreement would create a network of 17 national parks stretching across more than 1,500 miles, from Puerto Montt to Cape Horn, covering an area of land the size of Switzerland.[84]

This chapter has shown that the strategies employed by both Yvon Chouinard and Kristine and Doug Tompkins resulted in positive environmental benefits, but with some trade-offs and limitations. Patagonia continued to incorporate system-wide downsides, such as when the promise to provide the highest-quality outdoor products required the company to sell goods that are not 100 percent organic, recycled or resource-neutral in order to prioritize durability and reduce replacement. Sourcing from developing countries – more or less a mandatory element of any apparel business – exposed the company to the risk of working with counterparties that exploit their workforce. The vision was that as the company constantly improved its operations, shared its knowledge and thrived as a brand, it would become a role model. Patagonia has certainly been studied by high-profile large firms, but few large public companies have yet replicated the elements of the Patagonia sustainability strategy, which involved more than achieving greater cost-efficiency. This might be because a longer time is needed to make a full assessment.

The strategy of Doug and Kristine Tompkins might be seen as one-off, quixotic and paternalistic, but its positive environmental impact is very evident. The estimated sequestering and storage of 80 million tons of carbon was a significant contribution in terms of halting the pace of climate change. When that was combined with other environmental gains, which cannot be quantified at all, such as saving species from extinction, the net positive environmental impact was greater still. The couple also engaged in considerable environmental advocacy, which can only be seen as a major benefit for the natural environment, even if once again there are no metrics to capture the importance of such public voice. The natural environment would clearly benefit from a combined Tompkins–Chouinard approach on pollution and environmental destruction by actors not seeking their commercial exploitation. However, the broader take-away from the comparison of these strategies might be the positive potential for the application of entrepreneurial strategies and capabilities beyond seeking to make businesses more sustainable. Conservation is only one avenue in which this approach could be adopted.

NOTES

*   This chapter appeared in an earlier version as Jones, Geoffrey and Ben Gettinger (2016), "Alternative Paths of Green Entrepreneurship: The Environmental Legacies of North Face's Doug Tompkins and Patagonia's Yvon Chouinard," *Harvard Business School Working Paper* 17-034. The authors would like to thank Annelena Lobb and Mike Toffel for assistance and advice.

1.   Duane, "Rebel."
2.   Grant, "Esprit."
3.   Duane, "Rebel."
4.   Grant, "Esprit."
5.   Ibid.
6.   Duane, "Rebel."
7.   Chouinard, *Let*, 11.
8.   Ibid., 15.
9.   Ibid., 25, 31.
10. Ibid., 35.
11. Ibid., 30.
12. Ibid., 38.
13. Ibid., 65.
14. Reinhardt et al., "Patagonia," 2.
15. Ibid., 52–4.
16. Ibid., 2.
17. Baer, "Patagonia's."
18. Saverin, "Entrepreneur."
19. Ibid.; Drengson and Devall, *Ecology*; Naess, *Life's Philosophy*; Drengson, "Thought."
20. Grant, "Esprit."
21. Enders and Franklin, "Doug Tompkins."
22. Foundation for Deep Ecology, "History" webpage.
23. Foundation for Deep Ecology, "Grantmaking" webpage.
24. Tompkins Conservation, "Milestones" webpage.
25. Azócar Zamudio, *Tompkins*, 110, 113.
26. Ibid., 115.
27. Ibid., 116.
28. Pumalín Park and Project, "Pumalín's history" webpage.
29. Interview with Thomas Harrtung by Geoffrey Jones, April 18, 2017. Harrtung was a friend of Tompkins but he never discussed his financial strategies with him. On Harrtung's organic food business in Denmark, see Jones, *Profits*, 196–7.
30. Azócar Zamudio, *Tompkins*, 80–83.
31. Ibid., 174.
32. Ibid., 127–8, 130.
33. Ibid., 176.
34. Ibid., 178.
35. Ibid., 269–70.
36. Ibid., 208–10.
37. Ibid., 144.
38. Ibid., 146.
39. Conservación Patagónica, "Our history" webpage.
40. Saverin, "Entrepreneur."
41. Meakin, "Kris Tompkins."
42. Ball, "Patagonia clothing."
43. Chouinard, *Let*, 61.
44. Patagonia, "Environmental & social responsibility" webpage.
45. Chouinard, *Let*, 63.

46. Telephone interview with Rick Ridgeway by Ben Gettinger, April 4, 2016 (hereafter, Ridgeway interview, April).
47. Stevenson, "Patagonia's founder."
48. Reinhardt et al., "Patagonia," 3.
49. Ridgeway interview, April.
50. Nudd, "Ad."
51. Patagonia, "Worn Wear" webpage.
52. Ridgeway interview, April.
53. Chouinard, *Let*, 221–5.
54. Patagonia, *Annual Report*, 15.
55. Telephone interview of Professor Rattan Lal by Ben Gettinger, October 6, 2016. Lal is director of the Carbon Management and Sequestration Center, The Ohio State University, Columbia.
56. Conservation Land Trust, "Iberá Park" webpage; telephone interview with Rick Ridgeway by Ben Gettinger, August 15, 2016 (hereafter, Ridgeway interview, August).
57. Conservation Land Trust, "Corcovado National Park."
58. Parque Patagonia, "Threatened species" webpage.
59. Tompkins, "Rainforests," 16.
60. See Chapter 1; see Cheffins, "Team," for a recent review of the contingency of shareholder capitalism, which notes the prevalence of stakeholder capitalism even in the United States before the 1980s.
61. Marquis et al., "Scrutiny"; Jones, *Profits*, 290–94.
62. 1% for the Planet..
63. Stevenson, "Patagonia's founder."
64. Ridgeway interview, April.
65. Chouinard et al., "Sustainable Economy."
66. Azócar Zamudio, *Tompkins*, 140.
67. Saverin, "Entrepreneur."
68. Ibid.
69. See Chapter 1.
70. Dennis, "Proposed."
71. Tompkins, "Rainforests."
72. Mackinnon, "Strategy."
73. White, "Clothes."
74. Santen et al., "Leaving traces."
75. O'Rourke and Strand, "Patagonia."
76. Ridgeway interview, August.
77. Interview by Greg Dalton with Yvon Chouinard, October 27, 2016, accessed April 24, 2017 at https://climateone.org/audio/yvon-chouinard-founding-patagonia-and-living-simply.
78. White, "Clothes."
79. Ridgeway interview, April.
80. Quoted in Wieners, "Solving climate change."
81. Dauvergne and Lister, *Eco-business*, 2.
82. "20 Moments."
83. Enders and Franklin, "Doug Tompkins."
84. BBC News World, "North Face widow."

REFERENCES

1% for the Planet (n.d.), accessed January 19, 2018 at http://www.onepercent fortheplanet.org/what-we-do/our-approach.

20 Moments From The Past 20 Years That Moved The Whole World Forward, accessed January 19, 2018 at https://www.fastcompany.com/3052958/20-moments-that-matter.

Azócar Zamudio, Andrés (2007), *Tompkins: El Millonario Verde*, Santiago: Editorial La Copa Rota S.A.

Baer, Drake (2014), "How Patagonia's new CEO is increasing profits while trying to save the world," *Fast Company*, February 28, accessed March 11, 2016 at http://www.fastcompany.com/3026713/lessons-learned/how-patagonias-new-ceo-is-increasing-profits-while-trying-to-save-the-world.

Ball, Jena (December 2009/January 2010), "Patagonia clothing: Making a profit and meeting environmental challenges," *Mother Earth News*, accessed April 1, 2016 at http://www.motherearthnews.com/nature-and-environment/patagonia-clothing-zmaz09djzraw.aspx.

BBC News World (2017), "North Face widow Tompkins donates land for Chile parks," *BBC World News*, March 16, accessed April 16, 2017 at http://www.bbc.com/news/world-latin-america-39292600.

Cheffins, Brian (2015), "The Team Production Model as a Paradigm," *Seattle University Law Review*, **38**, (2), 397–432.

Chouinard, Yvon (2005), *Let My People Go Surfing*, New York: Penguin Press.

Chouinard, Yvon, Jib Ellison and Rick Ridgeway (2011, October), "The sustainable economy," *Harvard Business Review*, accessed May 14, 2016 at https://hbr.org/2011/10/the-sustainable-economy.

Conservacion Patagonica (n.d.), "Our history" webpage, accessed August 29, 2016 at http://www.conservacionpatagonica.org/aboutus_oh.htm.

Conservation Land Trust (n.d.), "Iberá park" webpage, accessed May 14, 2016 at http://www.theconservationlandtrust.org/eng/ibera.htm.

Conservation Land Trust (n.d.), "Corcovado National Park" webpage, accessed May 2016 at http://www.theconservationlandtrust.org/eng/corcovado.htm.

Dauvergne, Peter and Jane Lister (2013), *Eco-business: A Big-brand Takeover of Sustainability*, Cambridge, MA: MIT Press.

Dennis, Brady (2016), "Proposed national park is a multimillion-dollar gift wrapped up in distrust," *The Washington Post*, May 22, accessed September 18, 2016 at https://www.washingtonpost.com/national/health-science/proposed-national-park-is-a-multimillion-dollar-gift-wrapped-up-in-distrust/2016/05/22/0f036aa0-1d0b-11e6-b6e0-c53b7ef63b45_story.html.

Drengson, Alan (n.d.), "Some thought on the deep ecology movement," Foundation for Deep Ecology, accessed April 29, 2017 at http://www.deepecology.org/deepecology.htm.

Drengson, Alan and Bill Devall (eds.) (2008), *Ecology of Wisdom: Writings by Arne Naess*, Berkeley, CA: Counterpoint (distributed by Publishers Group West).

Duane, Daniel (n.d.), "Rebel with a cause: Yvon Chouinard on the passing of his lifelong friend, Doug Tompkins," *Men's Journal*, accessed March 1, 2016 at http://www.mensjournal.com/adventure/races-sports/rebel-with-a-cause-yvon-chouinard-on-the-passing-of-his-lifelong-friend-doug-tompkins-20160106.

Enders, Caty and Jonathan Franklin (n.d.), "Doug Tompkins: Life and death of the ecological visionary behind North Face," *The Guardian*, December 13, accessed March 1, 2016 at http://www.theguardian.com/us-news/2015/dec/13/douglas-tompkins-co-founder-north-face-chile-conservation.

Foundation for Deep Ecology (n.d.), "Grantmaking" webpage, accessed April 13, 2016 at http://www.deepecology.org/grantmaking.htm.

Foundation for Deep Ecology (n.d.), "History" webpage, accessed April 18, 2017 at http://www.deepecology.org/history.htm.

Grant, Tina (2000), "Esprit de Corps," in Tina Grant (ed.), *International Directory of Company Histories*, vol. 29, Farmington Hills, MI: St. James Press, 178–81.

Jones, Geoffrey (2017), *Profits and Sustainability: A History of Green Entrepreneurship*, Oxford: Oxford University Press.

Marquis, Christopher, Michael W. Toffel and Yanhua Zhou (2016), "Scrutiny, Norms, and Selective Disclosure: A Global Study of Greenwashing," *Organization Science*, **27**, (2), 483–504.

Mackinnon, J.B. (2015), "Patagonia's anti-growth strategy," May 21, *The New Yorker*, accessed April 13, 2016 at http://www.newyorker.com/business/currency/patagonias-anti-growth-strategy.

Meakin, Nione (2017, March), "Kris Tompkins battles on," *Celebrated Living*, accessed March 27, 2017 at https://americanwaymagazine.com/kris-tompkins-battles.

Naess, Arne (2002), *A Life's Philosophy: Reason and Feeling in a Deeper World*, Athens, GA: University of Georgia Press.

Nudd, Tim (2011), "Ad of the day: Patagonia," *Adweek*, November 28, accessed April 11, 2016 at http://www.adweek.com/news/advertising-branding/ad-day-patagonia-136745.

O'Rourke, Dara and Robert Strand (2017), "Patagonia: Driving Sustainable Innovation by Embracing Tensions," *California Management Review*, **60**, (1), 102–25.

Parque Patagonia (n.d.), "Threatened species" webpage, accessed May 8, 2016 at http://www.patagoniapark.org/threatened_species.htm.

Patagonia (2015), *Annual Report: Environmental + Social Initiatives*, Ventura, CA: Patagonia.

Patagonia (n.d.), "Environmental & social responsibility" webpage, accessed May 8, 2016 at http://www.patagonia.com/ca/patagonia.go?assetid=110489.

Patagonia (n.d.), "Worn wear" webpage, accessed April 8, 2016 at http://www.patagonia.com/us/worn-wear.

Pumalín Park and Project (n.d.), "Pumalín's History" webpage, accessed April 2, 2016 at http://www.parquepumalin.cl/en/pumalin_history.htm.

Reinhardt, Forest, Ramon Casadesus-Masanell and Hyun Jin Kim (n.d.), "Patagonia," *Harvard Business School Case* No. 711-020, Boston, MA: Harvard Business School Publishing, (rev. October 10 2010).

Saverin, Diana (2014), "The entrepreneur who wants to save paradise," *The Atlantic*, September 15, accessed March 19, 2016 at http://www.theatlantic.com/business/archive/2014/09/the-entrepreneur-who-wants-to-save-paradise/380116/.

Santen, Manfred, Kevin Brigden and Madeleine Cobbing (2016, January), "Leaving traces: The hidden hazardous chemicals in outdoor gear," *Greenpeace*, accessed March 8, 2016 at http://www.greenpeace.org/international/en/publications/Campaign-reports/Toxics-reports/Leaving-Traces.

Stevenson, Seth (2012), "Patagonia's founder is America's most unlikely business guru," *Wall Street Journal Magazine*, April 26, accessed April 2, 2016 at http://www.wsj.com/articles/SB10001424052702303513404577352221465986 612.

Tompkins Conservation (n.d.), "Milestones" webpage, accessed April 14, 2016 at http://www.tompkinsconservation.org/milestones.htm.

Tompkins, Douglas (January–February 1992), "Why Buy Rainforests?" *Buzzworm*, **4**.

Wieners, Bradford (2016), "Solving climate change with beer from Patagonia's food startup," *Bloomberg*, October 3, accessed October 22, 2016 at http://www.bloomberg.com/news/features/2016-10-03/solving-climate-change-with-beer-from-patagonia-s-food-startup.

White, Gillian B. (2015), "All your clothes are made with exploited labor," *The Atlantic*, June 3, accessed May 2, 2016 at http://www.theatlantic.com/business/archive/2015/06/patagonia-labor-clothing-factory-exploitation/394658.

PRIMARY MATERIALS

Interview by Geoffrey Jones with Thomas Harrtung, Boston, April 18, 2017.

Telephone interviews by Ben Gettinger with Rick Ridgeway, April 4, 2016; Rick Ridgeway, August 15, 2016; Professor Rattan Lal, October 6, 2016.

Postscript

This book has shown the deep and varied historical origins of endeavors to create for-profit businesses which were more sustainable and responsible than the prevailing norms. There is no comforting linear or upward trajectory in the story. Rather it is one of a patchy and uneven diffusion of a belief that a greener, more sustainable, business was needed, and was achievable. The uncertainties even over the very definition of sustainability and green business have been demonstrated in previous chapters. This is not a reason to dismiss the whole concept, but instead to address its complexity. Sustainability is a path whose ultimate ending cannot be precisely defined. The goal must not simply be for organic carrots or organic wines (or other green products) to capture the global market, but for companies and business systems as a whole to evolve in a sustainable fashion in all activities. The variety of mishaps and wrong paths taken evident here are not signs of failure, but rather represent the costs of discovering a new form of capitalism which addresses, rather than exacerbates, the environmental challenges and societal inequalities of the world.

The constraints, trade-offs and legitimacy challenges faced by the business leaders who have gone on this journey stand out. The problem was seldom one of identifying the challenge and proposing a solution, but rather of getting the solutions accepted and diffused. Collectively the individuals in this book, often motivated by philosophical and religious beliefs and sometimes by seeing products and services elsewhere which they wanted to emulate, offered alternatives to conventional norms, created new product categories and pioneered new technologies. Shibusawa and Bajaj articulated ideas of stakeholder capitalism and shared value as solutions to the sustainability challenges of their times, yet the concept never became mainstream. It is now the subject of renewed debates among management scholars and others today. Pioneering methods of recycling developed in wealthy cities in Germany in the early twentieth century, but most of the pioneering projects eventually stumbled, only to be picked up by later generations. Even today landfills, rather than recycling and recovery, remain the norm even in affluent countries such as the United States and Britain, let alone in emerging markets. A large parabolic solar energy system was functioning in Egypt by World War I, only for the technology to be put aside for decades. Today the potential for solar to provide energy for the developing world is again being widely discussed.

The challenge in developing more sustainable businesses was that however compelling the entrepreneurial vision, appropriate support from policy makers, and, especially, from individual consumers was necessary to progress far. Yet in waste management, energy, agriculture and other industries, governments were historically more interested in cost than the natural environment, and they were typically captured by conventional incumbents who could invariably provide goods and services cheaper than sustainable challengers because they did not account for environmental and societal externalities. Even as popular concerns about environmental sustainability grew, the willingness to pay a premium for sustainability by individual consumers was limited. As the trend toward buying vacations online emerged with the worldwide web in the 1990s, ecotourism businesses in Costa Rica learned that price rather than environmental sustainability drove consumer choice. Because sustainability involves systems-thinking, a profound and holistic mindset change seemed necessary – the kind envisaged by Rudolf Steiner and Arne Naess, or even reaching back to ancient religious and philosophical traditions such as Jainism and Confucianism.

Outcomes were varied between countries and categories because contexts varied so much. The prospects of the early solar energy industry were heavily dependent on the prices and availability of fossil fuel. It could only progress against fossil fuels when the latter were scarce, as in rural Denmark or Egypt before 1914, or when experts predicted future scarcities, as with the solar house movement in postwar America. New Zealand organic retailers battled against the context of the country's green and clean image. The Costa Rican ecotourism industry was able to grow in part because of the context of a country with political stability and an emergent national park system, quite unlike its Central American neighbors. The organic wine market in Sweden could eventually grow in part because there was a state-owned alcohol monopoly which resolved to promote the category.

Mobility and innovation offered paths out of constraints. Like the solar pioneer Frank Shuman, who started in Philadelphia and ended up in Egypt, entrepreneurs could and did move locations. Although the price of fossil fuels was an exogenous constraint for entrepreneurial solar cell businesses, the price differential was reduced by the technological innovations of Elliot Berman, Joseph Lindmeyer and Peter Varadi.

Innovation in organic wine-growing could and did greatly reduce the perceived quality gap between organic and conventional wines.

As sustainability is about systems, most progress was made through joint efforts and co-creation. In Germany, the early advances in waste management were the result of the invention of innovative systems combined with municipal legal ordinances that made the new endeavors, such as dust-free collection, profitable. Lobbying by organic farmers and others persuaded the Danish government to create an official label for organic food, which created a virtuous circle of future market growth. Meanwhile pioneering organic farmers and winemakers, ecotourism ventures, and companies such as Patagonia engaged actively with consumers to promote the mindset change which was so important to driving sustainability forward.

The journey to sustainability was challenging to businesses because it involved making choices about which activities should be prioritized and what needed to be left until viable solutions had been found. It has thus proved easier to define responsible and sustainable business by what it was not, rather than what it was. Businesses were faced by many awkward choices: deciding how many sulfites could be used in organic wines before they were not organic, or whether using water repellents in garments was the better choice for sustainability as it might reduce demand for new garments. In some cases, choices tipped over to full-scale greenwashing and the blurring of the whole concept of sustainability. Proponents of sustainable finance were clear that it meant providing an alternative to a conventional financial system which paid little regard to avoiding environmental degradation or helping disadvantaged social and ethnic groups, and which resulted in periodic massive financial crises. There was agreement among exponents that such an alternative finance needed to be more ethical, but not explicitly what ethics entailed or how trade-offs could be handled.

The complexities and trade-offs involved in seeking to make capitalism greener and more sustainable led to the decision of Doug and Kristine McDivitt Tompkins to leave business altogether, and focus on protecting, reforesting and rewilding huge areas of Argentina and Chile. This remarkable episode created, over two decades, a role model which national governments have now emulated, generating a virtuous circle of environmental gains, including saving whole species from extinction. The story signals the potential opportunity for entrepreneurial capabilities and vision to be applied to pursuing sustainability beyond business. Within business, the lesson of history is that making business sustainable is a hard journey with a lot of uncertainties and many variations, but it is a journey that is possible, and it is certainly one that is needed.

Index